STRATEGIC CORPORATE RESPONSIBILITY AND GREEN MANAGEMENT

CRITICAL STUDIES ON CORPORATE RESPONSIBILITY, GOVERNANCE AND SUSTAINABILITY

Series Editor: William Sun

Recent Volumes:

Lars Rademacher
MHMK (Macromedia University of Applied Sciences), Germany

Simon Robinson
Leeds Beckett University, UK

Greg Shailer
The Australian National University, Canberra, Australia

John Shields
The University of Sydney Business School, Australia

Jim Stewart
Liverpool John Moores University, UK

Peter Stokes
De Montfort University, UK

Ralph Tench
Leeds Beckett University, UK

Christoph Van der Elst
Tilburg University, The Netherlands

Wayne Visser
Antwerp Management School, Belgium

Suzanne Young
La Trobe University, Australia

CRITICAL STUDIES ON CORPORATE RESPONSIBILITY,
GOVERNANCE AND SUSTAINABILITY   VOLUME 16

STRATEGIC CORPORATE RESPONSIBILITY AND GREEN MANAGEMENT: PERSPECTIVES AND ISSUES IN EMERGING ECONOMIES

EDITED BY

ANANDA DAS GUPTA

Emeritus Professor, St. Josephs Institute of Management, India

United Kingdom – North America – Japan
India – Malaysia – China

Emerald Publishing Limited
Howard House, Wagon Lane, Bingley BD16 1WA, UK

First edition 2023

Reprints and permissions service
Contact: permissions@emeraldinsight.com

British Library Cataloguing in Publication Data
A catalogue record for this book is available from the British Library

ISBN: 978-1-80071-447-2 (Print)
ISBN: 978-1-80071-446-5 (Online)
ISBN: 978-1-80071-448-9 (Epub)

ISSN: 2043-9059 (Series)

Printed and bound by CPI Group (UK) Ltd, Croydon, CR0 4YY

ISOQAR certified
Management System,
awarded to Emerald
for adherence to
Environmental
standard
ISO 14001:2004.

Certificate Number 1985
ISO 14001

INVESTOR IN PEOPLE

CONTENTS

LIST OF CONTRIBUTORS

Divya Agarwal	Amazon Web Services, Singapore
Raji Ajwani-Ramchandani	Indian Institute of Technology, India
Rajesh Batra	IICA, India
Sonali Bhattacharya	Symbiosis Centre for Management and Human Resource Development, Symbiosis International (Deemed University), India
Nicholas Capaldi	Loyola University New Orleans, USA
Ananda Das Gupta	St. Josephs Institute of Management, India
Antonio Huerta-Estévez	Tecnológico Nacional de México/Instituto Tecnológico de Veracruz, Mexico
Aneel Karnani	University of Michigan, USA
José Satsumi López-Morales	Tecnológico Nacional de México/Instituto Tecnológico de Veracruz, Mexico
Ram Kumar Mishra	Institute of Public Enterprise, India
Kuruvilla Pandikattu, S. J.	XLRI – Xavier School of Management, India
Subhasis Ray	XIM University, India
Shulagna Sarkar	NLC India Ltd., India
Snigdha Shukla	NLC India Ltd., India
Pingali Venugopal	XLRI – Xavier School of Management, India

FOREWORD

Strategic Corporate Social Responsibility and Green Management: Perspectives in the Emerging Economies

In 2007 Professor John Ruggie, the architect of the United Nations Guiding Principles on Business and Human Rights (UN, 2008, 2011), pointed out with great vigour the 'fundamental institutional misalignment' between the drastic expansion and impact of global markets since the 1990s and the lack of capacity of societies to manage the adverse consequences of the markets. This 'creates the permissive environment within which blameworthy acts by corporations may occur without adequate sanctioning or reparation. For the sake of the victims of abuse, and to sustain globalization as a positive force, this must be fixed' (UN, 2007, p. 3).

Since then many initiatives have been taken towards addressing this fundamental institutional misalignment, not the least the United Nations Guiding Principles on Business and Human Rights (2011), inspiring multiple National Action Plans on Business and Human Rights and leading to legal provisions in numerous countries, particularly in Europe, and also in India with the Company Act 2013 on Corporate Social Responsibility.

It goes without saying that climate change and the COVID-19 pandemic have enormously aggravated this fundamental institutional misalignment. It is all the more important to raise the awareness of these multiple challenges, to support constructive initiatives, and to be critical about flawed and misguiding concepts and policies. This matters not only for states and international organisations but also for business organisations around the world in general and in emerging economies in particular.

Focussing on strategic corporate social responsibility (CSR) and green management in emerging economies, this volume, well arranged by the editor and co-author Ananda Das Gupta, offers valuable perspectives to these multiple challenges. Almost all contributions (except for the chapter on Mexican companies) address issues of great importance for India. They range from a very concrete and successful project in Chapter 1 (i.e. how technology enables solutions for women empowerment in India and waste management for combating COVID-19 and beyond) to a most-updated critical and constructive discussion on the macro-problematics of economic growth in Chapter 9 (i.e. green growth and regrowth pleading for progress with sustainability and responsibility). While Chapter 8 briefly informs about the detailed Indian legislation on Corporate Social Responsibility (in Company Act 2013/Section 135/Schedule VII), Chapter 3 criticises the concept of CSR that it does not avert 'the tragedy of the commons' by referring to the detailed case study of Coca Cola India. A spiritual foundation does not seem necessary according to Chapter 4 claiming that the main purpose of a market economy is to promote the 'Technological Progress', that is, to innovate and to grow. This chapter also sharply criticises the CSR movement for committing five 'sins' against the 'Technological Progress', while Chapters 5 and 6 intend to show that management practices – under certain conditions – can integrate social and environmental concerns into their business operations; Chapter 5 referring to the CSR model of e-Choupal for rural India, developed by ITC, one of India's foremost private sector companies; and Chapter 6 presenting the skill development efforts in India, especially needed in the COVID-19 pandemic, and how the CSR drive has been instrumental in addressing the skill gap in the country. Chapter 7 reminds the reader of the 54-year history of Auroville, located in Puducherry, that a spiritual foundation and a sustainable community building strategy are needed for a low carbon transition in developing economies.

Worldwide, the term CSR or Corporate Social Responsibility has been used in confusingly various ways and almost like a black box into which one can put almost any meaning. Fortunately, the CSR notion in the Indian Company Act 2013 is more specific. It includes especially nine policy activities from which the company Board – on the recommendation of its CSR Committee – may choose particular activities such as eradicating extreme hunger and poverty, promoting education, advancing gender equality and empowering women, and employment enhancing vocational skills. For the chosen activities, the company should spend, in every financial year, at least two percent of its average net profits.

These activities are discretionary and not necessarily linked to the company's strategies and core business activities. Therefore, this book – as the title says – explicitly focusses on 'strategic' CSR; this means, 'to link those largely discretionary activities explicitly intended to improve some aspect of society or the natural environment with their [the companies'] strategies and core business activities' (Waddock, 2018, p. 3272).

With this focus, the book offers more specific contributions in either critical or constructive perspectives as the short presentation of the chapters above can show. Still, two sets of questions are not yet raised and may stimulate further discussions, perhaps for a subsequent volume in this series.

The first set of questions relates to the notion of 'strategies and core business activities'. What does it precisely mean? What kind of purpose of the company is implied? Is it only about profit maximisation? Does it include – in addition to profit making – broader economic, societal and environmental objectives? While searching for 'win-win' solutions for business and society, what to decide when 'win-lose' solutions are unavoidable? Should then the benefit for business always win?

The second set of questions concerns the concept of 'responsibility' and its ethical foundation. The CSR literature uses this term abundantly, but rarely provides a conceptual explication and an ethical foundation. Often it is understood as a response to 'societal expectations'. I suggest drawing on the definition of responsibility developed by the German philosopher Walter Schulz (1972): Responsibility is self-commitment originating from freedom in worldly relationships. It involves two poles of human action: the interior *commitment* of the person to act responsibly and his or her *engagement* in concrete relationships with other persons, communities, non-human beings and nature. Responsibility is a relational concept and always 'anchored' in one or more actors (*who* is responsible?), concerns a concrete matter of *for what* one is responsible and relates to an authority or addressee *to whom* one is responsible (for example, stakeholders, tribunal, spouse or one's conscience). In a similar ('analogous') way, corporations as corporate actors are understood as moral actors who bear moral (or ethical) responsibility: they have the capacity to commit themselves to what they should do and to bear the consequences for what they do. (For further explanation, see Enderle, 2021, Chapters 1, 15, 16 and 17.)

In conclusion, responsibility not only in the legal but also in the ethical sense is necessary in our global and interconnected world. It is required from business enterprises of all sizes, from all social actors including non-governmental organisations, and from the states as well. As the Epilogue concludes, 'A stable nation providing good governance is thus a basic requirement for developing countries in their attempt to safeguard rights and interests of their poor and marginalized people'.

Georges Enderle
Professor Emeritus
Department of Marketing
Mendoza College of Business
University of Notre Dame
Notre Dame, IN 46556 Indiana, USA
Visiting scholar at Harvard University, Cambridge MA,
with Prof. Amartya Sen

REFERENCES

Enderle, G. (2021). *Corporate responsibility for wealth creation and human rights.* Cambridge: Cambridge University Press.

Schulz, W. (1972). *Philosophie der veränderten Welt* [*Philosophy in the changed world*]. Pfullingen: Neske.

United Nations (UN). (2007). *Business and human rights: Mapping international standards of responsibility and accountability for corporate acts. Report of the special representative of the secretary-general on the issue of human rights and transnational corporations and other business enterprises.* John Ruggie. Human Rights Council. Fourth Session, A/HRC/4/35.

United Nations (UN). (2008). *Promotion of all human rights, civil, political, economic, social and cultural rights, including the right to development. Protect, respect and remedy: A framework for business and human rights. Report of the special representative of the secretary-general on the issue of human rights and transnational corporations and other business enterprises.* John Ruggie. Human Rights Council. Eighth Session, A/HRC/8/5.

United Nations Human Rights Office of the High Commissioner (UN). (2011). *Guiding principles on business and human rights: Implementing the United Nations "protect, respect and remedy" framework.* New York, NY; Geneva: United Nations.

Waddock, S. (2018). Strategic corporate social responsibility. In R. W. Kolb (Ed.), *The Sage encyclopedia of business ethics and society* (2nd ed., 7 vols., pp. 3272–3273). Thousand Oaks, CA: Sage.

A TECHNOLOGY-ENABLED SOLUTION FOR WOMEN EMPOWERMENT IN INDIA AND WASTE MANAGEMENT FOR COMBATING COVID-19 AND BEYOND

Raji Ajwani-Ramchandani and Sonali Bhattacharya

ABSTRACT

Purpose: *COVID-19 not only has impacted adversely the health infrastructure, taking away lives of millions of people but it has also crippled the economy. The worst effected were food supply chain due to restrictions imposed on operations of shops and retail outlets. The consumers were suffering due to lack of supply. Similarly, agriculture produce were getting wasted due to lack of cold storage.*

Methodology: *In this case we have proposed how a mobile-based application solution during COVID lockdown can successfully transform the livelihood of rural farmers in the state of Maharashtra (India), a state worst affected by the pandemic.*

Result: *The technology-integrated supply chain model jointly developed by financial institutions, self-help groups (SHGs) and NGOs has enabled direct selling of fresh produces by rural women farmers to urban large residential societies at their doorsteps. It has provided a solution of municipality waste management by converting the waste to compost, getting them collected and used in the farmlands.*

Strategic Corporate Responsibility and Green Management
Critical Studies on Corporate Responsibility, Governance and Sustainability, Volume 16, 1–19
Copyright © 2023 by Emerald Publishing Limited
All rights of reproduction in any form reserved
ISSN: 2043-9059/doi:10.1108/S2043-905920230000016001

Implications: *It will help the urban consumers to have the continuous supply of fresh vegetables and fruits available at their doorsteps, and keep a track of transport of foods from farm to fork. The farmers will be able to get better price for their produce. The model will also contribute towards circular economy (CE) through citizen partnership.*

Keywords: COVID-19 Hotspot; technology-based fresh-produce value chain; self-help group federation; circular economy; humanitarian supply chain; mobile application

INTRODUCTION

India is the second largest producer of fresh fruits and vegetables. However, every year fresh produce worth nearly USD 2 billion (nearly 18% of the total production) is wasted due to the lack of adequate cold storage, refrigerated transport facilities (Bhosale, 2013) and a huge reliance on a broker-led network to coordinate the farm-food value chain (Pachouri, 2012). Farm produce that decomposes in landfills releases methane, a greenhouse gas which is at least 28 times more potent than carbon dioxide (Frischmann, 2019).

This scenario has been exacerbated due to the COVID-19 pandemic. The pandemic struck around harvest time period and affected the transport of fresh produce to the markets due to labour shortages, lockdown-related travel and transport restrictions (Bera, 2020).

Other unique challenges posed due to the COVID-19 situation are: need to maintain social distancing and avoid crowding in markets (Jayasimha, 2020), contact tracing (Ghosh, 2020) and a need to move towards cashless transactions, if possible, in order to avoid physical exchange of currency between people and kerb the circulation of contaminated notes (Sharma, 2020). In this case we proposed how a mobile based application technology created through joint efforts of NGOs, financial institutions and self-help groups (SHGs) during COVID-19 lockdown can enable rural farmers especially women to sell their products directly to large urban residential societies, hence ensuring better prices and better livelihood. Customers are also benefitted by getting fresh vegetables, fruits and groceries at their doorsteps, facilitated through a geographical information system (GIS)–based tracking system in the supply chain. The model has potential of contributing towards circular economy (CE) by enabling conversion of the organic components of the municipality solid wastes produced by these residential societies into compost and used by the rural farmers (Deakin & Reid, 2018). This case has taken the lens of inclusive innovation and humanitarian supply chain in the context of COVID-19 situation. In the next section, the theoretical concept of inclusive innovation and humanitarian supply chain which forms the base of our study is reviewed. We briefly describe the background of the study and its need in the present context. In section 'Research Methodology', we describe the step-by-step methodology and role of various stakeholders and technology in the model. In section 'Results and Discussion', we describe the impact of the model on the society, policymakers and environment. Finally, we discuss the implications of the study in the new normal.

LITERATURE REVIEW

Inclusive Innovation as defined by George, McGahan, and Prabhu (2012) is "the development and implementation of new ideas which aspire to create opportunities that enhance social and economic wellbeing for disenfranchised members of society".

The authors stress that inclusive innovation is valuable even when outcomes are not realised. Hence, any kind of innovation which contributes to the social, economic and environmental well-being and which is aimed at inclusivity of the base-of-the-pyramids can be called an inclusive innovation. Inclusive innovation can be looked from the lens of theory of resource assembly, deployment and development as creating an innovative logistic and supply chain which will enable to reach out to geographically dispersed population, such as the rural poor, at a low cost. Hence, it will include business solutions that enfranchise a previously disenfranchised section of the society. The responsible research and innovation theory of inclusive innovation demands that pros and cons of scientific and technological innovation should have direct linkage with social justice and development (Smith, Fressoli, & Thomas, 2014; Stirling, 2016). Inclusive innovations can be of three types: first, innovations meant for resolving specific local problem but with wider diffusion; second, appropriate to a situation but with transformative effects; and third, project-based solutions to achieve social justice goals with economic and political reasoning (Smith et al., 2014). Inclusive innovation encourages an open innovation ecosystem, where there is blending of grassroots innovation with corporate expertise in a reciprocative and responsible way. In grassroots level it has been found women are willing to adopt innovative technology, if they are part of some women development groups (Mohd Masdek, Nor, A'liah, & Rusli, 2018), and the level of adoption depends on their level of engagement with such groups. Kalkanci, Rahmani, and Toktay (2019) have looked into inclusive innovation as an integrative approach to resolve varied social issues in operational decision related to marginalised section of the society. In supply chain domain, inclusive innovation may include inclusive sourcing of resources including human resources, creating opportunities for livelihood, transparency in supply chain processes, and inclusive retail chain and distribution which targets base-of-the-pyramid as potential consumers providing them with quality goods and services at low cost and last-mile delivery innovations to reach remote places while partnering with or employing marginalised section of the society as service providers. The challenge is the trade-off that has to reach between profitability and inclusiveness. Humanitarian supply chain can be considered as a type of inclusive supply chain innovation. An example of such supply chain innovation is the direct cash transfer programme initiated in many countries targeting the 'have nots' (Heaslip, Kovács, & Haavisto, 2018). Corsini et al. (2020) have discussed that how innovations such as additive manufacturing or 3D printing can also be made to satisfy humanitarian supply chain goals by local sourcing and local manufacturing and satisfying humanitarian needs.

Humanitarian supply chain management (HSCM) include sustainable HSC; framework of agility, adaptability, alignment (Dubey & Gunasekaran, 2016); collaborative supply chain for humanitarian causes (Prasanna & Haavisto, 2018); humanitarian organisations' expectations regarding sustainability (Haavisto & Kovács, 2014); auction-based framework for procurement of goods (Alp Ertem & Buyurgan, 2011); flexibility and agility for humanitarian and logistics supply chain management (HLSCM) (Carroll & Neu, 2009); multiple-buyer procurement auctions for HSCM (Ertem, Buyurgan, & Rossetti, 2010); disaster relief logistics (Kovács & Spens, 2007); life cycle of disaster management (Goldschmidt & Kumar, 2016); HL preparedness (Jahre et al., 2016); decision support framework for disaster relief (Kumar & Havey, 2013); incentives and obstacles to consolidation of materials in HSC (Vaillancourt, 2016); and location selection and disaster relief network design (Timperio, Panchal, Samvedi, Goh, & De Souza, 2017). Pandemic like COVID-19 has thrown several challenges in the supply chain domain such as disruptions in the food and medical equipment supply chain in the public distribution network due to frequent proliferation of the disease which calls for development of a resilient supply chain (Singh, Kumar, Garza-Reyes, & de Sá, 2020). Some of the researches carried out on this regards are three-echelon stochastic optimisation model to optimally resolve the problems related to uncertainties in demand and supply (Salem & Haouari, 2017), developing a smart contract system for logistic service provider (Dolgui et al., 2020), game theoretic approach to resolve problems related to food, communication and logistic (Ivanov & Dolgui, 2020b), assessment of pre- and post-disaster supply chain performance based on agility and resilience (Altay, Gunasekaran, Dubey, & Childe, 2018) and associated risk (Ivanov & Dolgui, 2020a). Zlojutro, Rey and Gardner (2019) applied a multi-commodity network model to determine air traffic movement to determine spread of the disease. In this study, we have developed a conceptual resilient food supply network model between rural producer and urban consumer through mobile-based technology and blockchain-based collaborative network, which also contributes to CE.

Need for Connecting Farmers to Consumers Directly

The western state of Maharashtra has seen the maximum number of COVID-19 cases in the country (Government of India, COVID19 STATEWISE STATUS, 2020)[1] and has been grappling with trying to find solutions to fix the broken fresh-produce supply chain (Gupta, 2020). As per the Government of India's dashboard on 7 May 2020, the number of COVID-19 infected patients in Maharashtra was 14,541 out of a total figure of 52,952 for India. Large residential housing societies (mass clusters) have been directed by the state government[2] to arrange for the provision of grocery items within the society premises itself to comply with the lockdown order imposed by the Government of India. The need to maintain social distancing, usage of digital currency and minimum contact with the produce has been emphasised in order to flatten the pandemic curve. Thus, there is a need to conceptualise a supply chain approach that can help to connect the farmers with the final consumers in a manner that is transparent and reduces the time from farm to table.

Need for Technology-Based Fresh-Produce Value Chain

The pandemic and the surprise lockdown announced by the Indian government resulted in a panic-buying situation to stock up on fresh produce and grocery items amid speculations regarding the duration of the lockdown (India Today, 2020). Online green grocers were unable to meet the growth in the demand, and in many cases, delivery personnel were beaten up by the police or their work-places sealed resulting in a supply-chain breakdown (Economic Times, 2020). This resulted in makeshift arrangements cropping up to fulfil the need to ensure that a supply was made available in order to prevent people from leaving their homes in search of food items. The impact of COVID-19 on the fresh-produce value chain is shown in Table 1. The pandemic has forced a shift away from the conventional business practices that were intermediary-driven, physical location–bound spaces to a new way of doing business. In the post-COVID-19 world, customers and suppliers are more likely to choose meeting in a virtual marketplace using technology as a means to bridge the demand and supply gap. An application like Maha Savitri can help to provide market linkage to an SHG federation, enabling the members to benefit from the power of aggregation.

RESEARCH METHODOLOGY

The concept of the proposed mobile application was developed based upon the fieldwork of the author with the members of the SHG groups affiliated to the Gramin Mahila Swayamsiddha Sangh (GMSS) federation since 2011 (Ajwani-Ramchandani, 2017). Between 2013 and 2015 eight direct sales events were carried out in the vicinity of large housing societies (LHS) in Pune in order to gain an experience of the potential clients, requirements, logistical issues and the challenges faced by the members of the SHG group. The technology-based model has been conceptualised based on the experiences gained from those interactions.

Role of Self-Help Groups and Their Federation

SHGs were primarily seen as means of organising women for their empowerment at a village level and to mobilise collective action on various social issues such as dowry, domestic violence, alcoholism and access to potable water. The need to federate at a bigger level for financial reasons emerged since some of the groups faced shortage of funds for their internal lending. On the other hand, there were some other SHGs that had unutilised savings. These circumstances led to the idea of facilitating inter-lending between the groups through a federation.

The purpose behind establishing an SHG federation was to provide support and channelise the savings of rural SHGs by developing village-level clusters.

Table 1. Impact of COVID-19 on the Fresh-Produce Value Chain in Pune, Maharashtra.

Description	Pre-COVID-19 Scenario	Post-COVID-19 Scenario
Source of the fresh produce	Could be international/national or local	Local and national (to a limited extent because of interstate travel restrictions)
Production – consumption pattern	Linear: Grow–consume–throw	Circular approach possible: Grow–consume–recycle–rejuvenate
Supplier profile	Few large players having a strong distribution and marketing network	Multiple local players in close proximity to the customers
Logistics	Complex: Covering multiple modes of transport and large geographical distances	Relatively simple: Mainly road transport to cover short distances
Type of model	Intermediary-driven	Direct procurement options came about due to the pandemic
Usage of technology	Minimal usage as procurement, sales and monetary exchange was done manually	The concern associated with the pandemic led to the adoption of technology at the first and the last mile of the value chain
Mode of interaction between various value chain members	Physical interaction	Virtual – usage of phone and internet
Payment and Settlements mechanism	Mainly through physical currency (notes and coins)	Digital payments
Marketplaces	Physical spaces	Virtual spaces
Degree of transparency in the business operations	Low, due to lack of data	Relatively more transparent due to the availability of partial data
Food storage and cold chain infrastructure	Poor, resulting in a lot of wastage	Storage solutions had to be improved and in some cases conceptualised on a case-to-case basis in order to cope with passage of two ordinances that were passed during the COVID-19 period: The Farmers' Produce Trade and commerce (promotion and facilitation) Ordinance, 2020 or the FPTC

Source: Authors.

Each cluster is an association of 10–20 SHG groups. Each SHG group has about 10–20 members. The goal is to provide financial intermediation to each group at the federation level and to ensure that each group is able to meet the demand of its members.

GMSS started as an informal federation of five groups and worked that way for almost two years. Two leaders from each SHG were selected to represent their units. The rules of federation pertaining to membership fee and meetings were framed.

The number of groups increased to 20 by 1993. As the number of SHG groups increased, the funds pooled were found insufficient to meet the credit demand of all the members. Similarly, some groups faced a lot of difficulties in getting access to bank loans (Fig. 1). To overcome these challenges, linkages with external

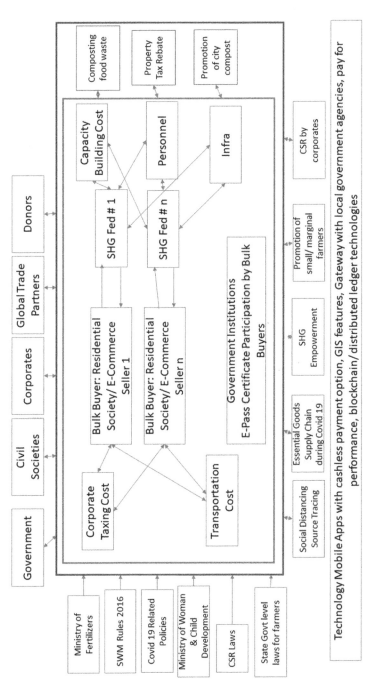

Fig. 1. Closing the Loop and Bridging the Supply Chain Gaps.
Source: Author.

agencies for accessing additional funds were established. The Friends of Women's World Banking (FWWB),[3] an institution engaged in financial services, initially gave credit to the informal unregistered federation by accepting a third-party guarantee. In order to facilitate further borrowing, FWWB suggested the need for creating a legal entity. Thus, the informal federation was formalised as GMSS, literally meaning 'Rural Women Self-Accomplishment Community' in 1993 by registering it as a society. Over the years, the power of aggregation has helped the members to solve a variety of problems mentioned above, existing at the village level.

The SHG federations started by *Chaitanya*[4] are located in various villages that lie along the Nashik + Mumbai Highway – such as Chakan, Bhosari, Kuruli, Chimbali, Rajgurunagar, Junnar and Ambegaon. The head office of GMSS is located in Rajgurunagar and this location is well connected to many LHS located in the Pune Metropolitan Region.

Chaitanya (the parent NGO) has spawned 37 SHG federations in Maharashtra and has a membership base of over 90,000 members in Maharashtra besides having 37 SHG federations operating in both Maharashtra and Madhya Pradesh (MP) (See Tables 2 and 3).

GMSS is the first SHG federation promoted in Maharashtra[5] and among the oldest women-centric SHG federation in India. It is a very lean organisation (staff strength of 20) that services the requirements of more than 8,400 members.

The Concept Behind Maha Savitri Mobile Application

The unique feature of the app is its emphasis on leveraging the power of aggregation possessed by SHG federations. The idea is to link the producers, that is, women farmers with *bulk* purchasers such as LHS and online green grocery start-ups (SUs) which sell to the households in the city (see Figs. 1 and 2). Technology acts as an enabler to "tie-up" the different stakeholders together, such as the farmers, SHG federation, customers and payment gateway providers, and to capitalise on some of the characteristics of the SHG model such as large membership base, relatively easy access to credit versus getting a bank loan, availability of the member's credit history and socio-economic markers.

Table 2. Summary of GMSS Membership and Loan Details as on 31 March 2020.

Particulars	Details
No of SHGs affiliated to GMSS	570
Village-level clusters	40
Members	8,475
Loan outstanding given to members	USD 407 thousand
Loans given to other SHG federations	USD 305 thousand
Total loans	USD 713 thousand

Source: GMSS.

Table 3. SHG Federations Promoted by Chaitanya in Maharashtra and Madhya Pradesh.

		SHG Federation Details as at September 2019				
Sr.No.	District	Federation Name	Year of Formation	Age of Federations	No of SHGs	No of Women Members
38	Madhya Pradesh	Damini Ujjain	2019	0	115	1,049
39	Madhya Pradesh	Sankalp Umariya	2018	1	457	5,027
40	Madhya Pradesh	Veerangana Umariya	2018	1		
		Less than 2 Years	*3*		*572*	*6,076*
7	Pune	Sakhi Maval	2016	3	121	1,452
		2–5 Years	*1*		*121*	*1,452*
9	Nandurbar	Jyoti Visarwadi	2011	8	184	1,957
10	Nandurbar	Dhartidhan Shahada	2011	8	176	1,957
12	Nagar	Rajmata Jijau Parner	2011	8	221	2,754
13	Nagar	Tarangana Akole	2011	8	230	2,680
14	Nagar	Veerangana, Kotul	2011	8	163	2,286
15	Nagar	Deokanya, Samsherpur	2011	8	174	1,885
16	Thane	Prerana Kudus	2011	8	173	2,125
17	Thane	Yashwanti Khodala	2011	8	151	1,627
18	Thane	Suryoday Wasai east	2011	8	146	1,763
19	Thane	Sankalp Wasai west	2011	8	146	1,980
22	Dhule	Agnishikha Songir	2011	8	203	2,536
23	Dhule	Deepshikha Malpur	2011	8	110	1,441
25	Nasik	Hirkani Sinnar	2011	8	240	2,957
27	Satara	Ankur Koregaon	2011	8	95	1,112
28	Satara	Yashodhara, Maan	2011	8	249	2,986
29	Yawatmal	Dnyaneshwari Kalamb	2011	8	150	2,003
30	Yawatmal	Aadhar Mahagaon	2011	8	145	1,550
31	Jalgaon	Neeranjana Bhusaval	2011	8	225	2,898
32	Jalgaon	Swapnapurti Kajgaon	2011	8	164	1,929
33	Kolhapur	Swawalambi, Shirol	2011	8	183	2,694
34	Kolhapur		2011	8	189	3,011

Table 3. *(Continued)*

		SHG Federation Details as at September 2019				
Sr.No.	District	Federation Name	Year of Formation	Age of Federations	No of SHGs	No of Women Members
		Yashaswi, Karveer				
35	Sindhudurg	Triveni Rajapur	2011	8	161	2,022
36	Amrawati	Tejaswini Warud	2011	8	175	2,498
37	Akola	Sanjeevani Telhara	2011	8	210	2,384
2	Pune	Sankalp Junnar	2009	10	318	4,022
3	Pune	Shivkanya Manchar	2009	10	232	3,099
4	Pune	Bharari Belha	2009	10	138	1,849
5	Pune	Vasundhara Daund	2009	10	65	1,228
6	Pune	Sankalsiddhi Shikrapur	2009	10	168	2,016
8	Nandurbar	Ajinkyatara Nandurbar	2009	10	231	2,770
11	Nagar	StreeShakti Supa	2009	10	264	4,156
20	Dhule	Veerangana, Sakri	2009	10	180	1,978
21	Dhule	Nakshtra Shindkheda	2009	10	166	1,910
26	Satara	Ekta Satara	2009	10	124	1,846
		5–10 Years	*34*		*6,149*	*77,909*
24	Nasik	Sahara Sinnar	2008	11	270	3,566
		10–15 Years	*1*		*270*	*3,566*
1	Pune	GMSS Khed	1989	30	594	8,545
		More than 15 Years	*1*		*594*	*8,545*
	Total				**7,706**	**97,548**

Source: Chaitanya.

In this model the village cluster is the node that connects various member women farmers with the federation (see Fig. 3). As indicated in Fig. 3, the distributed ledger mechanism can be used for tracking the provenance of the produce, the details of the farm and its location. Interactive features of GIS coupled with digital images can be used to improve user experience such as tracking the journey of the delivery truck from the field to the customer's doorstep, harvesting date and the packing date. Similarly, electronic payment methods can be linked via the app. Every SHG cluster can have a unique ID and name. Customer reviews/ratings for each SHG cluster can be shared in the public domain. The SHG federation will help with all the activities pertaining to the marketing of the produce from the farmers just like any middleman would do; however, there is a difference – in this case the SHG federation will earn a fee for their services.

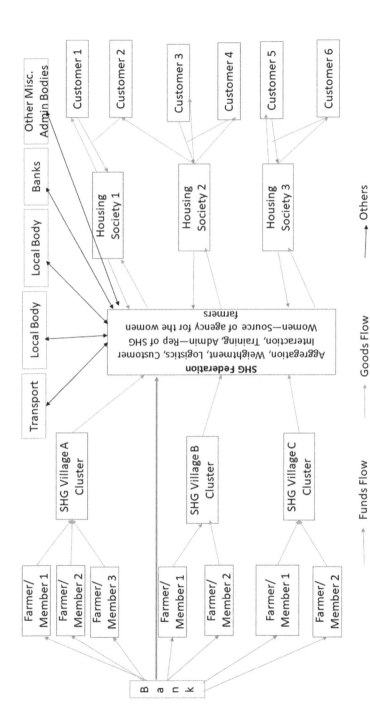

Fig. 2. Model: Maha Savitri Mobile Application. *Source:* Author.

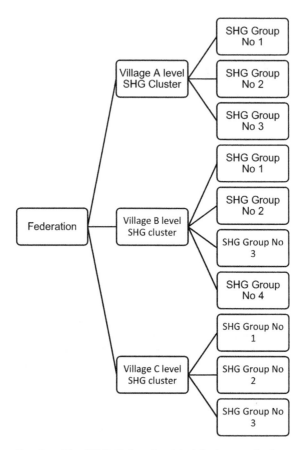

Fig. 3.   The SHG Federation Model. *Source:* Author.

The main benefit that will accrue to the farmers is that they will be able to earn a greater value for their labour by eliminating the broker/middleman (as shown in Fig. 4). This will shorten the farm-to-table value chain and ensuring fresh produce. From the customer's point of view, emerging technology like distributed ledger or blockchain can help trace the provenance of the produce, especially for crops cultivated using organic techniques. The SHG federation will earn a service fee for facilitating the sale and for handling any customer-related grievances. Some of the barriers that prevent women farmers undertaking entrepreneurial

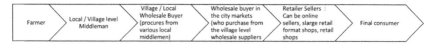

Fig. 4.   The Pre-COVID-19 (Current) Farm-to-Food Value Chain.
Source: Author.

activities are patriarchal norms prevalent in conventional Indian rural settings, language and communication barriers (Kabeer, 2016). This technology-based solution will help overcome these barriers.

The other feature of the mobile application is that it will help to connect the available transport options which are popular at the village level, such as small tempos, mini trucks, three wheelers and two wheelers with the SHG federation. Transport costs are a deterrent as they impact subsistence farmers by driving up the costs of agricultural activity (Gollin & Rogerson, 2014). However, by using local transport options and having a choice of the type of vehicle can help to control costs and create local employment opportunities for rural vehicle owners. At present, there is no electronic mechanism available to aggregate the demand and supply of transport options.

RESULTS AND DISCUSSION

Role of the Model in Food Supply Chain

The impact of COVID-19 is going to transform the way business models are configured given the fact that the number of infected cases are rising. India's case load surpassed Spain on 6 June 2020. With over 246 thousand cases, India has surpassed Spain, becoming the fifth worst-hit nation by the COVID-19 pandemic (The Indian Express, 2020). Now only the United States, Brazil and the United Kingdom have more cases than India. The Maha Savitri mobile app will continue to be relevant as it addresses the fundamental need of getting access to fresh and affordable vegetables that are sourced locally and have a short journey from the farm to the table. From the point of view of the government, supporting the Maha Savitri mobile app can solve multiple challenges such as generating stable livelihood opportunities in the rural areas, reducing forced migration and facilitating the implementation of the new farming ordinance.

Feminisation of Agriculture in India

As per India's economic survey for 2017–2018 (Government of India, 2018), due to the growing trend of urban migration by men, there is 'feminisation' of agriculture sector, with increasing number of women in multiple roles as cultivators, entrepreneurs and labourers. Focussing on SHGs has been recommended as a strategy to enable economic empowerment in the rural areas. The agriculture sector employs 80% of the economically active women and they comprise 33% of the agricultural labour force and 48% of the self-employed farmers (Patel, Chaudhary, & Chaudhary, 2018).

Policy Implications

On 4 June 2020, the government of India approved the Farming Produce Trade and Commerce (Promotion and Facilitation) Ordinance, 2020. This ordinance is expected to help farmers get better prices for their produce by allowing them to sell to any buyer who offers the best price. This ordinance has also recommended the usage of online platforms to facilitate the realisation of the best price by the farmer (Ohri, 2020). This move is expected to attract investment in cold chain storage in India and to help reduce wastage and promote livelihoods by enabling social distancing as farmers will be able to sell at their doorstep without having to travel to the wholesale markets.

Aggregation of the Large Membership Base Using Technology

Technology can help to link and aggregate the large pool of members (women farmers) who are already associated with GMSS (as shown in Table 1). Access to livelihood opportunities combined with credit can create a multiplier effect – as the income generated can help women members grow/diversify their business, augment savings, educate children particularly girls and overcome emergencies.

Scope of Cashless/Digital Payments for Customers

This mobile application has been conceptualised keeping in mind the need to facilitate business transactions in the post-COVID world, that is, the need to maintain social distancing and contact tracing. Digital payments have also been promoted as a solution by the government of India as a means to ensure transparency in business transactions and kerb the circulation of black money (Financial Express, 2020). Another advantage of this option is that, the payment from the customer will be collected at the time of placing the order. Returns will be permitted at the time of taking delivery of the order. This will be done by facilitating a visual inspection of the order for the customer by the salesperson. The salesperson will be masked and will wear gloves and sanitise her hands at regular intervals. Exchange of items will not be permitted so as to ensure minimal contact with the produce and reduce the possibility of spreading the virus. On-the-spot refund facility is expected to reduce consumer complaints, as the customer will be able to get a credit within one or two business days for the refund amount.

SMS Alerts/GIS-Based Tracking

This feature was conceptualised keeping the post-COVID-19 scenario in mind, wherein the need to maintain social distancing will continue to remain paramount to prevent transmission of the virus. This feature will prevent unnecessary crowding for all the concerned parties as it will be possible to track the movement of the delivery vehicle via the mobile app. Moreover, each customer will receive a SMS alert once their package is ready for delivery. This will save the waiting time for the customers and prevent crowding. Blockchain architecture can enable the verification of the entire data regarding the farmer, location of the farm, types and methods of crop cultivation. This can enable the customer to know the source of the food as well facilitate in contact tracing if required.

Reduction of Transport Costs and Benefits Returned to Rural Farmers

There are many small to mid-size vehicles available in rural areas such as tempos, autos and mid-size trucks which can be used for customer deliveries. Currently, there is no aggregator of such vehicles. Often times, these vehicles lose business if they are unable to get work through word-of-mouth referrals. Even that dries out during extreme scenarios such as the two-and-a-half month lockdown. Through this app, the SHG federation can seek quotes from interested parties which can result in a win-win for all the concerned entities. The opportunity to connect directly with the customers can help to open up alternate livelihood generation streams for the members and help to augment member/household income.

Incorporating Circular Economy Principles via the Maha Savitri App

In a CE system products and materials are used at their maximum value and functionality (Stahel & Reday, 1976). The CE approach adopts an elements[6] perspective and the aim is to set up closed loops in which the functionality of the elements is conserved as long as possible by avoiding breaking it down into its basic materials after each use (Murray, Skene, & Haynes, 2017).

Nearly 60–70% of the composition of the municipal solid waste in India is organic in nature and comprises food scraps, peels etc. (Sharholy, Ahmad, Mahmood, & Trivedi, 2008). This food waste can be converted into compost which is a rich source of nutrients for cultivating crops (Ramchandra, Bharath, Kulkarni, & Han, 2018).

A decentralised approach to managing Municipal Solid Waste (MSW) has been mandated by the Indian Solid Waste Management Rules (2016). LHS generating more than 100 kg of waste are designated as bulk waste generators and have to compost their food waste. The Maha Savitri application can help to unlock the potential in the organic and the recyclable components of the MSW as compost generated in the LHS can be donated to the farmers. This can create a virtuous cycle of healthy soils, nutritious food, clean air and cost savings for all the concerned stakeholders, viz, farmers, consumers, municipal authorities and policymakers.

CONCLUSION

The pandemic has upended conventional policy, governance and business models and forced businesses to rethink solutions. The post-COVID-19 era will require strengthening local value chains in order to continue with an uninterrupted supply of basic necessities such as food at affordable prices. In order to do so it is critical to integrate sustainable production initiatives with consumers by keeping in mind the constraints that have been posed due to the pandemic. Using technology as the connector can help in supporting sustainable livelihood for the poor while ensuring food security for the urban Indian populace. Integrating principles of CE to this approach can help to generate wealth from waste and create a workable solution, shorten the farm-to-food value chain and facilitate empowerment of women farmers as illustrated in the above case study. It has provided customers safe and secured supply of good quality commodities at their doorsteps during pandemic with reduced cost. Farmers were provided with direct sales opportunities, with better return and improved livelihood. The literature in CE is deficient in covering its application to the cities and the built environment and has focussed mainly on the industrial sector. According to Frischmann (2019), worldwide implementation of composting can reduce carbon emissions by 2.3 billion tonnes over the next 30 years. This is because food waste that decomposes in landfills releases methane which is a greenhouse gas which is atleast 28 times more potent than carbon dioxide. According to Project Drawdown (2019), the total food production worldwide would need to increase by 107 million tonnes annually by 2050. For this level of production to happen, more than billion acres of forests and grasslands will be required over the course of the next 30 years, resulting in the release of 84 billion tonnes of carbon dioxide equivalent in the atmosphere.

Food scraps and waste can be used as fertiliser on the cropland to improve soil health and productivity. However, on-site recycling of food waste can be viable only if the activity is systematically undertaken, supported by the community and recognised for its environmental benefits. This would help in 'closing the loop' thereby creating a circular process wherein what is otherwise considered as waste can become 'food' or input for growing fresh food thereby creating a virtuous cycle of opportunity instead of destruction.

NOTES

1. https://www.mygov.in/covid-19/.
2. https://timesofindia.indiatimes.com/city/mumbai/housing-societies-must-ensure-nobo dy-steps-out-government/articleshow/74880631.cms.
3. FWWB is an apex body in India which aims to empower impoverished women through entrepreneurial opportunities, agricultural finance, accessing renewal source of energy, improved water and sanitation facilities by financing various microfinance institutes and enterprises.
4. Chaitanya, literally meaning consciousness, is an NGO which promotes women-based microfinance institutions https://www.chaitanyaindia.org/.
5. http://indiastudyabroad.org/internship-at-chaitanya/.
6. Elements in this context refer to products, materials, packaging and other forms of goods that can somehow be re-utilised. The name is inspired from the Sanskrit word which symbolises the five elements of the material world, viz, air, water, fire, earth and the sky.

REFERENCES

Ajwani-Ramchandani, R. (2017). *The role of microfinance in women's empowerment: A comparative study of rural & urban groups in India.* Emerald Group Publishing.
Alp Ertem, M., & Buyurgan, N. (2011). An auction-based framework for resource allocation in disaster relief. *Journal of Humanitarian Logistics and Supply Chain Management, 1*(2), 170–188.
Altay, N., Gunasekaran, A., Dubey, R., & Childe, S. J. (2018). Agility and resilience as antecedents of supply chain performance under moderating effects of organizational culture within the humanitarian setting: A dynamic capability view. *Production Planning and Control, 29*(14), 1158–1174.

Bera, S. (2020, March 26). As buyers scramble for supplies, vegetables rot in India's biggest 'mandi'. Retrieved from Live Mint: https://www.livemint.com/news/india/as-buyers-scramble-for-supplies-vegetables-rot-in-india-s-biggest-mandi-11585161520729.html

Bhosale, J. (2013, November 28). India wastes fruits and vegetables worth Rs 13,300 crore every year: Emerson study. Retrieved from Economic Times: https://economictimes.indiatimes.com/news/economy/agriculture/india-wastes-fruits-and-vegetables-worth-rs-13300-crore-every-year-emerson-study/articleshow/26523928.cms?from=mdr

Carroll, A., & Neu, J. (2009). Volatility, unpredictability and asymmetry: An organising framework for humanitarian logistics operations? *Management Research News, 32*(11), 1024–1037.

Corsini, L., Aranda-Jan, C. B., & Moultrie, J. (2020). The impact of 3D printing on the humanitarian supply chain. *Production Planning and Control, 33*(6–7), 692–704.

Deakin, M., & Reid, A. (2018). Smart cities: Under-gridding the sustainability of city-districts as energy efficient-low carbon zones. *Journal of Cleaner Production, 173*, 39–48.

Dolgui, A., Ivanov, D., Potryasaev, S., Sokolov, B., Ivanova, M., & Werner, F. (2020). Blockchain-oriented dynamic modelling of smart contract design and execution in supply chain. *International Journal of Production Research, 58*(7), 2184–2199.

Dubey, R., & Gunasekaran, A. (2016). The sustainable humanitarian supply chain design: Agility, adaptability and alignment. *International Journal of Logistics Research and Applications, 19*(1), 62–82.

Economic Times. (2020, April 3). Issues faced by e-comm players during lockdown being resolved: DPIIT. Retrieved from Economic Times: https://economictimes.indiatimes.com/industry/services/retail/issues-faced-by-e-comm-players-during-lockdown-being-resolved-dpiit/articleshow/74965500.cms?from=mdr

Ertem, M. A., Buyurgan, N., & Rossetti, M. D. (2010). Multiple-buyer procurement auctions framework for humanitarian supply chain management. *International Journal of Physical Distribution & Logistics Management, 40*(3), 202–227.

Financial Express. (2020, January 3). If not for demonetisation, India would have had this much cash now; note ban slowed growth of cash. Retrieved from Financial Express: https://www.financialexpress.com/economy/if-not-for-demonetisation-india-would-have-had-this-much-cash-now-note-ban-slowed-growth-of-cash/1811761/#:~:text=The%20same%20also%20gave%20boost,eliminate%20fake%20I ndian%20currency%20notes

Frischmann, C. (2019, September 3). The climate impact of the food in the back of your fridge. Retrieved from The Washington Post: https://www.washingtonpost.com/news/theworldpost/wp/2018/07/31/food-waste/?noredirect=on

George, G., McGahan, A. M., & Prabhu, J. (2012). Innovation for inclusive growth: Towards a theoretical framework and a research agenda. *Journal of Management Studies, 49*(4), 661–683.

Ghosh, A. (2020, May 7). Mumbai positivity rate 15%, Centre stresses on contact tracing. Retrieved from The Indian Express: https://indianexpress.com/article/cities/mumbai/coronavirus-lockdown-mumbai-positivity-rate-15-centre-stresses-on-contact-tracing-6397627/

Goldschmidt, K. H., & Kumar, S. (2016). Humanitarian operations and crisis/disaster management: A retrospective review of the literature and framework for development. *International Journal of Disaster Risk Reduction, 20*, 1–13.

Gollin, D., & Rogerson, R. (2014). Productivity, transport costs and subsistence agriculture. *Journal of Development Economics, 197*, 38–48.

Government of India. (2018, January 29). Growing migration by men is causing 'feminisation' of agriculture sector, says economic survey. Retrieved from Press Information Bureau: https://pib.gov.in/Pressreleaseshare.aspx?PRID=1518099#:~:text=Economic%20Survey%202017%2D18 %2C%20tabled,roles%20as%20cultivators%2C%20entrepreneurs%2C%20and

Government of India. (2020, May 7). Covid19 statewise status. Retrieved from Government of India Covid19 dashboard: https://www.mygov.in/corona-data/covid19-statewise-status/

Gupta, M. (2020, April 11). Maharashtra takes food directly from farmers to housing societies. Retrieved from CNBC: https://www.cnbctv18.com/agriculture/maharashtra-takes-food-directly-from-farmer-to-housing-societies-5670951.htm

Haavisto, I., & Kovács, G. (2014). Perspectives on sustainability in humanitarian supply chains. *Disaster Prevention and Management, 23*(5), 610–631.

Heaslip, G., Kovács, G., & Haavisto, I. (2018). Innovations in humanitarian supply chains: The case of cash transfer programmes. *Production Planning and Control, 29*(14), 1175–1190.

India Today. (2020, March 24). Panic buying seen at shops after PM Modi's national lockdown announcement. Retrieved from India Today: https://www.indiatoday.in/india/story/pm-modi-coronavirus-national-lockdown-panic-buying-groceries-essential-items-1659291-2020-03-24

Ivanov, D., & Dolgui, A. (2020a). A digital supply chain twin for managing disruption risks and resilience in the era of Industry 4.0. *Production Planning and Control, 32*(9), 775–788.

Ivanov, D., & Dolgui, A. (2020b). Viability of intertwined supply networks: Extending supply chain resilience angles towards survivability. A position paper motivated by COVID-19 the outbreak. *International Journal of Production Research, 58*(10), 2904–2915.

Jahre, M., Kembro, J., Rezvanian, T., Ergun, O., Håpnes, S. J., & Berling, P. (2016). Integrating supply chains for emergencies and ongoing operations in UNHCR. *Journal of Operations Management, 45*, 57–72.

Jayasimha, K. R. (2020, April 4). Social distancing takes a back seat at markets. Retrieved from The Hindu: https://www.thehindu.com/news/cities/bangalore/social-distancing-takes-a-back-seat-at-markets/article31302590.ece

Kabeer, N. (2016). Gender equality, economic growth, and women's agency: The "endless variety" and "monotonous similarity" of patriarchal constraints. *Feminist Economics, 22*(1), 295–321.

Kalkanci, B., Rahmani, M., & Toktay, L. B. (2019). The role of inclusive innovation in promoting social sustainability. *Production and Operations Management, 28*(12), 2960–2982.

Kovács, G., & Spens, K. M. (2007). Humanitarian logistics in disaster relief operations. *International Journal of Physical Distribution & Logistics Management, 37*(2), 99–114.

Kumar, S., & Havey, T. (2013). Before and after disaster strikes: A relief supply chain decision support framework. *International Journal of Production Economics, 145*(2), 613–629.

Mohd Masdek, N. R. N., Nor, M., A'liah, N. A., & Rusli, R. (2018). Inclination towards the use of technology among rural women entrepreneurs in the agriculture sector. *International Journal of Business & Society, 19*, 56–65.

Murray, A., Skene, K., & Haynes, K. (2017). The circular economy: An interdisciplinary exploration of the concept and application in a global context. *Journal of Business Ethics, 140*, 369–380.

Ohri, N. (2020, June 03). India approves ordinance to allow farmers to freely sell produce. Retrieved from Bloomberg Quint: https://www.bloombergquint.com/economy-finance/india-approves-ordinance-to-allow-farmers-to-freely-sell-produce

Pachouri, A. (2012, December 28). *Economic inefficiencies in farm-market linkages in agriculture value chain in India: Problems and solutions.* Retrieved from ISAS Working Paper: https://www.files.ethz.ch/isn/158132/ISAS_Working_Paper_163_-_Economic_Inefficiencies_28122012163415.pdf

Patel, K. M., Chaudhary, M., & Chaudhary, M. (2018). Empowerment of tribal women of south Gujarat through agricultural by-products. *Gujarat Journal of Extension Education*, Special Issue on National Seminar: April 2018, 12–14.

Prasanna, S. R., & Haavisto, I. (2018). Collaboration in humanitarian supply chains: An organisational culture framework. *International Journal of Production Research, 56*(17), 5611–5625.

Ramchandra, T. V., Bharath, H. A., Kulkarni, G., & Han, S. S. (2018). Municipal solid waste: Generation, composition and GHG emissions in Bangalore, India. *Renewable and Sustainable Energy Reviews, 82*, 1122–1136.

Salem, R. W., & Haouari, M. (2017). A simulation-optimisation approach for supply chain network design under supply and demand uncertainties. *International Journal of Production Research, 55*(7), 1845–1861.

Sharholy, M., Ahmad, K., Mahmood, G., & Trivedi, R. C. (2008). Municipal solid waste management in Indian cities – A review. *Waste Management, 28*(2), 459–467.

Sharma, S. (2020, March 23). Digital India: Risk of coronavirus on currency notes, ATMs make banks recommend digital transactions. Retrieved from Financial Express: https://www.financialexpress.com/economy/digital-india-risk-of-coronavirus-on-currency-notes-atms-make-banks-recommend-digital-transactions/1906544/

Singh, R. K., Kumar, A., Garza-Reyes, J. A., & de Sá, M. M. (2020). Managing operations for circular economy in the mining sector: An analysis of barriers intensity. *Resources Policy, 69*, 101752.

Smith, A., Fressoli, M., & Thomas, H. (2014). Grassroots innovation movements: Challenges and contributions. *Journal of Cleaner Production, 63*, 114–124.

Stahel, W. R., & Reday, G. (1976). *The potential for substituting manpower for energy.* Report to the Commission of the European Communities, Brussels.

Stirling, A. (2016). Addressing scarcities in responsible innovation. *Journal of Responsible Innovation, 3*(3), 274–281.

The Indian Express. (2020, June 7). Coronavirus India LIVE Updates: Govt says 'fine tuning' strategy based on emerging knowledge, experience. Retrieved from https://indianexpress.com/article/india/coronavirus-india-news-live-updates-covid-19-tracker-latest-news-corona-virus-cases-deaths-in-india-state-wise-lockdown-today-update-6444777

Timperio, G., Panchal, G. B., Samvedi, A., Goh, M., & De Souza, R. (2017). Decision support framework for location selection and disaster relief network design. *Journal of Humanitarian Logistics and Supply Chain Management, 7*(3), 222–245.

Vaillancourt, A. (2016). A theoretical framework for consolidation in humanitarian logistics. *Journal of Humanitarian Logistics and Supply Chain Management, 6*(1), 2–23.

CORPORATE SOCIAL RESPONSIBILITY AND ITS IMPACT ON THE SUSTAINABLE DEVELOPMENT GOALS: A STUDY OF MEXICAN COMPANIES

Antonio Huerta-Estévez and
José Satsumi López-Morales

ABSTRACT

Corporate social responsibility (CSR) in Mexican companies is an incipient concept that, in recent years, has had greater participation in the planning of companies' organisational strategies. Similarly, Mexico, as an emerging economy, has managed to remain one of the main economies in Latin America and, together with companies and organised society, has developed public policies that allow compliance with the commitment of the 2030 Agenda and the achievement of its Sustainable Development Goals (SDGs). The objective of this work is to analyse the presence of CSR in Mexican companies and its relationship with the SDGs related to economic development, for which a content analysis of the websites of the hundred most important companies in Mexico, according to the 2019 ranking of Expansión *magazine, was performed. Finally, we establish that more than half of Mexican companies do not consider aspects related to CSR in their organisational development, contributing to the increase in the percentage of the population lagging behind in education, health and quality food and resulting in an increase in the levels of poverty and extreme poverty among the population of Mexico.*

Keywords: Emerging economies; corporate social responsibility; governance; sustainable development goals; agenda 2030; economic development

Strategic Corporate Responsibility and Green Management
Critical Studies on Corporate Responsibility, Governance and Sustainability, Volume 16, 21–38
Copyright © 2023 by Emerald Publishing Limited
All rights of reproduction in any form reserved
ISSN: 2043-9059/doi:10.1108/S2043-905920230000016002

INTRODUCTION

It is essential to evaluate countries' progress in economic and social matters over a period of time, and that in turn allows the identification of the needs that remain to be addressed. Factors such as the per capita national income and the human development index are generally used to classify countries into the developed and developing categories (Lopez-Correa & Patrinos, 2018). Countries that are classified as developing are also called emerging markets, although the term emerging economy is more commonly used, and these are the countries that are investing in increasing their productive capacity, leaving aside agriculture as the main base of their economy (Christy, 2021). The importance of emerging economies lies in their momentum in global economic growth. The rapid industrialisation of these countries, as well as their evolution to mixed economies, has prompted them to promote a better quality of life for their citizens, focussing primarily on areas such as education and health since these are intimately linked with human development (Lopez-Correa & Patrinos, 2018).

Countries such as Argentina, Brazil, Chile, Colombia, Peru and Mexico are considered to be the main emerging economies in Latin America since, in recent years, they have had a greater increase in capital investments due to various factors, such as the characteristics of the regions, low global interest rates and the slow recovery of the US economy, among others, making these countries attractive for investment (Lozano-Espitia & Melo-Becerra, 2012). In this context, Mexico stands as the main beneficiary of the economic rebound in the United States due to the close integration in economic matters of these two nations in addition to Mexico being the second commercial partner of United States (Saldívar, 2021).

The role played by Mexican companies is essential for Mexico to continue to be considered as one of the main emerging economies in Latin America; in addition, it should not be overlooked that Mexico, as a member of the United Nations (UN), participated in the preparation of the 2030 Agenda and its 17 Sustainable Development Goals (SDGs), in which the active involvement of society, the business sector and the government, through public policies and governance that favour the implementation of this agenda, is essential. This is why corporate social responsibility (CSR) is one of the key success factors for the achievement of the SDG agenda. It is understood that the efforts made by companies around CSR will present a better image to their clients, so companies focus their business strategies on CSR (Alvarado-Herrea & Schlesinger-Díaz, 2008).

In addition to this, the same society has been increasingly influential on issues related to social responsibility, which has led to a redesign of companies' function within society through the establishment of multiple programmes that direct their efforts to the benefit of society (García-Santos & Madero-Gómez, 2016). Although, in recent years, there has been legislation about companies' social responsibility for their environment, CSR should not only be understood as the obligations imposed on companies by law, since the truly important point about social responsibility is that it is based on the will to act for the benefit of society

(Martos-Molina, 2011). However, this is not easy since the constant changes of the environment around organisations in addition to the high complexity of social, economic and environmental problems are the greatest challenges that organisations face in achieving adequate remuneration for the development of societies (León, Baptist, & Contreras, 2012).

This empirical work aims to analyse the presence of concepts related to CSR in the mission and vision of the hundred most important companies in Mexico according to the 2019 ranking of *Expansión* magazine, which organises companies according to their annual sales, covering both for-profit companies and companies that offer a good service and that report income or sales. To carry out this work, a content analysis of the web pages of the organisations studied was undertaken. Subsequently, a literature review was conducted on the different factors involved in CSR, and the different existing definitions were identified for CSR, governance and the SDGs of the 2030 Agenda. Furthermore, their goals and their presence in the strategic planning of the state governments of Mexico were ascertained since this forms a fundamental part of the economic development of the nation. Finally, the results obtained and the conclusions are presented. In this way, it is possible to determine the relationship between companies' commitment to considering CSR in their mission and vision, their compliance with the SDGs regarding economic development and the impact on social rights indicators.

LITERATURE REVIEW

CSR has become an issue of the utmost importance in the daily practice of companies; however, a general and universal consensus cannot be reached because this concept has commonly been linked with the legal commitments and obligations on the part of companies in addition to the ethical ones (Saldarriaga-Ríos, 2013). CSR is an issue that has become the basis for the day-to-day running of companies, as evidenced by the increase in the use of the concept by companies regardless of the sector to which they belong or their size (López-Morales & Ortega-Ridau, 2016).

Currently, CSR is fundamental to the daily life of companies, and the increase in the presence of this term among companies of various sectors and sizes shows that, in the current era, its use by organisations has increased regardless of their type (López-Morales, Ortega-Ridaur, & Ortiz-Betancourt, 2017). A great diversity of works has been published regarding the role of CSR, business strategies, and their presence in the organisational culture of companies (their mission and vision) as well as its relationship with their finances and human factor. The work carried out by Mercado-Salgado and García-Hernández (2007) sought to describe CSR through four components – business ethics, preservation of the environment, quality of life at work and company–society linkage – and found that there is little or even no interest in a CSR culture among companies in the Toluca Valley in Mexico. CSR is a little-addressed area due to the lack of knowledge about the benefits that it brings to companies and that its application should be mandatory (Acosta-Véli, Lovato-Torres, & Buñay-Cantos, 2018).

Each business sector is different, and, for this reason, the influence of CSR on companies in various sectors is perceived differently. Companies with more years of consolidation and a larger size do not show a great interest in issues related to CSR in the food sector since only 20.4% of the companies belonging to this sector have indicated practices that favour CSR (Gaytán-Ramírez & Flores-Villanueva, 2018). Companies in the tourism sector have a good tendency to adopt strategic administration focussed on the management of CSR as they allocate resources to the practices of social actions, mostly aimed at their employees (Martos-Molina, 2018).

The concept of CSR cannot be alien to business strategies since it has an impact on organisations' customers and their satisfaction as well as the environment and the surroundings of the community in which organisations are located (Acosta-Véli et al., 2018). Various authors have carried out studies on the role of CSR in business strategies, specifically in the mission and vision of companies as well as in the impact that it exerts on the human factor. The most relevant definitions in the literature analysed for this work are presented below:

- CSR encompasses the economic, legal, ethical and voluntary or philanthropic expectations that society perceives organisations to have at any given time (Carroll, 1999).
- The corporate philosophy is embraced by an organisation to conduct itself for the benefit of its workers as well as their families and the community to which they belong; not only does it seek customer satisfaction but it also cares for the good of the community through its active involvement (Mercado-Salgado & García-Hernández, 2007).
- In some cases, CSR is seen by companies as a concept that extends beyond just initiatives promoted by marketing or public relations; rather, they identify it as a business opportunity that integrates values, people, community and the environment (Madero & Navarro, 2010).
- It is a concept that has been produced by progressive rationalisation derived from the analysis of the social effects of CSR in organisations and its impact on their financial situation (Calderon-Hernández, Álvarez-Giraldo, & Naranjo-Valencia, 2011).
- It is a concept that is conceived as a very particular method of business management, which is still in training (Volpentesta, 2012).
- It is a way of conducting business that makes the organisation an ally of and jointly responsible for the environment and the social development of its surroundings (Lopes de Oliveira-Filho & Moneva-Abadia, 2013).
- It is understood as the concept that should cause a company to seek social welfare and environmental protection and not only to worry about maximising its economic benefits (Tejedor-Estupiñán, 2015).

- It is a way to generate business in a more humane and transparent way, taking into account various sectors of the public as well as stakeholder theory, business ethics and corporate sustainability (Lizcano-Prada & Lombana, 2018).
- CSR is identified as a certain business strategy identified by a reactive attitude of the company for the benefit of the community and the environment, but it is also identified as a proactive attitude of a company whereby it develops programmes with certain socially responsible actions (Martos-Molina, 2018).

COMPANIES IN MEXICO

One hundred of the most important companies nationally were selected according to the ranking of *Expansión* magazine in relation to the level of annual sales, regardless of whether they provide goods or services and to which of the 27 different productive sectors, such as the financial, assembly, food and steel industries, among several others, they belong. Of the sectors involved in this analysis, 13% of the companies studied belong to the holding sector, this being the sector accounting for the largest number of companies, followed by the financial services sector with 12%. The sectors that represent the lowest percentages are airlines, cement and materials, entertainment, logistics and transport, restaurants, specialised trade, airport services, and glass and packaging, which only represent 1% of the total number of companies.

Once the companies had been catalogued by sector, a content analysis was performed, identifying the words, also known as CSR dimensions, that are expressed in their strategic planning (mission, vision and values) and that correspond to the related dimensions of CSR. These dimensions cover various topics that are directly related to the organisations' fields of action and their interaction with their environment, without overlooking elements such as the environment and laws. Due to this, CSR should be understood as a multi-dimensional concept (Husted & Allen, 2006; Sarmiento, 2008).

GOVERNANCE

Good governance must occur in the proper conducting of democracy to face the challenges posed by postmodernity, despite the lack of public resources (Olivos-Campos, 2013). Hence, governance is understood as the result of the relationships of different social actors with the development of public policies and the execution of processes that direct the attention to objectives allowing the visualisation of the country through cooperation between governmental and non-governmental entities (Martínez-Salvador & Martínez-Salvador, 2021). Governance is defined as the process that regulates the interaction between institutions and social groups of a private or public nature with the firm purpose of achieving objectives collectively through strategic alliances between the different entities that are involved in this process, in which the State must play the role of leader (Katsamunska, 2016; Ramos García, 2017).

To achieve the objectives set by the public administration, there must be more active and increasing participation by citizens to generate and evaluate public policies in association with the government to meet the demands of the population (De la Garza-Montemayor, Yllán-Ramírez, & Barredo-Ibáñez, 2018). In this sense, governance can also be defined as the set of strategies used by the government for the development of public policies that seek better decision-making through planning and the evaluation of results (Caso, 2011).

The term governance is used more frequently in relation to environmental aspects due to the greater participation of social sectors in environmental management; accordingly, there is a tendency to address environmental issues, such as water, with a governance approach that fosters solutions and points of agreement between the government, the private sector (companies) and society (Cáñez-Cota, 2018; Martínez & Espejel, 2015).

SUSTAINABLE DEVELOPMENT GOALS

The 17 SDGs, described in Fig. 1, detail the aspirations in terms of sustainable development for 2030 through the will of governments, companies and society at the global level. For companies, these SDGs represent a great challenge in the adoption of technologies that present sustainable solutions for the world because they are part of the 2030 Agenda, which addresses issues such as poverty, health, education and climate change as well as the degradation of the environment. The

Fig. 1.   The 17 Sustainable Development Goals (SDGs) of the United Nations. *Source:* https://www.un.org/sustainabledevelopment/. 'The content of this publication has not been approved by the United Nations and does not reflect the views of the United Nations or its officials or Member States'.

correct approach to these SDGs can lead companies, regardless of the sector to which they belong, to use them to formalise and redirect their business strategies to allow them to achieve goals that are capitalised in tangible benefits. The SDGs will help to reinforce the economic incentives of companies so that they use their resources more efficiently with the aim of having more sustainable alternatives in conjunction with the development of public policies and, thus, the commitment to customers, the social environment and the environment.

In recent decades, countries and societies have lived under enormous pressure resulting from various factors, such as the serious environmental deterioration to which the planet has been subjected, strong social conflicts and population growth (Pedersen, 2018). Due to this situation, during the second half of 2015, the UN developed the 2030 Agenda for sustainable development, which is made up of 17 SDGs and 169 goals for universal use. The main objective of this agenda is the inclusion of environmental sustainability through concepts that promote development, equality and human rights, among others (Gómez-Lee, 2019). They will help to achieve the fundamental objective of the 2030 Agenda, and, consequently, compliance with the SDGs requires concrete actions focussed on governments, companies and society in general (Caiado, Leal Filho, Quelhas, & De Mattos Nascimento, 2018). One of the areas contemplated in the SDGs is the environment, based on the study and analysis of climate change, pollution, and marine and terrestrial ecosystems, which include aspects related to food, water, health, energy, employment and infrastructure development (Nilsson & Persson, 2017).

METHODOLOGY

Success in achieving the objectives set out in all research work depends on the development of the correct methodology. For this work, a content analysis was carried out; this methodology allows the interpretation of reality through categories from the text to be analysed (Moraima-Campos & Auxiliadora-Mújica, 2008). This type of methodology is a very specific way of analysing ideas expressed in documents through the meaning of words or phrases and enables the internal structure of written information to be revealed (Lopez-Noguero, 2002).

Information about the mission, vision and values of the companies studied was collected by reviewing their web pages, taking into account the various categories related to CSR, such as sustainability, social responsibility, the environment, health, safety at work, education, community well-being, human rights, culture and society/population. The previously defined categories should be clearly expressed or implicitly considered, providing a clear idea of Mexican companies' commitment to issues related to CSR. Subsequently, an analysis was undertaken of the state development plans of the federative entities, commonly called states, that make up Mexico, establishing the presence of each of the SDGs, specifically those that are related to economic development, which are shown in Fig. 2.

Fig. 2.   SDGs Related to Economic Development. *Source:* https://
www.un.org/sustainabledevelopment/. 'The content of this publication has not been
approved by the United Nations and does not reflect the views of the United Nations
or its officials or Member States'.

The state development plan is the legal document in which the actions to be
implemented and developed by the state governments must be established within
the period corresponding to each administration. State governments' planning of
public policies aimed at achieving the SDGs represents a very important element
of the development and implementation of the 2030 Agenda (Ojeda-Medina,
2020). This will allow states, from the planning stage, to establish actions to
achieve the objectives of the 2030 Agenda and therefore the economic development of Mexico as an emerging economy. However, nothing can remain at the
planning stage; it is important that what is planned is carried out, and that is why,
in addition to analysing the state plans, the study took into consideration the
latest report on state governments' activities. With this information, it was
possible to determine the states' real contribution to the achievement of the
SDGs.

RESULTS

Companies' mission and vision are two key elements of their strategies since they
are considered to be fundamental in their strategic planning processes
(López-Morales & Ortega-Ridau, 2016). The first discovery of this work was that
there are companies that still do not contemplate their mission and vision within

an effective strategic plan; the mission is clearly described on the web pages of only 51% of the companies studied, while the vision is only found on the web pages of 41% of the companies. For the development of companies' mission, the dimensions that are most used are the environment, sustainability and social responsibility, while, for the development of their vision, the dimensions of sustainability and social responsibility continue to be evident. This highlights the absence of the environmental dimension in the companies' vision since it is understood that it is a concept that should be present in the pronouncement of companies' future perspective according to the current trends.

It is important to note that the companies belonging to the food, automotive/ auto parts, self-service trade, holding companies, financial services, and steel and metallurgy sectors are the ones that contemplate their vision the most in their strategic planning, with a total of 22 companies. When it comes to addressing their mission, companies belonging to the food, financial services, holding and assembly sectors are the ones that contribute the most in this area, with a total of 22 companies. These results clearly show that sectors such as food, financial services and holding companies are more aware of the importance of the mission and vision in their organisational strategy as well as their valuable contribution to social responsibility.

Another of the main actors in the implementation and fulfilment of the 2030 Agenda and its objectives is the state development plans, in which planning is established towards the achievement of the 17 SDGs. These state plans are broken down into guiding axes from which actions and programmes can be developed. Fig. 3 shows the areas most addressed by the states for the development of their guiding axes.

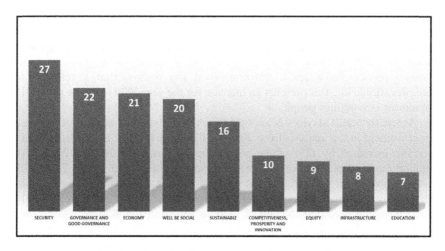

Fig. 3. Items by Strategic Axes. *Source:* Authors.

The economic and sustainability areas are two of the areas analysed for this work that have the largest presence in the strategic axes of the state plans, economy having a presence of 65.6% and sustainability a presence of 50%. The least present items are equity and infrastructure, with 28.12% and 25%, respectively. These items are those that are directly linked to the SDGs focussed on economic development. In general, it can be established that there is, at least on paper, adequate planning taking into account the 2030 Agenda and its SDGs for the economic development of the states and Mexico.

Planning without execution does not make sense, which is why, in addition to reviewing the state plans, a review was undertaken of each state's annual report for the year 2020 to determine whether they have already implemented actions and programmes that, through public policies, contribute to the achievement of the SDGs analysed in this study. Although there are actions focussed on the SDGs in most of the states, only the states of Chihuahua, Hidalgo, the State of Mexico, Morelos, Puebla, Veracruz and Yucatán, through their annual reports, clearly and in detail state how each of the actions carried out will contribute to the achievement of each of the SDGs. Table 1 shows the main actions and programmes established by the states in relation to each of the SDGs studied in this work.

These programmes and actions must be reflected in economic indicators that make it possible to establish that progress is being achieved in these matters. According to data from the National Council for the Evaluation of Social Development Policy (CONEVAL), between 2018 and 2020, the percentage of the population living in poverty rose from 41.9% to 43.9%, which means an increase of 3.8 million people by the end of 2020, as shown in Fig. 4.

On the other hand, there is a population in extreme poverty, which occurs when there are three or more types of social deprivation. This indicator also increased from 2018, when there were 8.7 million people, to 2020, when there were 10.8 million people, representing an increase of 1.5% of the population, as shown in Fig. 5.

The social rights that extreme poverty denies are the educational background, access to health services, access to social security, quality housing spaces, basic housing services and access to nutritious food. Fig. 6 shows that, in reference to the educational lag, this presents an increase for the year 2020 from the year 2018 of almost one million people.

Access to health services is another of the social rights that did not show an improvement in the analysis from 2018 to 2020 since the lack of access to health services increased by 12% of the population; that is, from 2018 to 2020, 15.6 million more people did not receive health services, as shown in Fig. 7.

The third of the social rights that presents an increase in its indicator is access to nutritious and quality food, which increased from 27.5 million people in 2018 to 28.6 million people at the end of 2020, as shown in Fig. 8.

However, there are three indicators that show a reduction in their values in the last two years. The percentage of the population in Mexico that lacked access to

Table 1. Main Programmes and Actions Implemented by State Governments.

SDG	Programmes and Actions Implemented
Affordable and clean energy	• Creation of photovoltaic parks that supply clean energy. • Operation of a wind farm and the installation of solar panels in homes and public schools for the production of clean energy. • Replacement of traditional public lighting with solar energy cells. • Sustainable Energy pilot project 'Light for Isolated Communities'. • Investment in infrastructure for the generation of clean and renewable electricity.
Decent work and economic growth	• Promote the development of micro, small and medium enterprises (MSMEs) that require financial support through loans to start a business. • Through INDEMIPYME, courses, technical advice and assistance offered to MSMEs to solve financing problems. • Promote the generation of formal and well-paid jobs and consolidate strategic economic development projects. • Employment Support Programme promoting the placement of unemployed people in an occupation or productive activity. • Promote the economic and social development of Indigenous communities and encourage the participation of young people in state entrepreneurship programmes in addition to mechanisms to promote investment and job creation.
Industry, innovation and infrastructure	• Infrastructure and equipment works in addition to construction works for pavements, sidewalls, sidewalks, drinking water and sewerage networks. • Creation of the fund for the promotion of the Development of science, technology and innovation in primary Education. • Promote the development of scientific and technological research in formal education institutions at all levels. • Pave streets to improve roads and safety in travel as well as introducing the electric power service and expanding the public lighting network for marginalised areas. • Encourage investment by companies in activities and projects related to research, technological development and innovation through the granting of economic incentives in addition to urban development and territorial planning programmes and the Urban Development Rules of the Territorial Planning Law.
Reduced inequalities	• Support programme for the vulnerable population to support and provide opportunities to aspire to better living conditions. • Construction of 'Specialized Areas for Attention to the Blind and Visually Impaired of the Center for Rehabilitation and Special Education'. • Inclusive and affordable land or Housing Programme to ensure the right to housing of low-income people. • Scholarships for people with disabilities. • Fund for accessibility in Public Transport for People with Disabilities in addition to financial support.
Sustainable cities and communities	• Construction of 84 bathrooms and building of 326 firm ceilings and firm floors; in addition, to reduce the lack of access to basic services in the home, implementation of the ecological stoves Programme. • Housing Programme for everyone and with everyone for the construction, expansion, and/or improvement of housing, investment of resources for the complete renovation of playgrounds with

Table 1. (*Continued*)

SDG	Programmes and Actions Implemented
	universally accessible spaces, as well as the construction, expansion, and conservation of highway sections and roads.
	• Reduce the strategic indicator referring to homes that do not have an electricity service in rural localities and urban neighbourhoods of high marginalisation, taking advantage of alternative energy from renewable sources.
	• State Modernisation Program for Public Registries and Cadastres. Strengthening of the Community cultural Development. Protect, preserve and disseminate the cultural heritage of the state. Design and implementation of public policies in the area of territorial and ecological planning and urban and metropolitan development.
	• Promotion of decent, sustainable and orderly housing for the most disadvantaged segments of the population, promoting sustainable land use planning in the entity that includes the inhabitants of rural and urban areas.
Responsible consumption and production	• Implementation of the State Strategy for Responsible consumption as well as the promotion and establishment of sustainable development programmes and projects through the regulations of the Solid Waste Law to reduce the impacts of single-use plastic.
	• Sustainable production with efficient use of the natural resources of the region, the productive reconversion of blackberries, pomegranates, table grape plants and apple trees to integrated producers, and, derived from the adoption of the sustainable development paradigm in the communities, the reconversion, reforestation and improvement of the environment in the state nurseries.
	• State Environmental Standard NAE-SEMA—DET-010/2019, which establishes the 'criteria and technical environmental specifications for the production of plastic bags for transport and single-use straws that are going to be distributed and/or commercialized in the state of Jalisco'.
	• Implementation of programmes and actions that are aimed at increasing the sustainable production, productivity, profitability and competitiveness of agri-food and livestock activities to generate jobs and income that improve the quality of life of the entity's agricultural and livestock producers.
	• Promote the virtuous circle of investment, employment and the satisfaction of consumption and savings needs of the Queretaro population by sustainably serving regional vocations and economic needs.

Source: Authors.

social security decreased from 53.5% to 52%. The lack of quality and housing spaces decreased by 1.7% between 2018 and 2020 from 13.6 million people to 11.8 million people, and the lack of access to basic services in housing decreased by 1.6 million people between 2018 and 2020, which represents a 1.7% reduction in the population.

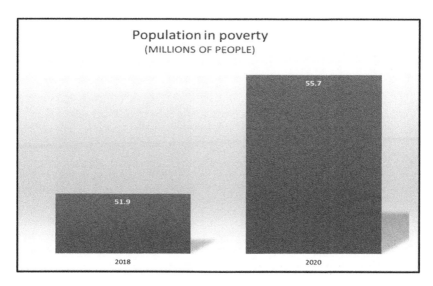

Fig. 4. People in Poverty. *Source:* Own elaboration based on data from CONEVAL. National Council for the Evaluation of Social Development Policy (CONEVAL). https://www.coneval.org.mx/Medicion/MP/Paginas/ Pobreza_2020.aspx.

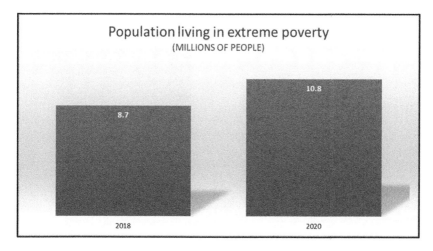

Fig. 5. People in Extreme Poverty. *Source:* Own elaboration based on data from CONEVAL. National Council for the Evaluation of Social Development Policy (CONEVAL). https://www.coneval.org.mx/Medicion/MP/Paginas/ Pobreza_2020.aspx.

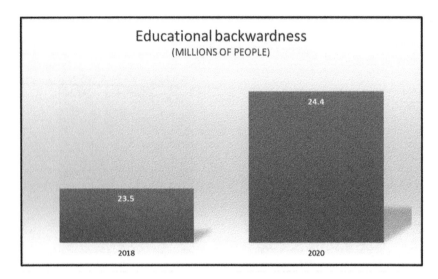

Fig. 6.   People in Educational Trait. *Source:* Own elaboration based on data from CONEVAL. National Council for the Evaluation of Social Development Policy (CONEVAL). https://www.coneval.org.mx/Medicion/MP/Paginas/ Pobreza_2020.aspx.

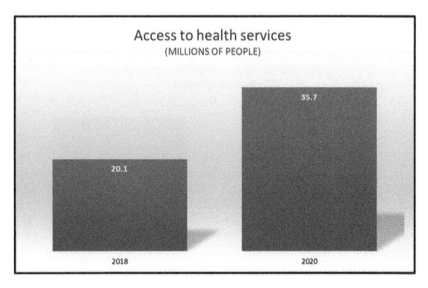

Fig. 7.   People With Deficiencies in Health Services. *Source:* Own elaboration based on data from CONEVAL. National Council for the Evaluation of Social Development Policy (CONEVAL). https://www.coneval.org.mx/Medicion/MP/ Paginas/Pobreza_2020.aspx.

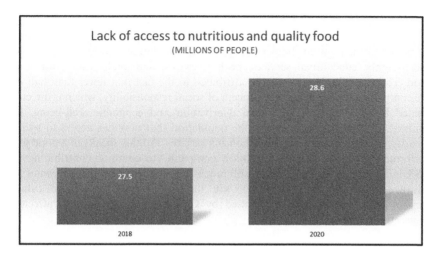

Fig. 8.   People With Deficiencies in Access to Nutritious and Quality Food.
Source: Own elaboration based on data from CONEVAL. National Council for the
Evaluation of Social Development Policy (CONEVAL). https://
www.coneval.org.mx/Medicion/MP/Paginas/Pobreza_2020.aspx.

CONCLUSION

Mexican companies show good progress regarding issues related to CSR, exerting
a positive impact on the Mexican economy. In recent decades, Mexico has been
characterised as a country with an emerging economy, and it has been adapting
to global economic crises and social or health crises, such as the pandemic caused
by COVID-19, which have not fostered economic growth. However, despite each
of these events, Mexico has managed to maintain its position as one of the main
emerging economies in Latin America. Public policies, especially those of local
governments, i.e. the federative entities that make up the Mexican Republic, have
encouraged companies to integrate CSR concepts increasingly into their planning
since, for example, through fiscal incentives, governments support companies that
bring people with disabilities into their ranks or that promote their employment.

Mexico, as a member of the UN, was among the initiating countries of the
2030 Agenda, seeking to achieve the 17 SDGs embodied in this agenda through
joint action with companies and organised society. Of these 17 SDGs, those that
refer to economic development (from 7 to 12) were analysed, and it could be
shown that all the states contemplate in their development plans programmes and
actions that suppose they are working in compliance with the SDGs, although
very few do so clearly and explicitly. Similarly, the annual reports refer to actions
that contribute to the achievement of the SDGs, although only seven states do so
explicitly in relation to the contribution of each action to the indicators that
measure the SDGs.

At the end of 2020, a slight advance can be seen in economic matters since, of the six indicators of social deprivation and economic well-being, only three registered an increase in the percentage of the population that lacked access to social rights: educational services, health services, and quality and nutritious food. These small advances can be attributed to the fact that fewer than half of the companies contemplated the concept of social responsibility, which is directly related to the indicators of social deprivation and economic well-being. In contrast, there was an increase in the population that now has access to social security, quality housing and basic housing services. All this speaks of a good job performed by public policies that allow companies to continue contributing to CSR in Mexico; however, there is still much to be undertaken for companies to advance with respect to CSR. Along with the very little progress, global catastrophes such as the pandemic caused by COVID-19 have seriously affected economies worldwide.

REFERENCES

Acosta-Véli, M., Lovato-Torres, S., & Buñay-Cantos, J. (2018). La responsabilidad social corporativa y su rol en las empresas ecuatorianas. *Lasallista de Investigación*, 105–117. doi:10.22507/rli. v15n2a8

Alvarado-Herrea, A., & Schlesinger-Díaz, M. W. (2008). Dimensionalidad de la responsabilidad social empresarial precibida y sus efectos sobre la imagen y la reputacion: una aproximacion desde el modelo Carroll. *Estudios Gerenciales*, *24*(108), 37–59.

Caiado, R., Leal Filho, W., Quelhas, O., & De Mattos Nascimento, D. (2018). A literature-based review on potentials and constraints in the implementation of the sustainable development goals. *Journal of Cleaner Production*, 1276–1288.

Calderon-Hernández, G., Álvarez-Giraldo, C. M., & Naranjo-Valencia, J. C. (2011). Papel de la gestion humanaen el cumplimiento de la responsabilidad social empresarial. *Estudios Gerenciales*, *27*(118), 163–188.

Cáñez-Cota, A. (2018). Influencia de estructuras de gobernanza internacionales en la política de agua en México. *Norteamérica*, *13*(2), 85–109.

Carroll, A. B. (1999). Corporate social responsibility evolution of a definitional construct. *Business & Society*, 268–295.

Caso, A. (2011). El Presupuesto Basado en Resultados (PbR) y el Sistema de Evaluación del Desempeño (SED) en México: Una Propuesta para Entidades Federativas. En I. N. Pública (Ed.), *La Evaluación de las Políticas Públicas en México* (pp. 313–341). Mexico: Distrito Federal: Secretaria de Hacienda Y Credito Publico.

Christy, J. (15 de Mayo de 2021). https://www.thebalance.com/. Recuperado el 1 de Noviembre de 2021, de. https://www.thebalance.com/top-emerging-market-economies-1979085. https://www.thebalance.com/top-emerging-market-economies-1979085

De la Garza-Montemayor, D. J., Yllán-Ramírez, E., & Barredo-Ibáñez, D. (2018). Tendencias en la administración pública moderna: la nueva gestión pública en México. *evista Venezolana de Gerencia (RVG)*, (81), 31–48.

García-Santos, J. J., & Madero-Gómez, S. M. (2016). La Evolución del Concepto de Responsabilidad Social Corporativa: Revisión literaria. *Conciencia Tecnológica*, (51), 38–46. Retrieved from http://www.redalyc.org/articulo.oa?id=94446004006

Gaytán-Ramírez, M. D., & Flores-Villanueva, C. A. (2018). Factores determinantes en la adopcion de practicas de responsabilidad social empresarial: un analisis sectorialen las franquicias mexicanas. *AD-Minister*, (33), 21–38. doi:10.17230/ad-minister.33.2

Gómez-Lee, M. I. (2019). Agenda 2030 de desarrollo sostenible: comunidad epistémica de los límites planetarios y cambio climático. *Opera*, 69–93.

Husted, B., & Allen, D. (2006). Corporate social responsibility in the multinational enterprise: Strategic and institutional approaches. *Journal of International Business Studies*, 838–849.

Katsamunska, P. (2016). The concept of governance and public governance theories. *Economic Alternatives*, 133–141.

León, M. d., Baptist, M. V., & Contreras, H. (2012). La innovación social en el contexto de la responsabilidad social empresarial. *Forum Empresarial, 17*(1), 31–63.

Lizcano-Prada, J., & Lombana, J. (2018). Responsabilidad social Corporativa (RSC): reconsiderando conceptos y enfoques. *Civilizar Ciencias Sociales y Humanas, 18*(34), 119–134.

Lopes de Oliveira-Filho, M., & Moneva-Abadia, J. M. (2013). El desempeño económico financiero y responsabilidad social corporativa Petrobrás versus Repsol. *Contaduría y Administración, 58*, 131–167.

Lopez-Correa, C., & Patrinos, G. (2018). Chapter 1 genomic medicine in developing and emerging economies: State-of-the-art and future trends. En C. Lopez-Correa & G. P. Patrinos, *Genomic medicine in emerging economies* (pp. 1–12). Londres (Reino Unido): Elsevier.

López-Morales, J. S., & Ortega-Ridau, I. (2016). Presencia de la expansion internacional en la mision y vision de las pricipales empresas privadas y estatales de America Latina. *estudios Gerenciales, 32*(140), 269–277.

López-Morales, J. S., Ortega-Ridaur, I., & Ortiz-Betancourt, I. (2017). Strategies of corporate social responsibility in Latin America: A content analysis in the extractive industry. *AD-Minister*, (31), 115–135. doi:10.17230/ad-minister.31.7

Lopez-Noguero, F. (2002). El Análisis de contenido como método de investigación. *Revista de Educación*, 167–179.

Lozano-Espitia, I., & Melo-Becerra, L. (2012). Flujos de capital y política fiscal en las economías emergentes de América Latina. *Borradores de Economía*, 1–37.

Madero, S., & Navarro, M. (2010). Como se muestra la responsabilidad social en México a traves de internet. Un analisis cualitativo. *EsicMarket*, 91–118.

Martínez-Salvador, L. E., & Martínez-Salvador, C. (2021). Dimensiones de la (in)gobernanza territorial en conflictos socioambientales. Un análisis desde la minería en México. *Región y sociedad, 33*, 2–28.

Martínez, N., & Espejel, I. (2015). La investigación de la gobernanza en México y su aplicabilidad ambiental. *Economía, Sociedad y Territorio, XV*(47), 153–183.

Martos-Molina, M. (2011). La responsabilidad social corporativa en la gestion hotelera. *Turismo y Sociedad, 12*, 169–184.

Martos-Molina, M. (2018). Responsabilidad social corporativa y turismo. ¿Realidad o Postureo? *Turismo y Sociedad, 22*, 25–44. doi:10.18601/01207555.n22.02

Mercado-Salgado, P., & García-Hernández, P. (2007). La responsabilidad social en empresas del vallede Toluca (México). Un estudio exploratorio. *Estudios Gerenciales, 23*(102), 119–135.

Moraima-Campos, M., & Auxiliadora-Mújica, L. (2008). El análisis de contenido: una forma de abordaje metodológico. *Laurus Revista de Educación, 14*(27), 129–144.

Nilsson, M., & Persson, Å. (2017). Policy note: Lessons from environmental policy integration for the implementation of the 2030 Agenda. *Environmental Science & Policy*, 36–39.

Ojeda-Medina, T. (2020). El rol estratégico de los gobiernos locales y regionales en la implementación de la Agenda 2030: experiencias desde la cooperación Sur-Sur y triangular. *Oasis*, 9–29.

Olivos-Campos, J. (2013). Gobernación municipal en México: alcances y desafíos. *IUS. Revista del Instituto de Ciencias Jurídicas de Puebla A.C.*, 118–147.

Pedersen, C. (2018). The UN Sustainable Development Goals (SDGs) are a great gift to business. *ScienceDirect*, 21–24.

Ramos García, J. M. (2017). Las entidades de la frontera norte y la Agenda 2030: retos para una gobernanza para el desarrollo. *Secuencia*, 228–256.

Saldarriaga-Ríos, j. G. (2013). Responsabilidad social y gestión del conocimiento como estrategias de gestión humana. *Estudios Gerenciales*, 110–117.

Saldívar, B. (26 de Mayo de 2021). https://www.eleconomista.com.mx/. Recuperado el 1 de Noviembre de 2021, de. https://www.eleconomista.com.mx/economia/Mexico-es-el-pais-emergente-que-mas-se-beneficiara-de-la-recuperacion-en-EU-Fitch-20210526-0055.html. https://www.

eleconomista.com.mx/economia/Mexico-es-el-pais-emergente-que-mas-se-beneficiara-de-la-recuperacion-en-EU-Fitch-20210526-0055.html

Sarmiento, N. (2008). ¿Bondad o estrategia? Tejiendo responsabilidad social en el mundo del carbón. *Colombia*, (67), 132–151.

Tejedor-Estupiñán, J. M. (2015). La responsabilidad social corporativa y su aporte a la economía. *Finanzas y Política Económica*, *7*(1), 11–14. doi:10.14718/revnanzpolitecon.2015.7.1.1

Volpentesta, J. R. (2012). Las acciones sociales en empresas con responsabilidad social. *Visión de Futuro*, *16*(2). Retrieved from http://revistacientifica.fce.unam.edu.ar/index.php?option=com_content&view=article&id=302

CORPORATE SOCIAL RESPONSIBILITY DOES NOT AVERT THE TRAGEDY OF THE COMMONS – CASE STUDY: COCA-COLA INDIA*

Aneel Karnani

ABSTRACT

'Tragedy of the commons' is a powerful concept to analyse a variety of problems related to environmental sustainability. The commons problem can be solved if individuals behave altruistically. In the business context, this chapter studies the proposition that corporate social responsibility (CSR) can avert the tragedy of the commons by examining one case study in depth: Coca-Cola's bottling operations in Rajasthan, India. In spite of choosing a context favourable to the proposition, the results indicate that CSR does not avert the tragedy of the commons. To address the major environmental challenges, it is essential to develop regulatory regimes with appropriate incentives and ability to enforce sanctions.

Keywords: Corporate social responsibility; tragedy of the commons; common-pool resource; environmental sustainability; tragedy of the commons; regulatory regime

In one of the most cited scientific articles ever written, Garrett Hardin outlined 'the tragedy of the commons', a powerful metaphor that the users of a commons are caught in an inevitable process that leads to the destruction of the very

---

*This chapter has been previously published in *Economics, Management, and Financial Markets*, Vol. 9(3), 2014. It has also been published in the form of a case study: 'Coca-Cola Bottling in Rajasthan, India: Tragedy of the Commons'. WDI Publishing, 2014. https://wdi-publishing.com/product/coca-cola-bottling-in-rajasthan-india-tragedy-ofthecommons/.

Strategic Corporate Responsibility and Green Management
Critical Studies on Corporate Responsibility, Governance and Sustainability, Volume 16, 39–58
Copyright © 2023 by Emerald Publishing Limited
All rights of reproduction in any form reserved
ISSN: 2043-9059/doi:10.1108/S2043-905920230000016003

resource on which they depend.[1] It is now a central concept in human ecology and the study of the environment, and can be used to view a variety of commons-related problems, such as population growth, environmental pollution, groundwater basins, forest management, climate change, fishing, wildlife habitats and traffic congestion. The prediction of the inevitable tragedy assumes that all individuals are inherently selfish. The tragedy of the commons, of course, can be averted if individuals behave altruistically, and voluntarily act in the interests of others in the wider community. Translating this to the business context, the tragedy of the commons can be averted if companies have a corporate social responsibility (CSR) to go beyond making profits and achieve some positive social goals.

This chapter studies the proposition that CSR can avert the tragedy of the commons by examining a case study in depth. I chose a case study – Coca-Cola's bottling operations in Rajasthan, India – that is favourable to the proposition. The company Coca-Cola, both globally and in India, vociferously proclaims to be socially responsible. Since water is the critical input to Coca-Cola's operations, it is not surprising that the company emphasises its water stewardship efforts, especially in the desert location of Rajasthan. In spite of choosing a context favourable to the proposition, the results indicate that CSR does not avert the tragedy of the commons.

Following Hardin's famous article, there is a vast literature on managing the commons. I provide a very brief overview of the critical concepts for solving the commons problem, and translate these ideas to the business context. There is also a vast literature on CSR, and the next section provides a brief overview of this concept, and links together these two fields. The rest of the chapter describes the case study and draws conclusions about the effectiveness of CSR for averting the tragedy of the commons.

THE TRAGEDY OF THE COMMONS

Hardin explained the tragedy of the commons using the fable of a pasture open to all. Each herdsman 'rationally' adds more sheep because his expected benefits are greater than expected costs, since he selfishly ignores the costs imposed on the others. Thus, individual decisions cumulate to tragic overuse and the potential destruction of the commons. Subsequent research has argued that it is necessary to distinguish between the intrinsic nature of the resource and the property regime under which it is held.[2] Common-pool resources (CPRs) are characterised by (1) difficulty of excluding beneficiaries through physical and institutional means and (2) subtractability, that is use by an individual reduces resources available to others. The literature identifies four types of property rights: open access (that is, no property rights), individual property, group property and government property.

Hardin has been criticised for confounding the intrinsic nature of the resource and the regime under which it is held. As Hardin later acknowledged, his argument applies to an open access CPR, or an 'unregulated commons'.[3] In the absence of rules for managing the CPR, the fundamental problem is free riding along two dimensions: overuse without concern for the adverse effect on others and a lack of contributions to maintain and improve the CPR. Solving CPR problems involves two distinct elements: restricting access and creating incentives for users to invest in the CPR.

Altruism

A critical assumption underlying Hardin's reasoning is that individuals are inherently selfish, 'locked into a system that compels' them to pursue their own best interest. It is ineffective for society to appeal to an 'individual exploiting a commons to restrain himself for the general good by means of his conscience'. Using Darwinian logic, Hardin argued that 'such an appeal is to set up a selective system that works towards the elimination of the conscience from the race'.

The tragedy of the commons, of course, can be averted if individuals voluntarily act in the interests of others in the wider community.[4] Many scholars have argued that this seems to the normal mode of human behaviour. Human beings are prone to altruism, or concern for others. According to the US Department of Labour, about 65 million people volunteered at least once in 2011, at the median rate of 51 hours per year. Most, if not all, of the world's religions promote altruism as a very important moral value. A stream of research on reciprocal altruism is based on the theory of repeated games and shows that 'cooperation based on reciprocity can get started in a predominantly noncooperative world, can thrive in a variegated environment, and can defend itself once fully established'.[5] Contemporary discussions of altruism are often based on evolutionary theories such as reciprocal altruism and kin selection.[6] Some evolutionary biologists go so far as to argue that 'morality is grounded in our biology'.[7]

However, the rational actor model that posits strict self-interest dominates the field of economics and is also influential in other fields including political science, sociology, ecology and psychology. As Adam Smith said 'we are not ready to suspect any person of being defective in selfishness'.[8] This rational actor model explains why market institutions facilitate an efficient allocation of private goods and is supported by much empirical research. It is not surprising that the bulk of research, especially in economics and political science, on solving CPR problems eschews altruism and focusses on property regimes.

Property Regimes

When a CPR is left to an open-access regime, that is, there are no enforced property rights, it results in degradation and destruction of the resource. In individual property regimes, resource rights are held by individuals who can exclude others; an example might be private ownership of grazing land bounded by a fence. For most CPRs, individual privatisation is not a feasible option in practice; as an extreme example, it would be impossible to privatise the earth's ozone layer. Accordingly, most research on CPR problems does not consider this a viable solution. In group property regimes, resource rights are held by a group of users who can exclude others and manage the CPR using various mechanisms such as communication, trust, reciprocity, reputation, sanctions and binding commitments. Elinor Ostrom, Nobel Prize economist, has studied a large number of commons problems in fisheries, grazing, forests and irrigation systems and shows how groups of users have developed local (as opposed to governmental) institutional arrangements to successfully manage CPRs.[9] User groups charac- terised by the presence of a community, small and stable populations, a thick social network and social norms promoting conservation do better at establishing effective group rights schemes. In government property regimes, resource rights are held by a government (central or a lower level) that can regulate the CPR and enforce incentives such as taxes and subsidies. For example, the government in Singapore imposes a toll on traffic in the central business district to control congestion. Empirical research has demonstrated that no property regime works well for all CPRs, and problems continue to exist in all property regimes. Elinor Ostrom has identified design principles associated with institutions that have successfully managed CPRs, with a special focus on group property regimes.[10]

The world's fisheries are in serious trouble due to overexploitation. In an open access regime, each fisherman has an incentive to 'race to fish' to outcompete the other fishermen, leading to eventual collapse of the fishery – the tragedy of the commons. In a widely cited study, Worm et al. estimated that about 27% of the world's fisheries were collapsed in 2003, and extrapolated the trend to predict that 100% of the world's fisheries could be collapsed by 2048.[11] The best way to protect the fisheries is to give the fishermen well-defined, long-term property rights to a share of the fish. In government-regulated fisheries, as in Iceland and New Zealand, this has taken the form of a tradable share of a fishing quota.[12] In other countries, especially developing countries, some fisheries are governed by a group property regime that gives rights over an expanse of coastal waters to a cooperative or fishing community, which then gives each licenced fisherman a fraction of the catch. Costello et al. studied 11,135 commercial fisheries around the world between 1950 and 2003 and found that the collapse rate was cut in half among the fisheries managed by government or group property regime compared to open access fisheries.[13] This supports the view that altruism does not effectively help avert the tragedy of the commons, whereas group and government property regimes are effective. Although the global rate of adoption of rights-based approach has increased since 1970, unfortunately the spread of such schemes has been very slow. The study identified only 121 fisheries (out of 11,135) managed using a share of the catch schemes in 2003.

Business Context

Neither Hardin nor most of the subsequent literature on managing CPRs explicitly analyse the situation when the users are modern corporations owned by shareholders and run by professional managers. Corporations are even less inclined to act altruistically to preserve the CPRs in open access regimes. According to neoliberal economic perspective, company managers have a fidu- ciary responsibility to their shareholders to maximise profits while conforming to the laws and norms of society.[14] The modern business corporation is 'the one important actor in our market economy that *does* match Hardin's depiction of the implacably rational, self-interested economic agent'.[15] So, it would seem that Hardin's dire prediction of the tragedy of the commons applies even more in an economic landscape populated by publicly traded companies.

The contrary, and more optimistic, view is that companies have a corporate social responsibility (CSR) and 'decide voluntarily to contribute to a better society and a cleaner environment'.[16] Thus, CSR is the corporate counterpart of altruism at the individual level, and will help avert the tragedy of the commons in a business context.[17] There is a vast literature on CSR, and simultaneously much controversy surrounding the concept.[18]

Corporate Social Responsibility

For CSR to move beyond empty platitudes, it is necessary to clearly distinguish between socially desirable activities that are profitable and those that are unprofitable for the firm involved.[19] Much of the contemporary literature on CSR emphasises its positive links to profitability.[20] The business case for CSR states that as companies behave more responsibly, they also become more profitable. One such recent article in the *Harvard Business Review* states 'executives behave as though they have to choose between the largely social benefits of developing sustainable products or processes and the financial costs of doing so. But that's simply not true'.[21] Another article in the *Harvard Business Review* proposes 'a new way to look at the relationship between business and society that does not treat corporate success and social welfare as a zero-sum game'.[22] Much of the popular business literature exhorting firms to be socially responsible is in this vein and assumes, at least implicitly, that all socially desirable behaviour is perfectly consistent with the firms' self-interest. This, of course, is contrary to the very concept of a CPR, which is characterised by a free-rider problem. The essence of a CPR problem is that in an open access regime the interests of one user are not congruent with the collective interests of society. Many contemporary societal problems clearly involve a CPR, and this view of CSR will not avert the tragedy of the commons.

For CSR to help avert the tragedy of the commons, it is necessary to define CSR as a company's responsibility to voluntarily undertake socially desirable behaviour that decreases the firm's profits.[23] Only then does CSR become the business equivalent of altruism at the individual level, and help avert the tragedy of the commons. It is an empirical question whether firms in fact do practice (and not just proclaim) CSR and help avert the tragedy of the commons. The case study described below examines this proposition in the context of Coca-Cola India's bottling operations in Rajasthan, India.

The alternative to CSR for averting the tragedy of the commons is a property regime to manage the CPR (see Table 1). Due to the very nature of a CPR (especially a large, complex CPR), it is rarely feasible to assign property rights to firms individually. Moreover, private ownership by large corporations of a CPR, which are often perceived as public goods, would be politically difficult in most

Table 1. Solving the CPR Problem.

Regime	Context of Individuals	Business Context
Open access	Altruism. Very few examples of success.	CSR. More research needed.
Private property	Individual(s) own the CPR (e.g. grazing land). Necessary condition: Technologically feasible to easily exclude others.	Firm(s) own the CPR. Unlikely to be technically feasible. More importantly, unlikely to be politically feasible.
Group property	Many successful examples, almost all at level of local communities. Necessary condition: 'thick' community capable of fostering trust, making binding commitments and enforcing sanctions.	Self-regulation. Unlikely to be successful without enforcement mechanisms, particularly for large, complex CPR. Difficult to develop a 'thick' community among firms.
Government property	Many successful examples. Necessary condition: Competent government.	Many successful examples. Necessary condition: Competent government. Particularly difficult if the CPR cuts across national boundaries.

democratic countries. Most examples of successful group property schemes have been in the context of very local communities, such as villages in Switzerland and Nepal.[24] People live in the same village for generations and intend to live there for generations to come. The use of community sanctions and social pressure was an important element of the group property regime, as were communication, trust, reputation and anticipation of future interactions. All these elements are difficult to establish in the business context, making group property rights a less viable solution. Ostrom et al. acknowledge that the 'humanity now faces new challenges to establish global institutions to manage biodiversity, climate change, and other ecosystem services', and that these challenges will be particularly difficult because of the scale of the problem, cultural diversity, complexity of interlinked CPRs, accelerating rates of change and need for unanimity. Thus, developing group property regimes in a business context with modern corporations will be rather difficult. It is not surprising that the success record of self-regulation by industries has been mixed at best.[25] Government property regime is in a sense the ultimate solution because the government has the legitimate power of coercion to enforce the rules. Hardin referred to this as 'mutual coercion, mutually agreed upon by the majority of the people affected'. It is the role and the responsibility of the government in a democratic society to manage the CPRs; a necessary condition for this to succeed, of course, is a competent government.

CASE STUDY: COCA-COLA INDIA

Social activists have long levelled various accusations against Coca-Cola, such as human rights abuses in Colombia, waste-disposal practices in India and groundwater depletion in India.[26] This chapter examines in depth only one issue: groundwater use at one location, Kaladera, in the state of Rajasthan in India. According to the *Wall Street Journal*, 'numerous NGOs both inside and outside India accuse Coke, among other 'crimes', of sucking local Indian communities dry through excessive pumping' of groundwater.[27] There were protests against Coca-Cola in Plachimada, Kerala, starting in 2002. There has been a long running legal dispute between the Kerala government and the company; the plant has been closed since 2004. There were similar protests that Coca-Cola bottling plants deplete the groundwater supply in Mehndiganj (Uttar Pradesh) and in Kaladera (Rajasthan). India Resource Center, a small NGO, has been a prominent critic of Coca-Cola India. Students Organizing for Labor and Economic Equality at the University of Michigan picked up on several accusations by social activists against Coca-Cola, and in 2004 formally requested the University of Michigan to cease doing business with Coca-Cola.[28] After a short suspension in 2006, the University resumed doing business with Coca-Cola, after the company agreed to the University's demand for an independent assessment, which was performed by The Energy and Resources Institute (TERI), a prestigious Delhi-based, not-for-profit, policy research organisation. The TERI report was a particularly useful source for this chapter.[29]

The in-depth case research in this chapter is based primarily on personal interviews. I visited Delhi and Rajasthan for two weeks in 2011, and interviewed several Coca-Cola India executives both at the country headquarters in Delhi and the bottling plant in Rajasthan, government officials at both the federal and state levels, local farmers and village leaders in Kaladera, and NGOs concerned about the water situation in India. All data and statements obtained from Coca-Cola India executives and used in this chapter were confirmed by the company in written emails, which are available from the author.

The Coca-Cola case was chosen precisely because the company vociferously proclaims its social responsibility. Muhtar Kent, Chairman and CEO, states, 'We support the United Nations Global Compact, and see our sustainability efforts first and foremost as the right thing to do – the continuation of responsible corporate citizenship that began in our earliest days as a company'.[30] It should be noted that Muhtar Kent does not make a 'business case for CSR', and instead defines CSR along the lines of this article. Coca-Cola India's website claims that 'The Coca-Cola Company has always placed high value on good citizenship. ... Coca-Cola India provides extensive support for community programs across the country, with a focus on education, health and water conservation'.[31] Several Coca-Cola India executives I met had business cards with some CSR slogan printed on the reverse side; here is one example: 'Live Positively is our commitment to making a positive difference in the world so that sustainability is part of everything we do. Forever'.

Given the nature of the company's products, it has appropriately focussed its sustainability efforts on water resources. Muhtar Kent states, 'At The Coca-Cola Company, we are transforming the way we think and act about water steward-ship. It is in the long-term interest of both our business and the communities where we operate to be good stewards of our most critical shared resource, water'.[32] The company claims that water stewardship 'is now clearly embedded in both our business strategy and our vision for sustainable business growth'.

WATER CRISIS

The world faces a water crisis. According to the United Nations Environmental Program, 200 scientists in 50 countries identified water shortage as one of the two most worrying problems for this millennium (the other was global warming).[33] The World Water Council believes that by 2020 we shall need 17% more water than available to feed the world. Today, one person in seven in the world does not have access to safe drinking water, and one in three lacks safe sanitation.[34] Compared to many other countries, India faces a more imminent water crisis. 'China's 1.33 billion people each have 2,117 cubic meters of water available per year, compared with 1,614 cubic meters in India and as much as 9,943 cubic meters in the U.S., according to the Food and Agriculture Organization of the United Nations. The 1.2 billion people in India, where farmers use 80% of available water, will exhaust their freshwater supplies by 2050 at the current rate, the World Bank estimates'.[35] The water crisis is predictably worse in the desert state of Rajasthan, where surface water is meagre and the entire state is princi-pally dependent on subterranean groundwater. Rajasthan has semi-arid to arid climate, and experiences frequent droughts (46 times during 1901–2002).[36]

The village of Kaladera (where the Coca-Cola plant is located), in the Jaipur district of Rajasthan, sits atop groundwater aquifers, which support many neighbouring towns and villages. The Kaladera watershed, comprising an area of 309 square kilometres, was officially designated as 'overexploited' – that is, the withdrawal rate exceeds the natural recharge rate – by the Central Ground Water Board in 1998.[37] The TERI study in 2006 independently confirmed that the annual extraction of groundwater is 'at least 1.35 times' the natural recharge rate; the government statistics indicate the exploitation ratio was 2.47 in 2004.[38] The groundwater level in Kaladera has dropped significantly from about 9 to 39 m below ground level in the last 20 years (see Fig. 1). The rate of decline, which averaged 0.5 m per year during 1984–1996, accelerated to 1.4 m per year during 1996–2006, according to the State Groundwater Department; Fig. 1 indicates further acceleration since 2006.

The decline in the water table has clearly had a negative impact on the people (mostly farmers) living in the Kaladera area. The farmers said their livelihood had been affected due to increased cost of irrigation: they had to dig deeper wells and purchase more powerful pumps. More land was left fallow because of inadequate water supply for irrigation. They felt that the crop yield levels had been reduced, although there was no hard empirical evidence. The women

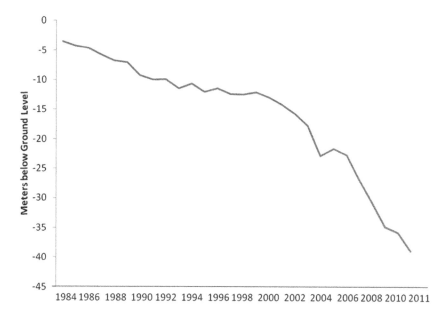

Fig. 1. Groundwater Levels in Kaladera Area. *Source:* Central
Groundwater Board (available at: http://gis2.nic.in/cgwb/Gemsdata.aspx), and
Rajasthan Groundwater Department.

emphasised that the water crisis had reduced their availability of water for
drinking and domestic purposes, and they had to spend more time and effort
fetching water. The women claimed that the yield of milk had gone down because
they could not provide enough water to their cattle.

Causes of the Water Crisis

Some of the stakeholders felt that one of the causes of the water crisis was
reduced rainfall in recent years, but the empirical data do not support this
explanation. The area has experienced mild to moderate droughts for eight of the
past 25 years, but this is not abnormal given the even longer-term pattern cited
earlier.[39] The problem is the high variance in annual rainfall. The Kaladera area
receives long-term average rainfall of about 600 mm per year, with a standard
deviation of about 175 mm.

The real cause of the water crisis has been the increasing extraction of
groundwater in the Kaladera area, which in turn is due to several factors. Water
demand has grown along with population growth in the region of about 2.6% per
year. Higher household incomes and changes in lifestyle increasingly involve
water-intensive activities. The pace of urbanisation, about 10–15% per decade,
has also contributed to the growing water demand. Although no quantitative
data are available, all stakeholders agreed that there has been a significant
increase in the number of bore wells both for agricultural and industrial purposes.

While there has been a gradual shift towards industrial and service sectors, this is still mostly a rural area, and agriculture continues to be the predominant occupation. The TERI study estimated that in the Kaladera area, total groundwater extraction is about 50 million cubic metres per year, and that agriculture accounts for about 91% of total groundwater extraction, and domestic and industrial uses for the remaining 9%. The gross area under cultivation and cropping intensity both have increased over the past three decades. Farmers increasingly utilise electric pumps, more powerful pumps, and deeper wells contributing to growing water extraction. Cropping patterns in the region have shifted towards cultivation of water-intensive crops like groundnut, mustard, wheat and millet. The problem has been exacerbated by the spread of free or vastly discounted electricity for farmers, who often pump out more water than needed. 'A favourite boon of politicians courting the rural vote, the low rates have encouraged farmers to pump out groundwater with abandon'.[40] Since electricity is unreliable and free, many farmers leave their pumps on all the time, thus wasting water, according to many of my interview subjects.

The Coca-Cola plant was established in 1999 in an industrial park operated by the Rajasthan State Industrial Development & Investment Corporation (RIICO), a state government agency. The Coca-Cola plant has four bore wells that are 100 m deep, but operates only two wells at a given time. It is not the only water-dependent factory in the park; others include Rajshri pulp, Oswal paper, Rajasthan liquors and MRK pipes. In its early years of operation, the Coca-Cola plant withdrew about 200,000 cubic metres of groundwater per year, which is about 0.4% of total groundwater extraction in the Kaladera area.[41] In recent years, Coca-Cola has reduced its water usage to about 100,000 cubic metres annually, and therefore might account for about 0.2% of total water extraction. Even at its current levels, Coca-Cola is one of the largest users of groundwater in the Kaladera area, and might be the single largest user. It is certainly perceived by the local people as the largest user of water. Coca-Cola's water consumption can be decomposed into the volume of beverages produced and the water usage ratio (defined as water consumed divided by volume of beverages produced). The production volume, of course, is driven by market demand in the region; the plant has always operated at about 30% or less of its installed annual capacity. The water usage ratio has come down steadily over the last 10 years from about 4.0 to about 2.0. While Coca-Cola has implemented various measures to improve its water efficiency, the largest factor driving down the water usage ratio is the shift from refillable glass bottles to plastic (polyethylene terephthalate) bottles, which significantly reduces the water needed to wash the bottles. Thus, the Coca-Cola plant has reduced its groundwater extraction by about half in the last several years, but at the expense of increasing the problem of non-degradable plastic bottles.

Coca-Cola's negative impact on the groundwater aquifer is compounded by the fact that its peak production, and hence its water extraction, occurs in the summer months April-June, which coincides with the acute water stress period in the region. At the localised level, defined as 2 km radius around the plant, the TERI study estimated that the Coca-Cola plant accounts for less than 2.7% of total water extraction 70% of the time, and less than 0.9% for 40% of the time. At its worst, in May 2004, the Coca-Cola plant alone accounted for about 8% of the total water extraction at the localised level.

Unregulated Commons

The law in India historically has been that access to and use of groundwater is a right of the landowner; there are no restrictions at all on who can pump groundwater, how much and for what purpose.[42] As result of the rapid expansion of groundwater use and the depleting supply, the central government has tried since the 1970s to persuade the states to adopt groundwater legislation. In general, water law in India is largely based at the state level. A few states (such as Kerala) only recently have adopted groundwater acts, but Rajasthan is not one of them.

The Planning Commission of the Government of India issued in 1997 a Report of the Expert Group on 'Ground Water Management and Ownership' that argued that 'since ground water is an open access resource, the tragedy of the commons often occurs where everyone tries to extract as much water as she can and degrades the resource'.[43] The report concluded, 'the Central Government has the obligation to see that groundwater use does not lead to environmental degradation'. However, there has been no action (except very recently – see the Epilogue at the end of this chapter). In response to my question about the lack of an appropriate regulatory regime, the chairman of the Central Ground Water Board replied, 'we are thinking about it'.

The state government of Rajasthan draughted in 1999 a State Water Policy to manage and regulate water resources. In its current version, the policy states that 'planning and development of water resources needs to be governed by the state's perspective' to ensure 'a judicious and equitable, and sound economic' allocation of water resources to different sectors: drinking water, irrigation, power generation and industrial, in that order of priorities.[44] 'Exploitation of groundwater resources should be so regulated as not to exceed recharging possibilities, and also to ensure social equity'. The policy advocates, 'water rates shall be so decided that it conveys the scarcity value of water to users and foster the motivation for economy in water usage'. The state government should prepare projects for artificial recharge of groundwater. All these recommendations are obviously sensible, but none have been enacted so far. Thus, in Rajasthan all landowners (homeowners, farmers and businesses) legally can extract as much groundwater as they like without concern for other users.

The Kaladera area was assessed to be 'overexploited' by the Central Ground Water Board in 1998. The Coca-Cola plant was established in the RIICO industrial park in 1999 and commenced production in 2000. The plant sunk four bore wells, and had permission for a maximum of five wells. It is not clear why RIICO gave this permission. The TERI report speculates about the lack of coordination between the Central Ground Water Board, the Central Ground Water Agency, the State Ground Water Department and RIICO. When I asked the head of the State Ground Water Department about the role of his department in the RIICO permission, he replied that he did not know since it was before his time, and he 'guessed' that his department had not been involved. Finally in 2004-05 RIICO refused to permit establishment of water-intensive industry in the area.

Plant Location

Since Coca-Cola claims to be socially responsible, one might expect that the company would not locate a water-intensive plant in a water-stressed area. I asked Coca-Cola India executives why the company had located the plant in Kaladera after the government had officially declared the area to be water 'overexploited'. Their response was 'consistent with our Company requirements, Environmental Due Diligence was conducted before we set up operations. The plant was set up after obtaining all necessary clearances from the relevant departments of the government. We do not share due diligence reports externally. These reports may contain sensitive information of both – business and legal nature'. The TERI study cites a similar response from the company on this topic. This lack of explanation, let alone a socially responsible explanation, reduces the credibility of Coca-Cola's CSR statements.

A plausible argument is that it is unfair to criticise Coca-Cola for its decision in 1999 to locate the plant in Kaladera, since that pre-dated the company's current emphasis on water stewardship. In 2002, in an effort to move towards more sustainable operations management, the company published its first environmental report.[45] In 2003, the company announced an Environment and Water Resources Department and appointed Jeff Seabright as a vice president to head the department. When asked to explain the firm's new global water strategy, Jeff Seabright told *The Economist* in 2005 that, 'water is to Coca-Cola as clean energy is to BP', using an unfortunate choice of analogy.[46] It is possible that awareness and actions about environmental sustainability at the Indian subsidiary lagged these initiatives at the global corporate level. The counterargument would be that the issue of water scarcity, especially in Rajasthan, was quite obvious even in 1999, and a socially responsible company would not have located a water intensive plant in that area, and that the current proclamations about water stewardship are just a public relations strategy in response to social activism – so-called 'greenwash'.

Even more curious than the state government permitting a Coca-Cola plant in a water-stressed area is the fact that the state government gave a tax incentive to Coca-Cola. Coca-Cola India executives stated that 'according to the tax incentive schedule of the Government of Rajasthan, Hindustan Coca-Cola Beverages [a wholly-owned subsidiary of the company] was entitled to sales tax incentive of an amount equivalent to the investment for setting up the green field plant amounting to Rs. 39 crores [about $9.1 million, in 1999]'. It would have been more logical for the Rajasthan government to exclude water-intensive businesses from the general economic development incentives. A profit maximising company would be expected to exploit the government's perverse incentive system. The fact that the government scheme set the incentive amount equal to the investment in the plant might also explain why Coca-Cola built a plant with so much excess capacity.

KALADERA PLANT

The TERI report recommended that Coca-Cola evaluate its options for the Kaladera plant, 'such as:

- Transport water from the nearest aquifer that may not be stressed (could be quite a distance form the existing plant)
- Store water from low-stress seasons (may not exist!)
- Relocate the plant to a water-surplus area
- Shut down this facility'.

In spite of the fact that Coca-Cola chose TERI to conduct the independent assessment, the company has rejected these four alternatives. Instead the company argues that its Kaladera plant is completely consistent with its CSR and water stewardship policies. First, the company argues that its plant's 'water consumption is very limited and has no impact or very minimal impact on the local ground water regime'. Second, the company claims it has built rain water harvesting structures around Kaladera that recharge the groundwater aquifers with 15 times the volume of the water extracted by the plant. Both these arguments are problematic.

Small User

The argument that Coca-Cola is a small user of groundwater is conceptually flawed. As Hardin explained in his seminal paper, each user of a CPR sees his impact on the resource as being small – that is the nature of a CPR.[47] The aggregate impact of all users thinking like this is exactly what leads to the tragedy of the commons. Aside from this, Coca-Cola's argument about being a small user is also empirically flawed.

Coca-Cola India cites a Central Ground Water Board study that the total groundwater extraction in 2005 was divided as follows: 95.06% for irrigation, 4.33% for domestic use, and only 0.61% for industrial use. These numbers are somewhat more 'favourable' to industrial use, and hence to Coca-Cola, than the TERI numbers (9% for domestic and industrial use combined). In a letter to the University of Michigan, the company stated 'Coca-Cola is a relatively small user of water in Kaladera; the plant taps far less than 1% of the area's available water'.[48] At the other extreme, Coca-Cola's external affairs manager for Northern India told a reporter that the Kaladera plant accounted for '3% of the area's groundwater'.[49] I estimated above that the Coca-Cola plant accounted for 0.2%–0.4% of total water extraction. Overall, the Coca-Cola plant probably accounts for somewhere between 0.2 and 1.0% of the total water extraction in the area.[50] The TERI report concluded that the plant's operations in Kaladera 'would continue to be one of the contributors to a worsening water situation and a source of stress to the communities around'. It is clearly true that agriculture accounts for the bulk of groundwater extraction, and this use alone exceeds the natural recharge rate of the Kaladera aquifers.

But that does not mean we should not pay any attention to the other lower usages of groundwater. Agriculture supports far more people and livelihoods than does industry in the Kaladera area, and it is necessary to 'normalise' the water usage by taking that into account. The Kaladera watershed in 2001 had a population of over 620,000 people, and more than 92,000 farmers. By comparison, the Coca-Cola plant, which is quite mechanised, employs about 70–250 people, depending on the season, with higher employment in the peak summer months. As a rough calculation, assume that domestic use accounts for 4% of total water consumption, Coca-Cola employs 150 people at its plant, and agriculture supports 92,000 livelihoods (ignoring the fact many family members usually work on the family farm – an assumption generous to Coca-Cola), then the plant would be 'entitled' to only 0.15% of total water usage. Thus, the Coca-Cola plant is not a low user of groundwater compared to this 'entitlement' calculated on a per person basis. Moreover, according to the government policy the priorities for water use are: drinking, agriculture, power generation and industrial, in that order. This would further reduce industry's, and Coca-Cola's, 'entitlement' of water. And within the industrial sector, it is unlikely that the Indian society would rate carbonated soft drinks as a high priority.

Rain Water Harvesting

Coca-Cola has built 140 rain water harvesting (RWH) structures (mostly recharge shafts dug into the ground) in the Kaladera area, but how much water they recharge into the aquifers is contentious. The TERI assessment found that, during field visits to randomly selected shafts they were 'all in a dilapidated state'. The company told TERI that maintenance of the structures had been included as a CSR target plan for 2007. I visited a RWH structure on the roof of a school, and all the pipes were broken making it impossible for it to collect any rainwater. I also visited a recharge shaft that was clogged up and could not function. However, I was taken to both these structures by India Resource Center, an anti-Coca-Cola NGO. The company told me these structures would be repaired before the rainy season, and showed me a recharge shaft that was in good shape. The company further said, 'for most rain water harvesting structures the ownership, and hence long term sustenance, lies with the communities where the structures are built'. This casts at least some doubt about the long-term functioning of the RWH structures.

More important is the issue of how much water the RWH structures recharge into the aquifers, even assuming proper maintenance. Coca-Cola does not actually measure the water going into the aquifers, contrary to what Jeff Seabright, Vice President Environment & Water Resources, promised to the University of Michigan on 11 January 2008, 'as part of our commitment going forward, we will install measuring devices that will verify the amount of water recharged'.[51] When I asked various Coca-Cola India executives why the company did not measure the water recharged, three executives gave three different answers: it is technologically infeasible (that is not true), it is too expensive (in that case, instal the metres on only a few shafts), and the villagers would steal the metres (in that case, find a way to lock down the metres) – none of these seem valid reasons to break the company's explicit commitment.[52] The company's external affairs manager told a reporter a yet different reason: a metre would require sending someone manually to check it after each rainfall – easy to do that in a country with cheap labour, and there are automatic metres.[53] Instead of actually measuring the recharge, the company uses a mathematical model to calculate the 'recharge potential' of the RWH structures. When I asked for the mathematical model and its assumptions with the intent of getting it examined by a hydrogeologist, the company responded, 'the calculations shown in the spread sheet are an internal document and not meant for external usage'. Coca-Cola has retained the consulting firm Golder to audit and assess the artificial recharge projects, but refused to share that report too. 'Their report is part of our company's internal programme and meant for internal audiences only'. There is thus absolutely no evidence to support the company's claim that it recharges 15 times the amount of water it withdraws. If nothing else, such lack of transparency is contrary to the spirit of CSR. It is also contrary to Coca-Cola's acknowledgement in the letter mentioned above, 'we are a user of water in a highly water-stressed area, and the burden of proof is on us to demonstrate that we can reconcile our operations with local community and watershed needs'. The company is not keeping its own explicit promises.

I interviewed Professor M.S. Rathore, a specialist in water resource management, and Director of the Center for Environment & Development Studies, Jaipur, Rajasthan, who asserted that there is 'no possibility' of Coca-Cola's RWH structures recharging so much water. The TERI report also concluded 'since the rainfall is scanty, the recharge achieved through such [rainwater] structures is unlikely to be meaningful'. Coca-Cola states that the cost of constructing a recharge shaft is about Rs. 20,000–22,000, which is equivalent to about $500. Thus the total cost of the 140 shafts would be about $70,000. By way of comparison, Coca-Cola India's annual revenues are probably in the order of $1.8 billion, and it plans to invest $2 billion in India over the next five years.[54] If the recharge shafts are so effective, one wonders why not build many more and reverse the decline in the water table.

CONCLUSIONS

The objective of this study is not to demonise Coca-Cola; nor should the company be canonised. The company is behaving like most profit-maximising firms. It is just unrealistic to expect companies to help solve CPR problems through voluntary CSR. That raises the question what can society expect of companies behaving in a responsible manner. Fortunately there are many situations where private interests and public welfare are aligned. There are many actions firms can take, and do, that simultaneously increase profits and social welfare. Executives should ensure that they undertake all such actions. Coca-Cola has reduced the water usage ratio at the Kaladera plant from 4.0 to 2.0. This win-win solution has helped reduce Coca-Cola's operating costs and also reduced the need for groundwater extraction. Switching to plastic bottles has reduced Coca-Cola's transportations costs while also reducing water used for washing bottles. The TERI assessment did not find pesticides above health standards in the process water used in Coca-Cola plants. Ensuring elimination of pesticides in its products is good for Coca-Cola's reputation and brand image and also good for public health. This is the so-called 'business case for CSR' or 'corporate shared value'.[55]

Responsible behaviour implies that executives are transparent about the social impact of their actions. Extravagant promises, lack of transparency and lack of accountability have led to a cynical view that the CSR programmes of many companies are merely 'greenwash'. Coca-Cola took a positive step when it agreed to a third-party independent assessment by TERI. But, it needs to go further to be truly responsible. Coca-Cola India makes strong claims about the quantity of water its RWH structures recharge into the aquifers, but is not transparent about how it arrived at its estimate. The TERI report recommended that Coca-Cola 'make its water programme more transparent to local communities and interested stakeholders, and accountable at the facility and country level'.

When private interests and public welfare are in conflict (as in CPR problems), government intervention is often necessary. Companies behaving in a responsible manner should not manipulate the political process to obstruct government intervention. Robert Reich, the former US Secretary of Labour, argues that firms wishing to enact CSR need only avoid lobbying and being involved in the political process.[56] As the Indian government struggles with how to regulate groundwater extraction, Coca-Cola and other companies should not use their lobbying resources to stymie the political process to the detriment of effective democracy.

Regulatory Regime

Underground aquifers are a perfect example of a CPR, characterised by difficulty of excluding users and subtractability. Privatisation of the Kaladera aquifers clearly is not a technically feasible option. The Kaladera watershed in 2001 had a population of over 600,000 living in many villages and towns, more than 92,000 farmers, over 25,000 irrigation pumps, spread over an area of 309 square kilometres. It is difficult to see how a 'thick' community would evolve here to develop a group property regime to 'self-regulate' the groundwater supply. This CPR problem is compounded by the fact that there are three types of users: households, farmers and factories, with differing interests and culture. In any case, a group property regime has not been developed. As the above discussion shows, the government has failed in its responsibility to develop regulations to manage and sustain the groundwater aquifers. Lacking a property regime, the only remaining alternative to avert the tragedy of the commons is altruism and CSR. There is no evidence of the farmers individually behaving in an altruistic manner.

Nor is there evidence that businesses, including Coca-Cola, have significantly restrained themselves from extracting groundwater. It is unfortunate, and not surprising, that the prediction of the tragedy of the unregulated commons is coming true for the Kaladera watershed.

The case study discussed above does not support the proposition that CSR will avert the tragedy of the unregulated commons. The case of Coca-Cola in Rajasthan is clearly favourable to the proposition since the company proclaims its CSR so vehemently. Coca-Cola is very profitable and could easily afford to pay for CSR activities. It is a consumer facing company with a very powerful brand; a favourable CSR image would enhance its reputation with consumers, and conversely the company would be susceptible to public pressure from social activists. CSR related to water resources is integral to the company's core business, and not some peripheral activity. A groundwater aquifer is a very localised resource with well-defined boundaries, making it easier to see the impact of one user's actions. If CSR is not effective in this benign context, there is little chance of, say, the cement industry significantly reducing air pollution through CSR, where the above favourable conditions are not present.

The lessons to be learnt from this case study are much broader than Coca-Cola and Kaladera. Unless we regulate the commons, tragedy looms for Kaladera, for Rajasthan, for India, and for the world, with regard to water and other CPRs. 'As per internationally accepted norms, a person needs 2,000 cubic meters of water per year. However, life can go on even at 1,000 cubic meters. But in Rajasthan we are already at 650 cubic meters mark. ... In few years, the availability will reach the absolute scarcity mark of 500 cubic meters. Previous studies have shown that migration begins at this mark', said Ram Lubhaya, principal secretary for water resources, state government of Rajasthan.[57] According to the 2012 draft of the National Water Policy, 'skewed availability of water between different regions and different people in the same regions is iniquitous and has the potential of causing social unrest'.[58] Many of the environmental challenges the world faces, from greenhouse gases to wildlife habitats, involve a common-pool resource. Asking companies to voluntarily act in the public interest will not be enough to solve these problems. It is essential to develop regulatory regimes with appropriate incentives and ability to enforce sanctions.

Epilogue

In pursuance of Supreme Court orders, the Government of India constituted the Central Ground Water Authority (CGWA) in 1997 for the purposes of regulation and control of groundwater development and management. The CGWA has not been particularly active till recently. On 15 November 2012, the CGWA introduced new 'Criteria for Evaluation of Proposals for Ground Water Abstraction'.[59] The CGWA categorises some parts of the country as 'notified' areas for the purposes of regulation of ground water development. The new CGWA rules state 'permission to abstract ground water through any energised means *will not be accorded* for any purposes other than drinking water' (emphasis in the original). The Govindgarh block, which includes Kaladera, was 'notified' on 13 August 2011.[60] In areas non-notified by CGWA, but declared over-exploited by CGWB, 'industries using water as raw material/water intensive industries like packaged drinking water, mineral water industries, distilleries, breweries, soft drink manufacturing industries, textiles, paper & pulp, etc. *shall not be granted NOC* [no objection certificate] for groundwater withdrawal' (emphasis in the original). The Kaladera area had been declared overexploited by CGWB back in 1998. The Coca-Cola plant in Kaladera clearly would not be permitted under the new rules.

NOTES

1. Hardin, G. (1968, December). Tragedy of the commons. *Science, 162*, 1243–1248.
2. Ostrom, E., et al. (1999, April). Revisiting the commons: Local lessons, global challenges. *Science, 284*, 278–282.
3. Hesse, S. (2006, July 26). Will common sense dawn again in time? *The Japan Times.*
4. Barclay, P. (2004). 'Trustworthiness and competitive altruism can also solve the "tragedy of the commons."' *Evolution and Human Behavior, 25*, 209–220.
5. Axelrod, R., & Hamilton, W. D. (1981). The evolution of cooperation. *Science, 21*(1), 1390–1396.
6. Trivers, R. L. (1971). The evolution of reciprocal altruism. *Quarterly Review of Biology, 46*, 35–57. Samir Okasha. 'Biological Altruism.' *Stanford Encyclopedia of Philosophy.*
7. Hauser, M. (2006). *Moral minds.* Harper Collins.
8. Smith, A. (1977). *A theory of moral sentiments.* 1804 (p. 446). Reprinted by Oxford University Press.
9. Ostrom, E. (1990). *Governing the commons: The evolution of institutions for collective action.* New York, NY: Cambridge University Press.
10. Elinor Ostrom. See footnote 9.
11. Worm, B., et al. (2006). Impacts of biodiversity loss on ocean ecosystem services. *Science, 314*, 787–790.
12. 'How to stop fishermen fishing.' *The Economist*, 25 February 2012.
13. Costello, C., et al. (2008). Can catch shares prevent fisheries collapse? *Science, 321*, 1678–1681.
14. Friedman, M. (1970, September 13). The social responsibility of business is to increase its profits. *New York Times.*
15. Rowland, W. (2009, Autumn). 'Corporate social responsibility and Garrett Hardin's "tragedy of the commons" as myth and reality.' *The Journal of Corporate Citizenship*, (35), 109–116.
16. European Commission. (2001). Green Paper – Promoting a European Framework for Corporate Social Responsibility. Retrieved from http://eur-lex.europa.eu/LexUriServ/LexUriServ.do?uri=CELEX:52001DC0366:EN:HTML. Accessed November 10, 2010.
17. Shultz, C. J., II & Holbrook, M. B. (1999, Fall). Marketing and the tragedy of the commons: a synthesis, commentary, and analysis for action. *Journal of Public Policy & Marketing, 18*(2), 218–229.
18. See, for example: Clive Crook. 'The good company,' *The Economist*, 20 January 2005. Daniel Franklin. 'Just good business.' *The Economist*, 17 January 2008. Vogel, D. (2005). *The Market for Virtue.* Brookings Institution Press, Washington, DC. Karnani, A. (2011, Winter). Doing well by doing good: the grand illusion. *California Management Review, 53*(2).
19. Karnani, A. (2011, Winter). CSR stuck in a logical trap. *California Management Review, 53*(2).

20. Vogel, D. (2005). *The market for virtue* (p. 19). Washington DC: Brookings Institution Press.

21. Nidumolu, R., Prahalad, C. K., & Rangaswami, M. R. (2009, September). Why sustainability is now the key driver of innovation. *Harvard Business Review, 87*(9), 56–64.

22. Porter, M. E., & Kramer, M. R. (2006, December). Strategy and society. *Harvard Business Review*.

23. Karnani, A. (2011, Winter). CSR stuck in a logical trap. *California Management Review, 53*(2).

24. Ostrom, E. (1990). *Governing the commons: The evolution of institutions for collective action*. New York, NY: Cambridge University Press.

25. Karnani, A. (2011, Winter). Doing well by doing good: the grand illusion. *California Management Review, 53*(2).

26. Thomas, M. (2008). *Belching out the devil*. New York, NY: Nation Books, 2008. Blanding, M. (2010). *The Coke machine*. New York, NY: Avery.

27. Stecklow, S. (2005, June 7). How a global web of activists gives Coke problems in India. *The Wall Street Journal, 7*, A1.

28. Hoffman, A., & Howie, S. (2010, July 25). 'Coke in the Cross Hairs: Water, India, and the University of Michigan.' Case 1-429-098. GlobalLens, William Davidson Institute at the University of Michigan.

29. *Independent third-party assessment of Coca-Cola facilities in India*. The Energy and Resources Institute, Delhi, 2008.

30. *2010/2011 Sustainability Report*. The Coca-Cola Company, 2011.

31. Company website: http://www.coca-colaindia.com/ourcompany/company_highlights .html. Accessed on March 7, 2012.

32. *The Water Stewardship and Replenish Report*. The Coca-Cola Company, January 2011.

33. Kirby, A. (2000, June 2). Dawn of a thirsty century. *BBC News*.

34. Karnani, A. (2011). *Fighting poverty together*. New York, NY: Palgrave Macmillan.

35. Thomas, C., et al. (2010, May 25). Coca-Cola, Intel, farmers battle for water in China, India. *Bloomberg*.

36. Rathore, M. S. (2005) 'State level analysis of drought policies and impacts in Rajasthan, India.' Working Paper 93. International Water Management Institute, Colombo.

37. See http://wrmin.nic.in/writereaddata/linkimages/anu11326762704.pdf. Accessed on April 2, 2013.

38. *Ground Water Scenario: Jaipur District*. Central Ground Water Board, Western Region, Jaipur, 2007.

39. Rathore, M. S. (2005). Groundwater exploration and augmentation efforts in Rajasthan—A review. Jaipur: Institute of Development Studies.

40. Sengupta, S. (2006, September 30). India digs deeper, but wells are drying up. *The New York Times*.

41. Company data based on personal interviews with Coca-Cola India executives, available in a written email.

42. Cullet, P. (2007). Water law in India. Working Paper 2007-01. International Environment Law research Center, Geneva.

43. Retrieved from http://planningcommission.nic.in/reports/genrep/rep_grndwat.pdf. Accessed on April 2, 2013.

44. 'State water policy.' Water Resources Department, Government of Rajasthan. Retrieved from http://waterresources.rajasthan.gov.in/5swp.htm. Accessed on March 7, 2012.

45. Hoffman, A., & Howie, S. (2010, July 25). 'Coke in the Cross Hairs: Water, India, and the University of Michigan.' Case 1-429-098. GlobalLens, William Davidson Institute at the University of Michigan.

46. 'Coca-Cola: In hot water.' *The Economist*, 6 October 2005.

47. Hardin, G. (1968, December). Tragedy of the commons. *Science, 162*, 1243–1248.

48. Coca-Cola's letter to the University of Michigan, 11 January 2008. Retrieved from: http://www.vpcomm.umich.edu/pa/key/pdf/MichiganTERILetter.pdf. Accessed on March 7, 2012.

49. Blanding, Michael. *The Coke machine* (p. 232). New York, NY: Avery, 2010.

50. As discussed earlier, Coca-Cola's share is larger at the 'localised' level of 2 km radius.

51. Coca-Cola's letter to the University of Michigan, 11 January 2008. Retrieved from http://www.vpcomm.umich.edu/pa/key/pdf/MichiganTERILetter.pdf. Accessed on March 7, 2012.

52. This is the only company statement in this article for which I do not have a written confirmation.

53. Blanding, M. (2010). *The Coke machine* (p. 258). New York, NY: Avery.

54. Coca-Cola does not publish the financial results for the Indian subsidiary. Articles in the business press in India estimate the Indian market for carbonated soft drinks to be about $3 billion, and Coca-Cola's market share to be about 60%.

55. Porter, M. E., & Kramer, M. R. (2006, December). Strategy and society. *Harvard Business Review*.

56. Reich, R. (2007). Supercapitalism: The transformation of business, democracy, and everyday life. New York, NY: Alfred Knopf.

57. Dey, A. (2010, May 19). Water crisis in Rajasthan to force migration, says study. *Times News Network*.

58. 'Skewed availability of water potential for social unrest: government.' *The Economic Times*, February 5, 2012.

59. Retrieved from http://cgwb.gov.in/CGWA/documents/Approved%20Guidelines%20for%20evaluation%20of%20proposals.pdf. Accessed on April 2, 2013.

60. See http://cgwb.gov.in/CGWA/Notified_areas.html. Accessed on April 2, 2013.

THE SINS OF THE CSR MOVEMENT: ERRORS IN CSR

Nicholas Capaldi

ABSTRACT

CSR, as a social and political movement, misunderstands the modern market economy. The purpose of corporations or publicly traded companies is not to reduce risk or liability but to promote risk. CSR distorts the role of corporate officers (not the distribution of company assets). It misunderstands the role of capital markets, promotes illegal and irresponsible behaviour on the part of some corporations, destabilises national and world economies, promotes the growth of the deep bureaucratic state and leads to crony capitalism. It encourages the false belief in a utopian social technology; inhibits economic and scientific growth; and misplaces the responsibility for failed states and cultural retardation.

Keywords: Agricentrism; social scientism; technological project; culture of personal autonomy; CSR; environment; climate change; imagination

THE FIVE ERRORS OF THE CSR MOVEMENT

Corporate Social Responsibility (CSR) is both a scholarly field and a movement. As a field of scholarship, it contributes a great deal of useful information about the functioning of specific corporations and even countries within the global economy and its challenges. As a movement, it often promotes a controversial political and social agenda. The purpose of this essay is to focus on the ways in which it undermines the local, national and the global economy, *modern economies*. It does so in presuming what I identify as *agricentrism (AC)* – a focus that reflects an agricultural world rather than an industrial and technological world. AC assumes a fixed earthly environment (biosphere) with an inherent structure and in which our duty is to respect and to conform to that external objective structure. Historically this reflects the fact that all previous civilisation required a

Strategic Corporate Responsibility and Green Management
Critical Studies on Corporate Responsibility, Governance and Sustainability, Volume 16, 59–68
Copyright © 2023 by Emerald Publishing Limited
All rights of reproduction in any form reserved
ISSN: 2043-9059/doi:10.1108/S2043-905920230000016004

predictable food supply, traditional agriculture responds to a specific locality of conditions (weather, soil etc.) and is carried out by a local community. AC encourages a very passive and almost worshipful attitude towards nature. It presumes that the 'environment' is identical to 'nature' and is restricted to the biosphere. There is a remarkable congruence here between the CSR movement agenda and the views of Pope Francis. (Capaldi, 2017).

As such, it is oblivious to the fact that humanity survives by controlling natural threats to the human race, that this control reflects a technological economy, that our environment extends to outer space and that the potential resources of this environment are infinite (Simon, 1981).

A caveat is in order here. No one denies that we should take the environment seriously that if a commercial action poses a threat to human health, then it should be prohibited or regulated (assuming the cure is not worse than the disease). The latest example is 'climate change'. With the understanding that 'climate change' is not identical to 'global warming', the 'earth's temperature' (a statistical construct) has risen one degree in the past century, that, at most, humans are responsible for no more than 10% of that increase, that we still do not have a comprehensive scientific understanding of weather (previous ice ages and periods of warming before the appearance of *Homo sapiens* and certainly before the Industrial Revolution), it is not clear or obvious what is the best public policy for dealing with this phenomenon (Lomborg, 2021. See also https://dailysceptic.o rg/2022/08/18/1200-scientists-and-professionals-declare-there-is-no-climate-emer-gency/).

AC presumes that wealth, like land, is finite, and the only challenge is how to distribute it. Advocates of AC are oblivious to how the Dutch created more 'land' through the use of dykes (see TP below) as well as ignoring fish farms.

AC is totally at odds with the dominant factor in modern economies, namely the Technological Project (hereafter the TP), an approach which reconstructs the environment to serve externally imposed human wants as well as needs. The TP originated in Western Europe in the sixteenth century, best expressed by Bacon and especially Descartes who asserted that our role is to become 'the masters and possessors of nature' (Capaldi, 2004). The TP is what gave rise to Western European domination (e.g. colonialism etc.). It is an example of what Schumpeter called 'creative destruction'. The TP has vastly improved the human condition by any measurement (I am writing this on my computer in an air-conditioned office, and it can be read simultaneously by scholars in India etc.).

The TP has also transformed the environment and in so doing has generated serious widespread problems (e.g. pollution, as well as serious social and political challenges – utopians are always disappointed to learn that benefits come with costs) – all of which are endlessly documented in the CSR literature. Advocates of TP, such as myself, respond (1) that its benefits exceed its costs, that historically it is too late to reverse this perspective (impossible otherwise even to feed the present world population to say nothing of the social and political fallout) and (2) that we therefore must use present and future technology to solve the problems created by past technology (funding research to develop clean energy, invest in research to develop varieties of crops and agricultural practices that deliver higher yields with a smaller environmental footprint). In any case, the world is now divided between developed and developing countries.

CSR has also helped to promote the climate debate. Because of its AC, CSR tends to lean towards abandoning the TP (unrealistic) or obstructing the TP with warmed-over socialism ('Greens'). As a consequence, Europe now sees '[S]oaring oil and natural gas prices. Electricity grids on the brink of failure. Energy shortages in Europe, with worse to come. The free world's growing strategic vulnerability to Vladimir Putin and other dictators. These are some of the unfolding results in the last year caused by the West's utopian dream to punish fossil fuels and sprint to a world driven solely by renewable energy. It's time for political leaders to recognise this manifest debacle and admit that, short of a technological breakthrough, the world will need an ample supply of carbon fuel for decades to remain prosperous and free' (WSJ 7/18/22).

AC is totally at odds with what makes the modern economy operate. The modern economy in its most prosperous and free forms reflects the *Lockean liberty narrative* (Capaldi & Lloyd, 2016). The narrative can be summarised abstractly in terms of the following diagram:

$$TP \rightarrow ME \rightarrow LG \rightarrow RL \rightarrow CPA \rightarrow TP$$

TP stands for the Technological Project.
ME stands for the Market Economy.
LG stands for limited government (restraining government on behalf of individual liberty)
RL stands for the 'rule of law'
CPA stands for the culture of personal autonomy.

The agricentrists believe that there is an external, objective and normative order in nature. This meant two things: human beings were obliged to use reason to discover that order and then to conform their behaviour to it. The moderns will argue that order is an internal human construct projected onto the world and that we are obliged to transform the world to conform to that internally generated vision of order. This is, philosophically speaking, the 'Copernican' Revolution (Capaldi, 1972) known as the 'technological project'. The Lockean narrative is the assertion of the claims that the technological project, that is, the transformation of the physical world of nature for human convenience, functions best in a free market economy which, in turn, requires a limited government subject to the rule of law, and all of the foregoing operate best within a culture that promotes personal autonomy. Finally, the TP is itself an expression of personal autonomy. Each of these concepts was individually articulated prior to Locke. So, for example, Descartes in the *Discourse on Method* advocated our becoming 'masters and possessors of nature'. What is significant about John Locke was that he was among the first, if not the first, to articulate and endorse a coherent version of the entire narrative.

The main purpose of a market economy is to promote the TP, that is, to innovate and to grow. Everything else, including the functioning of political and legal institutions, the role of other social institution, how we address social issues, all depend on the TP. Anything that detracts from the TP will negatively impact everything else.

THE TP DICTATES IMAGINATION AND PRIVATE PROPERTY

'Imagination' was a negative concept in the classical and medieval intellectual world, signifying the way in which the human mind failed to replicate the objective world. In the eighteenth century, the 'imagination' is a positive concept, and it is no accident that Hume and Kant first articulated this. Imagination cannot be predicted or reduced to a mechanical (AI) [difference between using robots on the assembly line and inventing the idea of an assembly line] or even organic model. There is no way to produce an algorithm telling us which people will make the best use of any resource or even identify that something is or could become a resource. This dictates a public policy of wide (not equal) private ownership of property to maximise entrepreneurship.

The function of a market economy is to maximise the interaction of creative people (many of whom do not have substantial private resources) with substantial resources – either by one person with lots of money or many people each with a small amount of money. Hence a corporation is not about minimising risk but of maximising risk, that is maximising the interaction of creative people with people willing to invest either small or large sums of money.

The modern market economy requires trial and error risk-taking. Creativity in the modern market economy encourages/requires individuals and groups to dream up projects that neither they nor others can either afford to or are willing to wholly subsidise. There is a whole new sub-discipline of 'managing' risk not eliminating risk.

Investment requires investors. In the AC mindset, wealth is finite. Developing countries therefore often do not understand why investors should be allowed to take profits out of their countries and perhaps why national debts (or interest thereon) do(es) not or should not have to be repaid.

CSR, hence, misunderstands what corporations are for and therefore misunderstand the role of investors. Investors are neither the owners nor greedy and expendable parasites but the life-blood of corporations. Investors also comprise many middle-class people who are saving for retirement, or to open a business, or to fund the education of their children etc. Again, commitment to AC hypostatises a world of a few owners opposed by masses of workers. Ironically, this repeats one of Marx's mistakes, namely, explaining the industrial social world as if it were a mere extension of the feudal agricultural world. CSR continues to imagine a world divided between the 'workers' (now including management) and the 'owners' (investors), failing to notice the extent to which 'workers' are investors through pension funds and private investing. Ironically, many of the scholars of CSR do not realize that their pensions are invested in the TP.

The arguments against 'profit' are a way of demonising 'shareholders' or investors. To what end? I suggest that this literature is originally motivated by the attempt to detach management in general and CEOs in particular from their obligations to investors. Freed of or weakening that obligation allows CEOs to become 'woke' capitalists. Ironically, Carl Rhodes (2022) argues that corporate leaders will undermine governments and non-profit organisations by assuming the role of public representatives and 'start directly taking on the provision of public goods and taking on responsibility for solving public problems' (p. 96). The risk is the gradual subversion of democracy by a plutocracy. For an example, see 'Bill Gates and the Secret Push to Save Biden's Climate Bill', https://www.bloomberg.com/news/features/2022-08-16/how-bill-gates-lobbied-to-save-the-climate-tax-bill-biden-just-signed?utm_campaign=news&utm_medium=bd&utm_source=applenews.

Although sometimes paying lip service to the importance of profit, the logic of CSR is ultimately to do away with it altogether OR to dictate when, where and how. Relying on an outmoded semantics, definitions of 'profit' refer to what is left after payment to employees and management (understood as employees), suppliers and R&D. Again, this presupposes the AC model of the landowner and the hired hands.

R&D expense could have been added to wages or lower prices to consumers. The fact is, R&D contributes to future investor rewards. Further, investors often invest in companies that do not pay immediate dividends in the hopes of greater future rewards for themselves as well as management, employees and customers. Management is often paid with stock options. None of this makes any sense in the old conception of 'profit'. Finally, maybe it does not even make any sense to talk about stockholders as 'owners' since this changes by the minute. In a manner of speaking, everyone involved is or potentially is an investor and this potential growth influences career choice and choice of employment.

Maximising shareholder wealth is not the purpose of the modern corporation. But, the TP is. Managerial decisions involve (1) a response to external factors and to (2) internal factors. The overarching external factors are the TP (competition, obsolescence), which, in principle, cannot be planned and is unpredictable, and the actions of others in a market (Hayek's thesis about why planning will not work). No firm will remain profitable and therefore in existence unless it accepts the constraints and discipline of both the TP and the free market economy. Profitability is crucial to most concerns much like breathing is to life. Breathing is not the goal of life but a necessary condition to continue on the journey much as profit is to the enterprise.

THIRD ERROR: (SOCIAL SCIENTISM)

The third error is social scientism (SS) – the belief that there can be social 'science' and a derivative social technology. Ironically, SS is analogous to the TP.

However, there is no such thing as a social science that discovers the underlying hidden structure of the social world because there is no such structure. (Capaldi, 1987). There are no social laws, only an unending series of alleged methodological innovations.

SS leads to the view that markets only require management + labour + government financing; marketing would become a subdivision of management; the world is to be run ultimately by university-trained graduates of the business school and the law school.

In the last 50 years, business schools have made themselves academically respectable but at the cost of driving business people out of the school. (Gordon & Howell, 1959, research sponsored by the Ford Foundation and the Carnegie Foundation). Business school faculty, including CSR scholars, think like academics and therefore do not understand how the real world of business operates. Part of the explanation is the nature of academic thinking.

Academic thinking has, of course, important virtues, but it is also narrowly rigid. Rooted in Euclid and Plato, all thinking is based on unassailable axioms and what can be strictly derived from the axioms. Everything, therefore, can be analysed and decontextualised into constituent parts. This is best exemplified in the dominance of professional academic philosophy by 'analytic philosophy' which has as one of its origins the attempt to formalise totally all of mathematics. Logicism is the theory that mathematics is reducible to logic (Frege, Russell). It effectively holds that mathematical theorems and truths are logically necessary or analytic. Unfortunately, this failed, as was shown by Godel's 'Incompleteness Proof' and Wittgenstein's analysis of rules in mathematics.

As we all know, the human brain has two sides: left (logical reasoning) and right (imagination). We all have different combinations of both. Left-brain dominance leads to a preference for order, Kuhnian 'normal science', routine, analysis, a focus on procedure, a system that can be mastered and in which there are authorities, and strict regulation. Right-brain dominance encourages novelty (easily bored), synthesis, search for new possibilities and de-regulation.

Large Bureaucracies (e.g. government, big corporations, academic institutions) are run by people who are left-brain dominant (lawyers, accountants, so-called 'bean counters'). They institutionalise routine, and they attract, hire and promote left-brain dominance individuals. This explains why bureaucracies cannot handle emergencies or crises (e.g. hurricane Katrina) but businesses (Walmart) can, why most intellectuals favour big government solutions and hate business people, why neo-classical economics cannot explain entrepreneurship but Austrian economics can, *why business schools run by left-dominance intellectuals favour large organisations and don't teach entrepreneurship or don't teach it correctly (insofar as it can be taught)*, Why the 'less gifted' (dropouts) may have greater success in the world of business than the 'more-gifted' (left-brain dominance), why generals are always fighting the last war, why regulators are always dealing with the last crisis, why all progress comes from 'bucking the system'.

The other problem with academic thinking is that it is subject to what is fashionable and self-serving. Since the 18th century, Enlightenment Project (EP) (Capaldi, 1998), the intellectual world has been dominated by the misguided belief that there can be a science of the social world in the same way that there is a science of the physical world, and that this alleged science provides for a potentially utopian social technology, housed in the academic social 'sciences'. As a consequence, newly minted PhDs in the business school all look like social science researchers. Unfortunately, there is no such thing as social science* only a continuous series of alleged methodological innovations resembling a carrousel in which the riders and tunes change but there is no real progress. *Academics like collegiality and oppose strong personalities; maintain discipline thru accreditation and an emphasis on process/ procedure, tenure and rigid rules for the achievement thereof.*

The latter includes publishing in the better (authoritative) journals defined as the ones with the highest (countable) rejection rates. In trying to create something analogous to physical science journals (usually based on confirmable research about external structures that actually exist), social science journals and business journals, based as they are on a false basic premise, often produce nothing of real use to the business world. Handling the newly and constantly emerging demands for ESR reports expands non-productive bureaucracies, again similar to the never-ending growth of academic bureaucracies. Surely, this adds to the cost of doing business.

Finally, there is no social technology and the belief that there is one leads to utopian expectations about the human condition and what the market economy can and cannot do. There may be serious discrepancies between what some individuals can accomplish (psychological and physical infirmities that we still do not understand) and what we expect modern economies to do. Perhaps many of the problems reflect human dysfunction and not market malfunction. (See Delsol, 2010): The ideas once held so dear – inevitable progress, the possibility of limitless social and self-transformation – are no longer believable. Delsol's portrait is engrossing. She explains how we have come simultaneously to embrace the 'good' but reject the 'true'; how we have sacralised rights and democracy; and how we have lost our sense of the tragic and embraced the idea of 'zero risk'.

FOURTH ERROR: ROLE OF GOVERNMENT AND REGULATION

Given its methodological orientation, one should not be surprised by its understanding of government and regulation. Its implicit orientation is that there are objective social truths that imply public policies, that the social truths are a sort of fact that all rational people can agree on or conform, and therefore some kind of participatory democratic socialism is the proper form of government (For a contrary view, see Idowu, 2010). There is no hesitancy on the part of some CSR scholars to argue that their research should lead to specific public policy implemented and regulated by the government. There is a growing literature on the politicisation of science literature.

Moreover, the very structure of commercial organisations is seen along political lines. For example, the executive is the CEO, the legislature is the board of directors, with the directors chosen not only by shareholders and investors but by employees, and numberless other interest groups (stakeholders of which there is a potentially infinite list). Instead of projecting commercial insights such as the value of competition onto politics (US model as understood by its founders such as James Madison), it projects a typical European 'democratic' social consensus politics onto corporate structure (analogous to academic Senates with representation by the administration, the faculty, students, support staff, groundskeepers etc.). This used to be called industrial democracy. Another example would be suggesting that all investment decisions be made by the appropriate government experts instead of individual investors. Those who make this suggestion seem unaware of Hayek's arguments about why markets cannot be planned and predicted.

For some time, over the last decade or so, it has moved considerably from voluntary decisions at the level of individual organisations to mandatory schemes at regional, national and international levels. How and why is a set of social policies advocated by the UN (where impoverished, undemocratic, and corrupt 'developing' countries are a majority) better than decisions made at national levels? And which nations do we have in mind?

Developing countries → UN → redistribution

Since when is China a 'developing' country? How do the 'Paris Accords' improve global climate if all it does is shift the concentration of pollution to 'developing' countries?

During the 2020 Presidential election in the United States, private corporations (Google, Facebook, Twitter) and newspapers and TV stations owned by large multinational corporations (e.g. Amazon) deliberately censored information in order to influence the outcome. No doubt, many academics ignored this because they favoured the outcome. But, think about it! Is helping to 'rig' the outcome of an election an example of CSR designed to address a host of social issues? Once 'government' becomes the major source of investment, this may incentivise corporation to pursue renewable energy but it may also incentivise corporations to divert government largesse to wasteful or corrupt ends (an aberrant form of 'greenwashing' in which we pretend to research for renewables). How is this different from crony capitalism? Is crony socialism different from crony capitalism? Democratic socialism inevitably reverts to capitalism as in Sweden or to eliminating the 'democratic' part because periodic elections lead to regime changes and the inability to engage in long-range public policy planning. Will demonising fossil fuels lead to major shortages? Social problems? Destruction of needed economic growth? Misdirected research?

Last, but not least, is the misunderstanding of the role of the legal system. The concept of the 'rule of law' in the Anglo-American legal tradition limits government in the interest of protecting individual rights. The 'rule thru law' of the Continental legal tradition, which is the model for the rest of the world, understands that law is a tool for politics not a way to limit government. Listing the legal jurisdictions of the 'rule of law' (United Kingdom, United States, Canada, Australia, New Zealand, Hong Kong and Singapore) should answer most readers' questions as to which is most likely to improve economic development. (Capaldi & Nedzel, 2021).

FIFTH ERROR: HOLISTIC CULTURE

Economic growth, the TP, requires a culture that permits/encourages individual autonomy. As numerous scholars have pointed out, these cultures are largely restricted to northwest Europe and its derivatives (United States and Australia).

> The extraordinary change from an agrarian economy to an industrial world, first achieved in England...the civilisation is based ultimately on the individual...but how could it escape, for the first time in history, agrarian constraints?...all other Eurasian societies moved towards 'caste'. This hierarchy-with-mobility is an essential basis for modernity...They placed the relationship with their married partner before that to their parents or children...The English family system soon became unique in Europe and later spread to America...The central feature of modernity is the development of associations based on 'contract' rather than communities based on birth and blood...with the King under the law...The legal system is the key to modernity. The unique mixture of Common Law and Equity, with judge-made, precedent-based law, with the presence of juries and the assumption of innocence until proven guilty...There was equality before the law and the rule of law...History shows that great economic achievement in the modern world is only sustainable in cultures that have escaped from the collective identity imposed by traditions rooted in agrarianism. (MacFarlane, 2014).

> The importance of extricating oneself from a holistic culture has been a central theme in contemporary literature as seen in the work of V. S. Naipaul. (Capaldi, 2022).

Periodically and ritualistically, CSR scholars celebrate the economic and technological advances in holistic cultures. Recall that in the 1960s the *Soviet Union* succeeded in putting a man into orbit before the United States. The Soviet Union no longer exists. In the 1980s, scholars celebrated Japan's economic accomplishments, and the management literature was full of articles of how lifetime employment should become a universal model. We now see stagnation in Japan and the inability to produce flexible workforces capable of adopting the latest technology (Maitland & Umezu, 2006). In the twenty-first century, *China* has been touted as the paragon of non-Western industrialisation. China's achievement has been based on terror, slave labour, total disregard for the environment, bending all of the rules, privileges by being classified as a so-called 'developing' economy, bribery, theft of intellectual property, industrial espionage and outsourcing R&D through so-called Confucian institutes in the United States and the United Kingdom. The day of reckoning is upon us (Peterson, 2019).

REFERENCES

Capaldi, N. (1972). The Copernican revolution in Hume and Kant. In L. W. Beck (Ed.), *Proceedings of the third international Kant congress* (pp. 234–240). Dordrecht: Reidel.

Capaldi, N. (1987). The future of the social sciences. The Faculty of Arts and Social Sciences of the National University of Singapore. ISBN 9971 49 026 9.

Capaldi, N. (1998). The enlightenment project in 20th century philosophy. In J. McCarthy (Ed.), *Modern enlightenment and the rule of reason* (pp. 257–282). Washington, DC: Catholic University of America Press.

Capaldi, N. (2004). The ethical foundations of free market societies. *Journal of Private Enterprise*, *XX*(1 Fall), 30–54.

Capaldi, N. (2017). A Critique of Pope Francis' Laudato si. *Seattle University Law Review, 40*, 1261–1282.

Capaldi, N. (2022, August). V.S. Naipaul and the universality of individual freedom. *The Postil.* Retrieved from https://www.thepostil.com/v-s-naipaul-and-the-universality-of-individual-freedom/

Capaldi, N., & Lloyd, G. (2016). *Liberty and equality in political economy: From Locke versus Rousseau to the present.* London: Edward Elgar.

Capaldi, N., & Nedzel, N. E. (2021). CSR in the USA and UK versus CSR in Europe and Asia. In D. Crowther & S. Seifi (Eds.), *The Palgrave handbook of corporate social responsibility* (pp. 1071–1101). London: Springer.

Delsol, C. (2010). *Icarus Fallen: The Search for meaning in an uncertain world.* Delaware: Intercollegiate Studies Institute.

Gordon, R. A., & Howell, J. E. (1959). *Higher education for business.* New York, NY: Garland Publishing.

Idowu, S. (2010). Corporate social responsibility – A capitalists or socialists ideology? *SSRN.* Retrieved from https://ssrn.com/abstract=1564749

Lomborg, B. (2021). *False alarm: How climate change panic costs us trillions, hurts the poor, and fails to fix the planet.* New York, NY: Basic Books. Retrieved from https://dailysceptic.org/2022/08/18/1200-scientists-and-professionals-declare-there-is-no-climate-emergency/

MacFarlane, A. (2014). The invention of the modern world. *Fortnightly Review*, iv–xi. Les Brouzils, France.

Maitland, I., & Umezu, M. (2006). An evaluation of Japan's Stakeholder capitalism. *The Journal of Private Enterprise, 22*(2), 131–164. ISSN 0890-913X, ZDB-ID 1107843-1.

Peterson, R. (2019). Confucius institutes. Academic Questions (Summer 2019). Retrieved from https://www.nas.org/academic-questions/32/2/the-confucius-institutes

Rhodes, C. (2022). *Woke capitalism: How corporate morality is sabotaging democracy.* London: Bristol Press.

Simon, J. (1981). *The ultimate resource.* Princeton, NJ: Princeton.

CAN CORPORATE SOCIAL RESPONSIBILITY MAKE BUSINESS SENSE? FRAMEWORK BASED ON ITC E-CHOUPAL

Pingali Venugopal and Divya Agarwal

ABSTRACT

Corporate Social Responsibility (CSR) has been in practice in India even before it was mandated by the Companies Act, 2013. While the objectives of CSR varied from philanthropy, being socially responsible to improving the corporate image, the relationship between financial performance and CSR has not been established. Also only a few companies are aligning their CSR activities with their corporate goals. This chapter builds a framework for integrating business with its CSR activities. The first part of the chapter describes how the concept of CSR evolved over years in general and specifically in India. It also discusses the current status of CSR in India. The second part of the chapter uses a well-known CSR model of e-Choupal to build a framework to integrate CSR with business.

Keywords: Business and CSR; concept of CSR; current status of CSR; procurement model; e-Choupal; strategic CSR

INTRODUCTION

The underlying philosophy of Corporate Social Responsibility (CSR) is the responsibility of business to society at large. A lot of the emphasis has been placed upon businesses and businesspeople to act in a more socially responsible manner and to acknowledge that shareholders are only one of a number of business stakeholders (Letza, Sun, & Kirkbride, 2004). Though some articles state that there is a direct relationship between corporate social performance and

Strategic Corporate Responsibility and Green Management
Critical Studies on Corporate Responsibility, Governance and Sustainability, Volume 16, 69–81
Copyright © 2023 by Emerald Publishing Limited
All rights of reproduction in any form reserved
ISSN: 2043-9059/doi:10.1108/S2043-905920230000016005

corporate financial performance (Moure, 2011) and some articles wrongly equate CSR with irresponsible corporate actions (Jones, Ryan, & Tench, 2009), the debate of the relationships between financial performance and CSR has been inconclusive (Margolis, Elfenbein, & Walsh, 2007; Orlitzky, Frank, & Sara, 2003). This chapter discusses ITC e-Choupal as a business case whereby social responsibility can be converted to gain competitive advantage and social capital (Nahapiet & Ghoshal, 1998) by integrating CSR with the company goals. The chapter is divided into two parts. The first part discusses about CSR as a concept and CSR in India. The second part discusses the case of ITC's e-Choupal to build the framework.

PART I

CSR: THE CONCEPT

UNIDO (2022) defines corporate responsibility as management practices which integrate social and environmental concerns into their business operations. UNIDO states that properly implemented CSR would help build 'competitive advantages, better access to capital and markets, increased sales and profits, operational cost savings, improved productivity and quality, efficient human resource base, improved brand image and reputation, enhanced customer loyalty, better decision making and risk management processes'.

Carroll and Brown (2018) detailed how the concept of CSR was conceptualised over the years. In 1953 Bowen defined social responsibility as 'the obligations of businessmen to pursue those policies, to make those decisions, or to follow those lines of action which are desirable in terms of the objectives and values of our society'. In 1978 Frederick differentiated between CSR_1 focussing on accountability and CSR_2 focussing on responsiveness. In 1973, Keith Davis defined CSR as 'the firm's consideration of, and response to, issues beyond the narrow economic, technical, and legal requirements of the firm'. In 1979 Carroll proposed responsiveness towards social issues. Wartick and Cochran (1985) defined it as 'a business organization's configuration of principles of social responsibility, processes of social responsiveness and policies, programs and other observable outcomes as they related to the firm's societal relationships'. In 2008, Matten and Moon defined CSR as 'policies and practices of corporations that reflect business responsibility for some of the wider societal good. Yet the precise manifestation and direction of the responsibility lie at the discretion of the corporation' (all definitions quoted so far in this paragraph were quoted from Carroll & Brown, 2018). The European Commission (2001) defined CSR as 'a concept where companies integrate social and environmental concerns in their business operations and in their interaction with their stakeholders on a voluntary basis'. The European Commission in 2015 included the Sustainable Development Goals as part of CSR (Munro, 2020).

Moon (2014) states that all the definitions highlight that corporates need to conduct themselves ethically, be accountable, compensate for negative impacts and add to societal welfare. Key CSR issues identified by UNIDO (2020), include:

- environmental management
- eco-efficiency
- responsible sourcing
- stakeholder engagement
- labour standards and working conditions
- employee and community relations
- social equity
- gender balance
- human rights
- good governance and
- anti-corruption measures.

KPMG's International Survey of Corporate (Social) Responsibility Reporting 2005, which surveyed more than 1,600 companies worldwide, identified the following top 10 motivators of CSR:

- Economic considerations
- Ethical considerations
- Innovation and learning
- Employee motivation
- Risk management or risk reduction
- Access to capital or increased shareholder value
- Reputation or brand
- Market position or share
- Strengthened supplier relationships
- Cost savings

The Aflac survey of 2016 (quoted in Carroll & Brown, 2018) found that irresponsible companies could lose 39% of its customer base and 75% of its consumers could take negative actions. Davidson et al. (2018) provide a framework to understand the contextual elements of CSR for different countries. These include history of the country, religious ideologies, social norms, geopolitical issues governing the country, political structure, level of economic development, local institutions and safety net.

CSR IN INDIA

India is the first country to make CSR mandatory. Government introduced various regulations from 2010 to mandate CSR. The Company Act 2013 requires companies, who have a net worth greater than INR 5 billion or an annual turnover of greater than INR 10 billion, to spend at least 2% of their average profit for the past three years on CSR. Companies (Amendment) Act, 2019, also requires that the unspent money, if any, during a financial year be transferred to a fund as specified in the schedule IV of the Act and that amount be utilised within the next three years. The law also has a monetary penalty and or imprisonment for noncompliance.

India has, however, had a long rich history of close business involvement in social causes for national development (Kumar, Murphy, & Balsari, 2001). Spirituality and corporate social responsibility have had a strong connection in India. 'The link between the "karma" as espoused by sacred Indian texts and initiatives anchoring corporates as responsible citizens has been amply evident in India since the early days' (Sagar & Singla, 2004). Fig. 1 shows the different stages of CSR in India.

Societal expectations in India are that businesses should be involved in wider issues of societal and national concern while continuing to conduct their business responsibly (Gupta, 2007). Chavan, Gowan, and Vogeley (2022) found non-governmental organisations and corporates collaborate effectively to implement CSR activities.

As per the National CSR portal, Government of India in 2020–2021, 17,007 companies spent Rs. 24,865.46 crores for CSR undertaking 36,865 projects in 14 sectors, an increase from Rs. 14,344.87 crores in 2016–2017 covering 22,968 projects. 82% of the CSR spent during 2020–2021 came from non-PSU companies with 9,374 companies spending more than the mandatory two percent in 2020–2021, an increase from only 1701 companies which spent more than 2% in 2015. For example, D. B. Corp Ltd., a leading media conglomerate with a strong presence across print, radio and digital segments, has spent Rs. 6.99 crores during 2021–2022 towards CSR activities which is approximately 4.91% of its net profit (Kumar, 2022).

In 2020–2021, the maximum amount on CSR was spent in Maharashtra (Rs. 3,306.72 crores) followed by Gujarat (Rs. 1,397.26 crores). Amongst the sectors, health and sanitation received the maximum during 2020–2021 at Rs. 8,706 crores, followed by education with Rs. 8,020.82 crores, rural development with Rs. 1,818.3 crores and environment and animal welfare with Rs. 1,273.38 crores (National CSR portal).

CSR AND CORPORATES

Gupta (2007) estimated that India has over 200,000 private sector trusts, a large number set up by Indian businesses for contributing to social causes. Activities

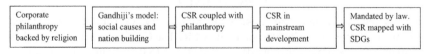

Fig. 1. Stages of CSR in India. *Source:* Author using information from Mishra (2020) and Narayanan and Singh (2022).

included areas of education, healthcare services, rural infrastructure, development, community welfare, environment protection, relief and emergency assistance, preserving art, heritage, culture, religious and a host of other issues.

Social businesses based on models of micro credit, self-help and stakeholder centred management have grown to become large and successful businesses promoting stakeholders' interests. They have also been able to decentralise management to ensure empowerment and participation of the poor. Examples include Amul Milk Cooperative, Sewa India and Tilonia.

Large number of corporate houses and companies in India are doing significant work in CSR, including corporate philanthropy. For example, CSR programmes at the Tata group of companies extend across a wide spectrum including rural development, community development and social welfare, family initiatives, tribal development and water management. Again, as part of the Aditya Vikram Birla Group's Social Reach, the Birla group focusses on health, education including adult education and rehabilitation of the handicapped persons. Table 1 shows the top 10 companies in terms of their CSR spent.

Some companies are also integrating CSR as part of their long-term business strategy. Arthur Page, Vice President AT&T and former Advisor to US President said (Sagar & Singla, 2004) 'All business in a democratic country begins with public permission and exists by public approval'. Smith and Huang (2022) found that some companies are aligning CSR with their corporate goals. For example, Project Sakthi of HUL was based on leveraging the pre-existing SHGs (self-help groups), which had a widespread presence in the various villages in India. A woman who would be a member of the SHG would be chosen by HUL to be a 'Shakti-entrepreneur'. She would be made the HUL distributor and would receive the stock at her doorstep, which she would sell to both the consumers directly and the rural retailers. This would lead to women empowerment as the woman would be able to make a living. The Tata Business Excellence Model integrates social responsibility into the framework of corporate management wherein social responsibility is encapsulated as a key business process.

Table 1. CSR Spent Top 10 Companies.

Company (Rank Based on 2020–2021 Spent)	2020–2021 (in Rs. Cr)	2016–2017 (in Rs Cr)
Reliance Industries	922	649.26 (rank 1)
Tata Consultancy Services	674	380 (rank 3)
Tata Sons	545.83	
HDFC Bank	534.03	305.42 (rank 4)
ONGC	531.45	504.91 (rank 2)
IOCL	445.09	213.99 (rank 9)
NTPC	418.87	277.81 (rank 6)
Infosys	361.42	289.44 (rank 5)
ITC	355.43	275.96 (rank 7)
Wipro	246.99	186.31 (rank 10)
Oil India		216.74 (rank 8)

Source: Author using information from National CSR Portal.

The next part of the chapter discusses the case of ITC e-Choupal and builds a framework to integrate business into the CSR activities.

PART II

ITC E-CHOUPAL

ITC e-Choupal model is much talked about in India as a model tailor-made to tackle the challenges posed by the unique features of the rural India, characterised by fragmented and dispersed farms, weak infrastructure and the involvement of numerous intermediaries, among others. It constituted a unique rural digital infrastructure network to share information and empower the farmer community (Appendix 1). The model also facilitated the purchase of farm produce from the farmers' doorsteps at a pre-determined price. This chapter studies e-Choupal from the perspective of integrating CSR with the business of the company.

e-Choupal is the largest initiative among all internet-based interventions in rural India started in June 2000. ITC's vision is to create a network of 20,000 e-Choupals, thereby extending coverage to 100,000 villages representing one-sixth of rural India. But news reports in 2010 quote the architect of the model stating that 'expansion of e-Choupals stopped in 2007' (Appendix 2).

Is this an issue of sustenance or is it a pause?

E-CHOUPAL MODEL

The traditional foodgrain procurement model operates out of the Mandi. The Mandi is central to the functioning of the agricultural output marketing channel and is part of the Government of India regulated marketing system. It acted as a delivery point where farmers brought their crop for sale to traders. It is part of the legislation in India that all agricultural produce have to be sold through the regulated markets. The trading was facilitated by the commission agents called Adatiyas (the brokers who bought and sold produce). The Kachha Adatiyas were 'pure purchasing agents' who only bought on behalf of others. On the other hand, the Pukka Adatiyas financed the trade as representatives of distant buyers and sometimes even procured produce on their own account.

The decision of the farmer on when and at what price to sell the produce was based on local information within the village. It was here that the role of middlemen came in by providing/blocking information to the farmers. Very often, to avoid peak-season crowds, the farmer would go to the Mandi the night before. Peak-season Mandi volume ranged from 2,000 to 5,000 metric tons of wheat per day. This could result in situations wherein the market price maybe different (maybe lower) by the time the farmer's turn to sell comes. Since they cannot take the produce back, the farmers are forced to sell at the prevailing (lower) prices.

It was in this backdrop that ITC initiated the e-Choupal project (appendix 1). A choupal is usually headed by a village elder and is a forum for interaction, information gathering and business. It is here apart from other things farmers discussed issues related to their crops and problems/solutions related to their produce. ITC used this concept to implement its model, a gathering around the internet connected computer (e-Choupal). The model intended to offer CSR benefits to the farmers to raise their living standard by offering them information, expertise and a fair price for their produce.

It should be noted that the farmers were at no obligation to sell to ITC. They could sell to the open market if they get a better price or to ITC if ITC's price was higher than the market price.

Sustenance of the Model: Issues

The model could raise the following questions:

- So, what is the benefit for ITC?
  A farmer would sell only if ITC's price is higher than the market price. This raises the question of the feasibility of procuring raw materials for ITC's agri-business at a high price.
- Does it make business sense?
  As a CSR it could make sense, but how long and at what scale should the CSR model continue to procure raw materials at a higher price than what ITC would have got from the open market.
- Does providing information and advice on farming practices build trust with ITC or make it an obligation for the farmers to sell to ITC? Are there reasons other than price which would make a farmer sell to ITC even if ITC's price is lower than the market?

These questions would require an understanding of the role of the middleman in the procurement process. In rural India, the middleman, apart from procuring farm produce, plays an important role of providing money to facilitate agricultural production. Over 80% farmers depend on the middleman for purchase of agricultural inputs. Studies have shown that the formal sector provides only around 27.5% of the credit requirement of the farmers and the rest is met by the middlemen (Agricorner, 2011). Moreover, the credit to the farmers goes beyond agricultural needs. Middlemen give credit for social (family functions) also. And this credit is without any documentation and waiting time.

So, if a farmer shifts to e-Choupal, he would be breaking his ties with the middleman and runs the risk of not getting credit from the middleman in the future.

Sustenance of the e-Choupal model would require ITC to shift the farmers from the middleman by building a collaborative growth model, mutually benefiting both the farmer community and ITC, wherein the farmers could benefit through enhanced farm productivity and higher farm gate prices and ITC could benefit by building a competitive advantage.

Table 2. Procurement Model.

	Low Value Crop/Addition	High Value Crop/Addition
Low Price differentiation	Traditional agricultural regulated market	Medicinal plants
High Price differentiation	Fruit and vegetable procurement	Milk processing plants

Source: Author.

THEORETICAL FRAMEWORK

Procurement should ideally be an economic activity benefiting both the parties without any bias. The different examples of procurement are depicted in Table 2. Companies working towards building CSR activities should therefore develop long-term strategies which mutually benefit both the parties.

For e-Choupal to be successful the benefit for the farmers from the company has to increase without creating a conflict with the existing system, as selling to e-Choupal could mean redefining the social and financial relations with the middlemen. The company can expect the farmers to sell only if the company can create a confidence that they would be able to take care of their needs from a long-term perspective. The stages of building a long-term perspective are shown in Table 3.

In stage 1, the company should aim at reducing conflict and build confidence. ITC has adopted the price discovery option to build the confidence. ITC is only providing information and opportunity of higher prices for the farmer's produce. There is no obligation for the farmer to sell to ITC. It also involved the middlemen as part of the initiative to avoid the conflict.

> Status: It had reached out to over four million farmers in over 35,000 villages through 6100 kiosks across ten states (Madhya Pradesh, Haryana, Uttarakhand, Karnataka, Andhra Pradesh, Uttar Pradesh, Rajasthan, Maharashtra, Kerala and Tamil Nadu) (ITC Portal).

In stage 2, the relationship building activities could be taken up wherein the farmers are trained in growing specialised crops which would provide higher value to the farmer. Though there may not be price differences between different procuring agencies for their higher value crops, the farmer could get a higher value as they are growing specialised crops.

> Status: As part of the echoupal initiative, ITC has also initiated 'Choupal Pradarshan Khet (CPK)'. This initiative provides information about the latest and best agricultural practices (agricultural extension services) to help farmers increase productivity. The services are

Table 3. Stages of Building a Long-Term Commitment.

	Low Value Crop/Addition	High Value Crop/Addition
Low Price differentiation	Current situation	Build relationship. Training, Income enhancing activities. Crop diversification
High Price differentiation	Reduce conflict. Build confidence. Information based. Price discovery.	Win-Win. Commitment. Build export opportunities.

Source: Author.

customised to the local needs. As per the company portal with 91,900 CPKs the company has been able to reach eleven lakh farmers.

Finally, a win-win situation is where a commitment from both the sides is developed. Here the company should be able derive a higher price for the specialised crops by value added processes (e.g. Amul) or building export markets. This is when value addition would benefit both the farmer and the company.

Status: This is a time-consuming process, and the company needs to create a minimum base before it can start stage 3. So, the company needs to consolidate, and this could be the reason for the company to hold on expansion of e-choupals temporarily (Exhibit 2).

While the e-Choupal could have a greater focus on CSR, the business benefit to ITC could accrue from stage 3 when ITC also gains from value-added products/export marketing. In addition, the business model of the company goes beyond the procurement through e-Choupal, where the business model includes building a FMCG superhighway (Choupal Sagar) to cater to the needs of the farmers benefiting from the e-Choupal. Choupal Sagars are multi-purpose hubs that not only take care of the procurement of agricultural commodities but also sell products and services to the farmers.

FMCG SUPERHIGHWAY

ITC had also set up the ITC Choupal Sagar. These are rural supermarkets where everything from a mere safety pin to things as big as a tractor would be sold for the convenience of the rural population. This was done to ensure a one-stop shopping experience to the villagers who otherwise had to travel to the nearby towns or cities for purchasing goods. Choupal Sagar also made quality products available to the farmers. Choupal Sagars also used to conduct Choupal Mahotsavs and Choupal Haats. Choupal Mahotsavs are three-day events to provide a multi-brand consumer engagement platform which provides entertainment, information and shopping at ITC Choupal Sagars. Health camps are also conducted during the Mahotsavs. The Choupal Haats provide companies an opportunity to understand the needs of the target audience and offer solutions. The Choupal Haat platform includes consumer engagement, product demonstration, sampling, retail seeding, lead/enquiry collection and tracking of leads/enquiries.

So the company, while raising the income of the farmers through CSR, is providing a platform for them to purchase branded and good quality goods and services at Choupal Sagar (superhighway). The underlying assumption is that the higher income derived from the benefits of e-Choupal will increase their aspiration to replicate the behaviour of their urban counterparts (Pingali, 2012), that is purchase good quality products and aspirational brands.

Companies wanting to enter the rural markets could sell their products through the 'super highway'. For example, Motorola used this route to cater to the non-metro markets (Balakrishnan, 2017). The bargaining power of ITC would help it to procure brands at a lower price and gain from its margins. That would complete the journey from CSR to a business model.

The farmers will gain by getting higher incomes from better agricultural practices and getting aspirational products close to their places and ITC would gain by getting high quality farm produce for its agribusiness division and good returns for brands sold from the Choupal Sagar (business model).

Status: ITC's Agri Business has set up 24 Choupal Saagars across the three states.

- Uttar Pradesh: Hathras, Chandouli, Hardoi, Budaun, Bahraich, Gonda, Pilibhit and Jagdishpur (Fuel Station only).
- Madhya Pradesh: Sehore, Vidisha, Itarsi, Chindwara, Dewas, Dhar, Mhow, Ujjain, Nagda, Ratlam and Mandsaur.
- Maharashtra: Wardha, Yavatmal, Amravati, Washim and Parbhani.

The multi-category hypermarkets offer a wide range of apparels, footwear, grocery, consumer durables, electronics and household items and other items. Aspirational brands available at Choupal Saagars include Classic Polo, Duke, Donear, DCot, Integriti, Chota Bheem, Adidas, Red Chief, Bata, Relaxo, Nilkamal, Bombay Dyeing, VIP, Welspun, American Tourister, Hawkins, Milton and Singer (Company information https://www.itcabd.com/rural-marketing.aspx).

The success of Choupal Sagar would depend on (1) establishment of Choupal Sagar at places catering to the intended target group and (2) the e-Choupal is able to raise the farmers' income, as the supermarkets may be unviable till then. Again, this would need a pause for consolidation.

As part of CSR ITC would not only help farmers through their e-Choupal (CSR), but it could also benefit its agribusiness division through developing and marketing value added products or export marketing. In addition, the Choupal Sagar would help ITC gain from the retail business. Mukerji (2020) also highlights the business side of the e-Choupal model by stating that the company gained by strategically integrating supply chain, lowering transaction costs, increasing sourcing efficiency and product differentiation.

IMPLICATIONS FOR STRATEGIC CSR

Porter and Kramer (2006) state the relationship between business and society need not be a zero-sum game. Anlesinya and Abugre (2022) found that strategic CSR contributes significantly to business value creation. The case study suggests that the path from a CSR perspective towards a business model should be seen as a 'gradual' process that requires vision, commitment, integration, innovation, competence, management systems and resources (Ragusa, 2011).

Burke and Logsdon (1996) identify 'centrality, visibility, appropriability or specificity, voluntarism and proactivity' as the dimensions of strategic CSR and managing them effectively would create business value. They define centrality as 'a measure of the fit between a CSR programmes and the firm's mission and objectives'. Specificity or appropriability means that the firm should be able to gain business value from CSR. Proactivity refers to the firm's responsiveness to the stakeholders' expectations.

Siltaloppi, Rajala, and Hietala (2021) discuss the management practices that need to be considered to manage the challenges companies would face while integrating CSR with the corporate goals. The companies could therefore look at integrating their corporate goals with CSR.

REFERENCES

Agricorner. (2011, February 2). Can the role of middleman be eliminated? Retrieved from http://www.agricorner.com/can-the-role-of-middleman-be-eliminated/. Accessed on June 6, 2012.

Anlesinya, A., & Abugre, J. B. (2022). Strategic CSR practices, strategic orientation and business value creation among multinational subsidiaries in Ghana. *Society and Business Review*, *17*(2), 257–279.

Balakrishnan, R. (2017). Hello again. MOTO: A look at the smartphones Brand revival. Retrieved from http://timesofindia.indiatimes.com/articleshow/57042292.cms?utm_source=contentofinterest&utm_medium=text&utm_campaign=cppst

Burke, L., & Logsdon, J. M. (1996). How corporate social responsibility pays off. *Long Range Planning*, *29*(4), 495–502.

Carroll, A. B., & Brown, J. A. (2018). Corporate social responsibility: A review of current concepts, research, and issues. In *Corporate social responsibility* (business and society 360, Vol. 2, pp. 39–69). Bingley: Emerald Publishing Limited.

Chavan, M., Gowan, S., & Vogeley, J. (2022). Collaborative corporate social responsibility praxis: Case studies from India. *Social Responsibility Journal*. ahead-of-print No. ahead-of-print.

Davidson, D. K., Tanimoto, K., Jun, L. G., Taneja, S., Taneja, P. K., & Yin, J. (2018). Corporate social responsibility across Asia: A review of four countries. In *Corporate social responsibility* (business and society 360, Vol. 2, pp. 73–132). Bingley: Emerald Publishing Limited.

European Commission. (2001). *Green paper: Promoting a European framework for corporate social responsibility*. COM 366. Brussels: European Commission.

Gupta, A. D. (2007). Social responsibility in India towards global compact approach. *International Journal of Social Economics*, *34*(9), 637–663.

ITC Portal. Retrieved from http://www.itcportal.com/about-itc/newsroom/press-reports/PressReport.aspx?id=258&type=C&news=e-choupal-reach. Accessed on November 22, 2010.

Jones, B., Ryan, B., & Tench, R. (2009). Corporate irresponsibility and corporate social responsibility: Competing realities. *Social Responsibility Journal*, *5*(3), 300–310.

Kumar, R. (2022). DB corp spends more than 4% of its net profit on CSR in FY 2021–22. Retrieved from https://indiacsr.in/db-corp-spends-more-than-4-of-its-net-profit-on-csr-in-fy-2021-22/

Kumar, R., Murphy, D. F., & Balsari, V. (2001). *Altered images: The 2001 state of corporate responsibility in India Poll*. TERI-India. A TERI Report, New Delhi.

Letza, S., Sun, X., & Kirkbride, J. (2004). Shareholding versus stakeholding: A critical review of corporate governance. *Corporate Governance*, *12*(3), 242–262.

Margolis, J., Elfenbein, H., & Walsh, J. (2007). *Does it pay to be good? A meta-analysis and redirection of research on the relationship between corporate social and financial performance*. Harvard Business School, Boston, MA. working paper.

Mishra, S. (2020). Evolution of corporate social responsibility: Two sets of explanation. *Social Responsibility Journal*, *16*(8), 1341–1356.

Moon, J. (2014). *Corporate social responsibility: A very short introduction*. Oxford: Oxford University Press.

Moure, R. C. (2011). Is there any relationship between organizational charts and corporate social responsibility? The EU-15 banking case. *Social Responsibility Journal*, *7*(3), 421–437.

Mukerji, M. (2020). *Re-examining strategic and developmental implications of e-Choupal, India*. doi:10.1002/isd2.12132

Munro, V. (2020). CSR historical and emerging themes and related terms. In *CSR for purpose, shared value and deep transformation* (pp. 15–51). Bingley: Emerald Publishing Limited.

Nahapiet, J., & Ghoshal, S. (1998). Social capital, intellectual capital and the organisational advantage. *Academy of Management Review*, *23*(2), 242–266.

Narayanan, S., & Singh, G. A. (2022). Will legalizing corporate social responsibility get businesses to participate in welfare activities – The case of India. *Society and Business Review*. ahead-of-print No. ahead-of-print.

Orlitzky, M., Frank, L. S., & Sara, L. R. (2003). Corporate social and financial performance: A meta-analysis. *Organization Studies, 24*(3), 403–441.

Pingali, V. (2012). Urban orientation of rural consumers: Implication for consumer goods distribution. *International Journal of Rural Management, 8*(1–2), 107–119.

Porter, M. E., & Kramer, M. R. (2006). Strategy and society: The link between competitive advantage and corporate social responsibility. *Harvard Business Review, 84*(12), 56–68.

Ragusa, R. (2011). Integration of company responsibility, the learning process: The autogrill case. *The Journal of Management Development, 30*(10), 1000–1016.

Sagar, P., & Singla, A. (2004). Trust and corporate social responsibility: Lessons from India. *Journal of Communication Management, 8*(3), 282–290.

Siltaloppi, J., Rajala, R., & Hietala, H. (2021). Integrating CSR with business strategy: A tension management perspective. *Journal of Business Ethics, 174*, 507–527.

Smith, K. T., & Huang, Y.-S. (S). (2022). A shift in corporate prioritization of CSR issues. *Corporate Communications: An International Journal.* ahead-of-print No. ahead-of-print.

UNIDO. (2020). What is CSR?. Retrieved from https://www.unido.org/our-focus/advancing-economic-competitiveness/competitive-trade-capacities-and-corporate-responsibility/corporate-social-responsibility-market-integration/what-csr#:~:text=Key%20CSR%20issues%3A%20environmental%20management,%2C%20and%20anti%2Dcorruption%20measures. Downloaded. Accessed on August 22, 2022.

UNIDO. (2022). What is CSR. Retrieved from https://www.unido.org/our-focus/advancing-economic-competitiveness/competitive-trade-capacities-and-corporate-responsibility/corporate-social-responsibility-market-integration/what-csr

Wartick, S. L., & Cochran, P. L. (1985). The evolution of the corporate social performance model. *The Academy of Management Review, 10*(4), 758–769.

APPENDIX 1

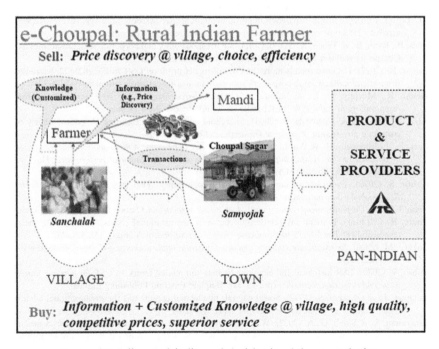

Source: https://www.alcindia.org/cdm/view/module-on-marketing.

APPENDIX 2

E-CHOUPALS: DEVESHWAR'S DREAM GETS HAZY, BUSINESS STANDARD, ISHITA AYAN DUTT | KOLKATA 18 AUGUST 2010

ITC's showcase project has stopped growing after 2007. ITC Chairman Y. C. Deveshwar wanted to do a Walmart with e-Choupals, which leveraged the internet to empower small and marginal farmers by linking them directly with buyers. It was his showcase project and Deveshwar made sure he walked the talk. But 10 years after the launch of the project, both the walk and the talk are showing signs of faltering. Launched in 2000 with six installations, the number of e-Choupals grew to 6,500 in 2007, and at one point of time, ITC was opening six such choupals a day.

E-CHOUPALS: DEVESHWAR'S DREAM GETS HAZY REDIFF.COM: 18 AUGUST 2010

ITC Chairman Y. C. Deveshwar wanted to do a Wal-Mart with e-Choupals, which leveraged the internet to empower small and marginal farmers by linking them directly with buyers. It was his showcase project and Deveshwar made sure he walked the talk. But 10 years after the launch of the project, both the walk and the talk are showing signs of faltering. Launched in 2000 with six installations, the number of e-Choupals grew to 6,500 in 2007, and at one point of time, ITC was opening six such choupals a day.

The largest such online initiative for farmers made for numerous case studies, including at the Harvard Business School and C. K. Prahalad's 'The Fortune at the Bottom of the Pyramid'.

The target then was to have 20,000 e-Choupals, covering 100,000 villages, by 2010. Three years later, however, much of the zing is missing, as the number has remained stagnant at 6,500. 'The ten-year old boy stopped growing after age seven,' said an industry insider. S. Sivakumar, chief executive of the agribusiness division of ITC and architect of the e-Choupal, said for all practical purposes, expansion of e-Choupals stopped in 2007. No new e-Choupals are being set up at this time.

ENABLING SKILL DEVELOPMENT IN THE PANDEMIC – THE CSR PERSPECTIVE

Shulagna Sarkar, Snigdha Shukla and Ram Kumar Mishra

ABSTRACT

The pandemic has affected people across the world. Businesses have been impacted and in a way have affected the employment scenario worldwide. The skill development initiative is playing a major role in bringing back the affected to the mainstream. Skill development efforts have always been a true solution to income generation especially in context to developing the underprivileged segment of the nations. Numerous countries are enabling skill development through the corporate social responsibility (CSR) practices. India is one such country which has undertaken lot of effort in enabling Skill Development by encouraging impact-based CSR practices. It would be interesting to understand the impact of pandemic on work and how the skillsets are expected to change with the change in the working environment. The chapter mainly focusses in identifying the workplace changes with special reference to Education, Information technology, Retail, Mining and Power Generation sectors in the Indian context. It has also attempted to share the existing skill gap in fulfiling the organisation's expectations and the strategies addressing the skill gap. The chapter also shares best practices in skill development and focusses mainly on understanding the impact of such efforts. The chapter uses case study as a methodology and includes qualitative data analysis of impact interviews. The chapter uniquely attempts to share the policy, programmes, outcomes and major road blocks especially in context to skill development in the Indian scenario and how CSR drive has been instrumental in addressing the skill gap in India.

Strategic Corporate Responsibility and Green Management
Critical Studies on Corporate Responsibility, Governance and Sustainability, Volume 16, 83–97
ISSN: 2043-9059/doi:10.1108/S2043-905920230000016006

Keywords: Skill development; CSR; COVID-19; unemployment; skill enhancement; countries

INTRODUCTION

The world has been witnessing numerous unanticipated transformations not just in workspace but also in an individual's life. In the Indian scenario, limited skill set for an individual or business operation acts as a big hindrance. Businesses are forced to transform themselves to more technology-driven, demanding and dynamic roles. One of the primary challenges by Indian businesses is the shortage of technical, specific and general employability skills. The skill deficit in the country has put skill development as an urgent national priority. With the advent of pandemic and rising technology intervention there is a raised anxiety among the working group world across.

A well-educated population, equipped with the relevant knowledge, attitudes and skills is essential for the economic and social development of any nation in the twenty-first century. Education is the most potent tool for socioeconomic mobility and a key instrument for building an equitable and just society. Education provides skills and competencies for economic well-being. India has a population of 1.3 billion at present, of which about 0.8 billion is of the working age. We generally boast of our demographic dividend as one of our strengths, but this strength is on the other hand the greatest challenge for the country. Irrespective of the large working population, research by CII and its partners reveal that there is a huge gap in the quality of skills availability to that of the required. In fact for about 3/4th Indian businesses, one of the primary challenges faced is the shortage of technical, specific and general employability skills. The large working population of the country is both a strength and challenge as a number of research studies reveal that there is gap in the quality of skills availability to that of the required.

The chapter attempts to share a larger picture of the skill development in a global front. An attempt has been made in identifying the workplace changes with special reference to Education, Information technology, Retail, Mining and Power Generation sector in the Indian context. It is also attempted to share the existing skill gap in fulfilling the organisation's expectations and the strategies addressing the skill gap. The chapter also shares best practices in skill development and focusses mainly on understanding the impact of such efforts. The chapter uses case study as a methodology and includes qualitative data analysis of impact interviews. The chapter uniquely attempts to share the policy, programmes, outcomes and major road blocks especially in the context to skill development in the Indian scenario and how CSR drive has been instrumental in addressing the skill gap in India.

COVID-19 SCENARIO – A WORLD VIEW

The novel coronavirus (COVID-19) pandemic has created an unprecedented health emergency situation across the world for the past 3–4 months. The resultant preventive and curative measures have seen the day-to-day business coming to a grinding halt or significantly slowing down various industries, creating tremendous stress on world economy. It's no different in India. The novel coronavirus pandemic has resulted in an unimaginable loss of human lives also leading to loss to the global economy unprecedented in an era of global peace. COVID-19 has impacted people and in a way has encouraged both the organisations and employees to react in varied ways. Not only are the numbers upsetting but also the speed at which the challenges have emerged across the world is intimidating (Refer Table 1).

SKILL DEVELOPMENT – A GLOBAL VIEW

Governments in every country have the responsibility to set up the overall framework that shapes the education system and defines its operation. They determine the organisation and structure of the system. Factors like years of compulsory education, students' age for entry in school, grade levels, courses offered, teachers' qualifications, provision of compulsory education (public and/ or private actors), choices of schools available, mechanism of financing education, standards by which education providers are held accountable, etc. play a major role in determining the accessibility and quality in accessibility of education of the country. World Economic Forum (WEF, 2020) data clearly indicate that 93% of the world's workers resided in countries which are practicing 'workplace closure' as a strategy to prevent the spread of coronavirus. The report clearly indicates that only 30% of the businesses are focussing on re-skilling and up-skilling programmes.

Automation, artificial intelligence, machine learning and a global pandemic – It is definitely not surprising that professionals are in fear of losing jobs. As

Table 1. COVID-19 Spread Across the World.

S.No.	Country, Other	Total Cases	Total Deaths	Total Recovered	Deaths/ 1M Pop	Population
	World	347,282,497	5,604,853	276,824,461	719.1	
1	USA	71,394,579	887,643	44,191,512	2,657	334,019,477
2	India	38,903,731	488,911	36,301,482	349	1,401,087,479
3	Brazil	23,757,741	622,647	21,851,922	2,897	214,907,717
4	France	16,001,498	128,347	10,063,579	1,960	65,498,037
5	UK	15,709,059	153,490	11,957,439	2,243	68,440,290
6	Russia	11,044,986	325,433	10,000,577	2,229	146,031,742

Source: Created by Authors based on Worldometer Statistics, 22nd January 2022.

businesses across sectors strive to achieve digital transformation within a record time, the workforce needs to grow with these changes. Entrepreneurs and professionals are looking at new implications, and that's where re-skilling comes in handy. Having a limited skill set for any employee or business owner could be a big hindrance, especially as businesses gear up for demanding and dynamic roles. For unicorn startups and new entrepreneurs, re-skilling and up-skilling are not buzzwords anymore. It is estimated that a mere 4.69% of the total workforce in India has undergone formal skill training of any sort compared to 68% in the United Kingdom, 75% in Germany, 52% in the United States, 80% in Japan and 96% in South Korea.

India is adding about 12 million people to the job market every year, whereas a very small percentage of the workforce has undergone skill training of any form. India has a population of 1.3 billion that is expected to reach 1.48 billion by 2030. India will be the largest contributor to the global workforce, with working-age population (15–59) likely to swell from 749 million to 962 million over 2010 to 2030 (UNESCO, 2012). By 2025, the average age in India will be only 30 years, compared with a median age of 40.6 in China, 39 in Australia and 50.5 in Japan (Statista, 2022). For details on Skill development efforts during pandemic with varied country perspective (Refer Table 2).

Table 2. Skill Development Efforts During Pandemic – Country Perspective.

Country	Key Practices to Enable Skill Development	Indian Efforts
United States	• Core skill community formed to focus on high-growth sectors. Building stockpile of technological devices • Education emergency relief of around 6 billion USD. • Outreach, prevention, education and non-discrimination (OPEN) guidelines for education sector stakeholders	• Full stipend for 2.4 lakh apprentices during the lockdown period with an overall planned outlay of INR 36 crore by the Ministry of Skill Development and Entrepreneurship (MSDE) • 33 National Skill Training Institutes under Directorate General training proposed to be used as quarantine centres
South Korea	• Main components of the programme include technical vocational and education (TVET). • Main actors of skills development assistance are KOICA and EDCF who are in charge of grant aid/technical cooperation and soft loans, respectively. (Chun & Cheol Eo, 2012)	• Introduction of virtual classrooms and promotion of e-learning in schools in disadvantaged and inaccessible places by the Department of Education, of one of the largest Indian states • Extension of training batches for enroled candidates for National Skill Development Corporation (NSDC) courses on Skills India Portal
United Kingdom	• Funds under Innovate UK to be utilised • Launched COVID-19 self-employment income support scheme to support apprenticeship and grant payout • New session plan to be released by quarter end • Special attention to job-creating sectors	
China	• China has around 13,093 schools offering vocational secondary education The MOHRSS is responsible for the following training providers – Technical schools also known as Skilled Worker Schools	

Table 2. *(Continued)*

Country	Key Practices to Enable Skill Development	Indian Efforts
	(SWSS) are the main providers of training for skilled workers. • Loan staffing of workforce in cross-sectors. (Mehrotra, 2014)	
France	• Learning Nation label created and broadcast on TV to promote skill development • Counselling telephone cells for parents of students • Facilitating prompt reallocation of employment to essential activities during the emergency	
Australia	• Task force to monitor the impact • Cash inflow, communication and collaboration to stabilise vocational sector • Wage subsidy up to 50% to apprentices	

Source: Authors.

PANDEMIC AND SKILL DEVELOPMENT – INDIAN PERSPECTIVE

The COVID-19 pandemic has severely affected the job market across the world. This is a major concern for people and the governments throughout the globe, but even more concerning is the fact that the conditions are not expected to improve very soon. The pandemic-induced lockdown and physical distancing measures have caused not only unexpected disruption in the provision of education and training but also sparked innovation, in particular, in distance learning. Initially the pandemic had put a complete full stop to the training and skill development and thus shifted the world a few years in the backward direction, but technology came as a saviour and all this led to an unprecedented shift towards digitisation as organisations across the world re-imagined their business models and working patterns.

While access to learning and skills development was maintained in some contexts through a rapid shift to distance learning in technical and vocational training and education, the pre-existing social, economic and digital divides deprived the most underserved and marginalised groups of continued learning and put them at risk of falling further behind, compared to the privileged class which has access to all the facilities and resources. This condition is more or less similar across the globe, but economic and financial status of the individuals as well as the nation as a whole also play a key role in determining the resources available, and thus the accessibility to required skill development training programmes.

With only a few exceptions, the increased adoption of distance learning solutions by technical and vocational training and education programmes has definitely not facilitated the acquisition of required and necessary practical skills. Business shutdown and severe decline in profits has negatively affected employment and prospects of decent work. This also caused wage cuts as well as number of offers of paid trainings and apprenticeship placements in enterprises. Lack of fully operational distance-learning platforms and educational resources, disruptions to assessment and certification, and a general decline in the quality of training caused demotivation among learners and teachers and, together with rising economic hardship, increased the likelihood of people dropping out of education. Industries re-invented their business or market, the skills which employers looked out for has also undergone a shift. While on one hand the pandemic made a lot of companies realise the need to have professionals with advanced and specific skill sets, and on the other hand the pace of up-skilling and re-skilling the workforce has slowed down drastically.

The disruptions due to the COVID-19 pandemic are varying in nature across various industrial sectors. While the workforce of some industries like healthcare and pharmaceuticals were over-burdened with work, people from sectors like aviation, tourism and hospitality struggled a lot even to earn enough for their livelihood. As cited by (CMIE, 2020) report on unemployment for India, just in the matter of two months since the pandemic arrived in the country for the first time, the unemployment rate shot up to a record high, and in April 2020, it reached up to 23.52%, causing great economic turmoil (Refer Fig. 1). This social and economic turmoil was further reflected in the GDP growth of the subcontinent for the year 2019–20. The annual GDP growth percentage of India was shot down to its most negative value of −7.252% for the year 2019–20 as per the World Bank report.

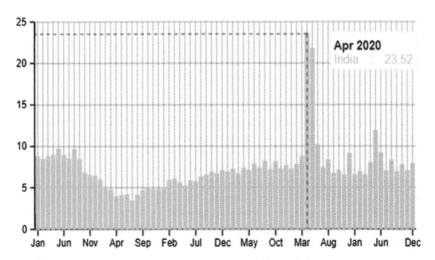

Fig. 1.   Unemployment Rate – CMIE Series (UER ≥ 15). *Source:* Centre for Monitoring Indian Economy Pvt. Ltd.

According to the World Bank (2020) report, India is one of the youngest nations in the world today with around 67.265% of its population in the age group of 15–64 years and over 62% of its population in the working-age group of 15–59 years. Apart from this, around 54% population comes under the below 25 years age tab. India's burgeoning young and energetic workforce of more than 830 million people can be an invaluable asset not just for India but also for the senescent developed world, provided it is nurtured as per the requirements and prepared well for the future. It is the responsibility of the government to make efficient and judicious use of such an extraordinarily large pool of manpower.

According to the World Economic Forum's Future of Jobs Report, 50% of all employees will need to re-skill by 2025 as the adoption of technology increases. It is thus very important for the employees as well as for the business leaders to keep learning, unlearning and re-learning things with a pace comparable to the pace of changing technology.

The time when companies are struggling to stay afloat doesn't seem to be very appropriate for employee up-skilling and re-skilling. The crisis of 2020 as its effects, have been uneven. Government has taken a lot of measures to curb the crisis, but still there are a lot of challenges to bridge the voids already created by this pandemic. As cited by the KPMG report Ramaswamy et al. (2020), some key challenges that the Skill Sector in India is facing are as given in Table 3.

SECTORAL PERSPECTIVE TO SKILL DEVELOPMENT

Workplace changes with special reference to Education, Information technology, Retail, Mining and Power Generation sector in the Indian context have been shared in Table 4.

Table 3. Mitigating Key Challenges to the Skill Availability.

S.No	Key Challenges	Strategic Efforts to Address Challenges
1.	Mobilising labours post migration due to the COVID-19 lockdown	Increasing reach to the labours, creating awareness, building support and winning trust back.
2.	Low focus on capacity development and training due to increased costs with more need for training requirements.	Adequate opportunities to train and build capacities in association with grassroot level NGOs who will enable wider reach of
3.	Limited availability of IT infrastructure for conducting online training	available infrastructure for providing needed training.
4.	Reduced debt serviceability of skills service providers	Encouraging smaller Skill development agencies for skill development. Providing adequate training to youth, women, and other marginalised groups.
5.	Reduced or diminishing CSR funds for skill-development initiatives	Encouraging MoUs with corporate to engage in skill development initiative. Partnering
6.	Lack of employment and apprenticeship opportunities due to deferment of recruitment by industry	through apprenticeship programmes to make available skilled workforce at affordable payment option.

Source: Authors.

Table 4. Sectoral Perspective to Skill Development.

Sector	Impact of Pandemic	New Skill Sets Required
Education	• Distinctive rise of e-learning, digital classes • Increased accessibility to international experts and speakers • Rise in computer courses, language classes, and online skill assessments	• Digital Skills, specially basic computer literacy have become mandatory for learners as well as for the teachers
Information Technology	• IT services predominantly new services and developments to be impacted due to cost cutting • With surge in remote working, usage of remote connectivity tools and networking to witness surge in demand. • Mobile application development and Media Development to experience growth	• Re-skilling, up-skilling to be critical in job retention enabling existing workforce to work on wider set of technologies. • Local businesses need to emerge with online stores to sustain • Wider online search skills needed with acclimatisation to newer apps and technology experience.
Retail Sector	• Increased shift towards online shopping • Change in consumers' purchasing expectation and overall lifestyle • Increased demand of health and hygiene related products	• Leveraging technology like digital payment methods, data-driven insights • Need for augmented reality to make online purchasing experience better
Mining	• Suspension of mineral production • Loss of wages on account of absenteeism and pandemic restrictions, unemployment, and declined sale of minerals in the market • New mineral deposit exploration affected	• Large-scale automation and usage of artificial intelligence becomes important, as mechanised mines with fewer staff need not slow their operations to the same extent as labour-intensive mine sites. • Re-training and up-skilling workers forced out of the mining. Labour market due to the crisis has become essential to ensure their transition to other economic sectors
Power Generation	• Loss of revenues and liquidity crunch for Indian DISCOMs due to reduction of demand from the commercial and industrial customers • Deviation in demand and supply patterns at a temporal and locational level	• Need for more skilled and trained people in industry • Need to undertake measures like smart metring, smart grid technology • Adopting renewable sources of energy • Adoption of Blockchain in managing distributed energy resources • Artificial Intelligence

Source: Authors.

   Though each sector is unique in its operation and challenges associated differ considerably, there is a high need for collaboration between public and private sectors for skill development initiatives. As there is a low participation of women compared to men in the workforce, the skill development initiatives catering to equi-gender also differ and mostly the skills-based courses for women differ widely. There is a dearth of standardisation of skill trainings when compared to the global standards and the nature of skills essential for a large number of jobs is not properly documented. In fact, there are a large number of companies that do not follow structured job analysis techniques leading to poor documentation of jobs. Table 5 reflects the workforce impact of Covid-19 pandemic across sectors.

Table 5. Workforce Impact of the COVID-19 Pandemic Across Sectors.

Sector	Impact
Aviation, Hospitality, Tourism	**HIGH**
Transport and Logistics	
Construction and Engineering	
Consumer Durables and Electronics	
Textiles and Apparels	
IT and Telecom	
Automobiles and Auto parts	
Financial services sector	
Agriculture and Horticulture	
Healthcare and Pharmaceutical	**LOW**

Source: Created by Authors based on information available at KPMG Covid-19: Skills sector Impact.

GOVERNMENT OF INDIA – EFFORTS TO ADDRESS SKILL GAP

In order to address the skill gap across the nation in the pre-pandemic period, the Government of India had set up the Ministry of Skill Development & Entrepreneurship (MSDE) and various schemes under its compass such as Pradhan Mantri Kaushal Vikas Yojana (PMKVY), Skill India, SANKALP and National Skill Development Mission (NSDM) etc. The MSDE has set up institutional mechanisms at three tiers to help in making this mission successful; a Governing Council at the apex level for policy guidance, a Steering Committee and a Mission Directorate. The Mission Directorate will be supported by three additional institutions that will help the Directorate to facilitate proper and smooth functioning by working horizontally:

- National Skill Development Agency (NSDA) – The NSDA anchors the National Skills Qualifications Framework (NSQF) and allied quality assurance mechanisms for synergising skill initiatives in the country. It acts as the nodal agency for State Skill Development missions. Also, it has the responsibility to raise extra-budgetary resources for skill development and training from various national and multi-national agencies including the private sector.
- National Skill Development Corporation (NSDC) – NSDC is one of its kind, with multiple stakeholders involved in catalysing the skill development initiatives across the country. Its stakeholders include many private players, non-profit organisations, Central and State Government of India, various schools/universities, etc. It aims at upgrading the skills of the citizens at par with the international standards, by developing and designing the frameworks for standards, curriculum and quality standards. The NSDC also enhances, supports and coordinates private sector skill development initiatives, based on

the PPP (Public–Private partnership) model and prioritises those initiatives having multi-dimensional effects over others with one-off impact.

• Directorate General of Training (DGT) – The DGT is a National Level apex organisation for coordination and development of the programmes related to vocational trainings, including women-centric vocational trainings. Industrial Training Institutes and under the direct control of Central or State Governments, the DGT has the authority to frame the overall policies, norms and common standards and procedures. It also functions to assist Scheduled Caste/ Scheduled Tribes and people with disabilities by enhancing their capabilities for getting jobs or for self-employment.

The Government of India has already launched many campaigns including 'Make in India', to develop the Indian subcontinent into a manufacturing hub and to increase the job opportunities for the people living here. The government also launched the 'Skill India' programme under the same mission to complement the 'Make in India' campaign as it considered the genuine inability of the industries, businesses and service sectors, to recruit unskilled and inexperienced manpower for the jobs.

The goal of *Make in India* with *zero defect* (quality) and *zero effect* (on the environment) stands as a herculean task for the existing government. As a vision statement, there could not be anything more appropriate for India when the data by World Bank for 2013 said India ranked 132nd out of 185 economies in Doing Business. The Make in India programme includes major new initiatives creating opportunities in 25 different sectors designed to facilitate investment, foster innovation, protect intellectual property and build in best-in-class manufacturing infrastructure ultimately aiming to transform *India* into a global manufacturing hub. The 'Make in India' vision though very appropriate yet lately awakened stands questioned due to several reasons like deficient infrastructure, inhospitable business environment, corruption, problems with access to timely and adequate credit, land acquisition, high burden of taxation and restrictive labour regulations and inadequate availability of quality workforce.

Irrespective of the large working population, research by CII and its partners reveal that there is a huge gap in the quality of skills availability to that required. In fact for about 3/4th Indian businesses, one of the primary challenges faced is the shortage of technical or specific skills. The other challenges are shortage of general employability skills such as teamwork, communications and others faced by 2/3rd businesses followed by lack of applicants and required work experience faced by over 61% businesses, respectively. The research also revealed that employability in the skill pool seems to decline with an increase in age.

It is high time that thought leaders are encouraged to strategise in strengthening the employability skills in India. Rapid action is needed from academia as well as the Government to impart the desired skills to the talent pool so that they are fit for employment in industries. 'Collaboration' amongst the Academia, Students, Employers and Government holds the key to resolve the Big Indian Talent Conundrum.

With the advent of the fourth industrial revolution, the skill requirements in all the sectors have changed greatly, forcing the industries, the Government and the academia to focus on developing new-age skills including analytical ability, critical thinking, design thinking, creativity, innovation, sustainability, complex cognitive skills and most importantly, the technical skills needed for the jobs. The Ministry of Tribal Affairs partnered with Facebook India to launch the 'Going Online as Leaders' (GOAL) programme initiative to digitally skill 5,000 tribal youth in the country (USAID India, 2020)

The COVID crisis has further accelerated the process of transition to the automation revolution. When it comes to enabling the skill development for the future workforce, it requires two types of changes: up-skilling, in which the employees develop new skills to perform better or fit more into their pre-existing or current roles, and re-skilling, in which the staff or the employees develop capabilities to fit into an entirely new job or role. According to different industry reports and National Policy for Skill Development and Entrepreneurship (2015), as much as 40% of vacancies at the entry level don't get filled due to paucity of skilled manpower.

If the skill development is not paced on par with the number of available jobs in the country, a skill gap would emerge to cripple the entire demand and supply of talent in the nation. This is already evident in various jobs roles related to AI, ML, Cloud infrastructure, Biotechnology and Energy sectors. When India is emerging as a global leader in industry and scientific advancement, the skill gap should be addressed in every nook and corner of the country. A skill gap analysis conducted by the National Skill Development Corporation (NSDC) in 2014 reports an incremental requirement of 109.73 million skilled manpower by 2022 across 24 key sectors.

The reflection on skill availability and skill shortages in India in 2019 revealed several new-age jobs and highlighted that people are unable to find a suitable match due to skill gaps across sectors. According to the International Labour Organization (ILO), India is staring at a 29 million skill deficit by 2030. Owing to the skill shortage, 53% of Indian businesses could not recruit in 2019–2020. On the other hand, India is expected to have talent surplus of 245 million workers by 2030 (Ferry, 2018). Bridging the skills gap between work and education is necessary to sustain the productivity and growth of the economy. Further addition of under-educated and unskilled people into the workforce will reduce the overall quality of the workforce.

As revealed by the Wheebox (2021) India Skills Report, the youth employ-ability in the Indian subcontinent stood at 45.9% consisting of highly employable resources, which is significantly lower than the previous year. The emergence of skill gap, which is exacerbated by the COVID-19 pandemic, is the prominent reason that youth employability reduced to 45.9% from last year's 46.2%. As the ways of working and technology are evolving faster every day, there is an evident gap between the education system and the skills required in the real world.

As per a 2019 UNICEF report on learning outcomes projections for South Asian countries, more than half of Class-12 passed young Indian students will lack the skills to find jobs by 2030 (GBCE, 2019). The prominent reasons behind this are outdated and low-quality course contents and sub-optimal vocational training provided to the school students, which do not provide them with adequate skill levels, thus making them incompetent for employment. India loses out to the Maldives (46%), Nepal (46%) and Pakistan (40%) who are projected to see even fewer young students reach the right level of learning and skills to tackle the jobs of 2030 (UNICEF, 2019).

According to a (APAC report, February 2021) prepared by the consulting firm AlphaBeta and commissioned by Amazon Web Services (AWS), India's present workforce comprises only 12% digitally skilled employees. The report estimates that the number of employees requiring digital skills in the country will need to increase nine-fold by 2025, and an average Indian worker will need to develop seven new digital skills by 2025 to balance the demand-supply curve and to keep pace with the technology. This would amount to a large figure of nearly 3.9 billion digital skill trainings from 2020 to 2025. Even in non-technology sectors like education and manufacturing, there is a huge demand for more digital workers, to support constant growth and innovation. This report also highlights the top five in-demand digital skills in India, which are: cloud architecture design, software operations support, game/websites/software development, large-scale data modeling and cybersecurity skills.

It is estimated that around 39 to 58% of the worldwide work activities in the operationally intensive sectors could be automated using currently demonstrated technologies. As the automation in operations across various sectors will increase, it will cause a subsequent shift in the job roles for tomorrow. The sectors will then need people who can handle the automated equipment, and do the jobs that cannot be done by machines. In future, demand in the job market is expected to decline for physical or manual skills in repetitive and predictable tasks, as well as for the basic literacy and numeracy skills. In contrast, demand for techno-logical skills, complex cognitive skills and other high-level social and emotional skills is expected to rise in the coming decades (Table 5).

Interestingly, the pandemic revealed a huge skill gap in the IT sector alone. Major businesses have begun to shift to the technology demands of the day. The skill gap in the IT sector can be addressed by increasing practical exposure to the latest technologies that gained popularity in the last 5 years. With a tremendous shift towards remote working specially in the corporate sector, demand for social skills, along with technological skills has increased manifold, as while working remotely every employee needs to be adaptive, collaborative, self-disciplined, motivated and accountable. The cloud computing giants Microsoft and Amazon continued their investments in India even during the crisis. According to India Skills Report 2021, skill gap is found to be maximum in the fields of Data Science, Artificial Intelligence and Natural Language Processing. Data analysis skills were found to be the most important by the employers from automotive and core (oil and gas, power, steel), manufacturing and e-commerce (rating >3.5 on a scale of 4). Similarly, human-centred design is given quite an emphasis from manufacturing, pharma and IT sector employees. The essential skills to overcome the skill gap in the Indian context include Communication, Collaboration,

Table 6. Top Five Essential Skills.

Technical Skills	Soft Skills
Python Programing	Problem-solving
Neural Networks	Communication
Cloud Computing	Active learning, resilience, flexibility
Supply Chain	Digital Dexterity
General statistics	Analytical and Critical thinking

Source: Authors.

Decision-making, Problem-solving, Critical Thinking and Digital Literacy (Refer Table 6). It was also suggested that being able to manage the distribution of tasks along with processing information relevant to decision-making is equally important to enhancing employability skills.

Industries have adopted several measures to adapt with the inclusion of new-age technology for access, efficiency and control, while a skill gap emerges in time to address the future of up-skilling and re-skilling initiatives in the Indian subcontinent.

CSR AND SKILL DEVELOPMENT

CSR contributes to governmental resources and delivery mechanisms either to supplement these, i.e. to chip in, or as a substitute, to fill up 'governance gaps' especially where governments are weak, corrupt and under-resourced, and institutions are weak (Blowfield & Frynas, 2005; Matter & Moon, 2008; Visser, 2008).

The Schedule VII of the CSR Act mentions skill development as one of the activities to be undertaken. The Government has mounted several initiatives to ensure better education – extending from the Sarva Shiksha to The Right to Education (RTE) Act, 2009. India has also taken up the Sustainable Development Goals (SDGs), as well as initiated various schemes and programmes including girl child focus, scholarships, single-teacher schools, teacher training and more. In terms of SDGs, SDG#4 (Quality Education) and SDG#3 (Good Health and Living) have witnessed the highest CSR expenditure (Niti Ayog, 2021). Education remains the most preferred area for CSR expenditure with 27% companies spending 31% of overall CSR expenditure, which is around INR 5,700 crores FY18-19. While there is a high spend on education, separately skill development has not received much attention. The biggest challenge that India's public education system faces today is that the tremendous success in achieving nearly 100% access to schooling has not translated to quality learning (Fig. 2).

Fig. 2. Forms of Skill Development Effort in India. *Source:* Authors.

CONCLUSION

The skill deficit in the country has put skill development as an urgent national priority. Companies can play a significant role in skill development. The CSR leaders can invest in a number of opportunities in skill development through their CSR initiatives. Though education as a whole receives high attention, CSR separately is not able to draw attention to skill development especially to building vocational skills. While, on the other hand, the government has promoted numerous schemes to support skill development and address skill gap, there is a gap when it comes to collaboratively addressing the issue. Various stakeholders to the issue of skill gap including government, corporates and grassroot level NGOs need to join hands to address the skill gap. This is more prominent at present because of the pandemic spread; the companies are not able to considerably focus on hiring and recruitment freezes has led to low focus on skill development.

Hence, CSR project models must incorporate capacity building training programmes for youth, women, poor and marginalised individuals and groups through NGOs, volunteers, corporates and professionals, networking and partnership for skills development and employability enhancement programmes, developing entrepreneurship EDP training, skill development and employability workshops. These initial steps are what will help the country in fulfiling the dreams of Make in India and help us to take advantage of our demographic dividend.

REFERENCES

APAC. (2021). *Unlocking APAC's digital potential: Changing digital skill needs and policy approaches.* Retrieved from https://aws.amazon.com/blogs/publicsector/new-report-asia-pacific-workforce-applying-digital-skills-increase-five-fold-2025/. Accessed on December 22, 2021.

Blowfield, M., & Frynas, J. G. (2005). Setting new agendas: Critical perspectives on corporate social responsibility in the developing world. *International Affairs, 81*, 499–513.

Chun, H. M., & Cheol Eo, K. (2012). *Aid for skills development: South Korea case study.* Unescdoc Digital Library. Retrieved from https://unesdoc.unesco.org/ark:/48223/pf0000217875

CMIE. (2020). Centre for monitoring Indian Economy Pvt. Ltd.: Unemployment rate in India. Retrieved from https://unemploymentinindia.cmie.com/. Accessed on December 5, 2021.

Ferry, K. (2018). *Future of work: The global talent crunch.* Retrieved from https://www.kornferry.com/content/dam/kornferry/docs/pdfs/KF-Future-of-Work-Talent-Crunch-Report.pdf. Accessed on November 20, 2021.

Global Business Coalition for Education (GBCE), The Education Commission. (2019). *The 2030 skills scorecard.* Retrieved from https://gbc-education.org/wp-content/uploads/2019/09/GBC-Education-2030-Skills-Scorecard.pdf. Accessed on November 29, 2021.

Matter, D., & Moon, J. (2008). "Implicit" and "explicit" CSR: A conceptual framework for a comparative understanding of corporate social responsibility. *Academy of Management Review, 33*(2), 404–424.

Mehrotra, S. (2014) *China's skill development system: Lessons for India, IAMR report No. 2/2014,* Planning commission GoI.

Niti Ayog. (2021, April). *Social impact assessment of corporate social responsibility in India, FY14-15 to FY19-20.*

NPSDE. (2015). *National policy for skill development and entrepreneurship* (pp. 1–4). Retrieved from https://archive.pib.gov.in/documents/rlink/2015/jul/p201571503.pdf. Accessed on November 24, 2021.

Ramaswamy, N., Vilvarayanallur, M., Ghosh, D., Katiyar, A., Maheshwari, A., Singh, K. P., … Srivastava, J. (2020). COVID-19: Skills sector impact – How should India respond? Retrieved from https://assets.kpmg/content/dam/kpmg/in/pdf/2020/04/covid19-skills-sector-impact.pdf. Accessed on January 5, 2022.

Statista. (2022). Median age of the population in India 2015. Retrieved from https://www.statista.com/statistics/254469/median-age-of-the-population-in-india/. Accessed on January 22, 2022.

UNESCO. (2012). *Global education digest, education at a glance report, OECD 2014, NSDC, economic times Jul 5 2014, eleventh five year plan 2007–2012.*

UNICEF Press Release. (2019). More than half of South Asian youth are not on track to have the education and skills necessary for employment in 2030. Retrieved from https://www.unicef.org/press-releases/more-half-south-asian-youth-are-not-track-have-education-and-skills-necessary. Accessed on January 20, 2022.

USAID India. (2020). Country development cooperation strategy. Retrieved from https://www.usaid.gov/india/cdcs. Accessed on December 20, 2021.

Visser, W. (2008). Corporate social responsibility in developing countries. In *The Oxford handbook of corporate social responsibility.* Oxford Handbooks.

WEF. (2020). *Resetting the future of work agenda: Disruption and renewal in a post-COVID world.* Retrieved from http://www3.weforum.org/docs/WEF_NES_Resetting_FOW_Agenda_2020.pdf. Accessed on October 25, 2021.

Wheebox. (2021). *India Skills Report 2021: Key Insights into the post-covid landscape of talent demand and supply in India.* Retrieved from https://indiaeducationforum.org/pdf/ISR-2021.pdf. Accessed on January 04, 2022.

SUSTAINABLE COMMUNITIES AND CONSCIOUSNESS – THE MISSING LINK TO A LOW CARBON TRANSITION IN DEVELOPING ECONOMIES

Subhasis Ray

ABSTRACT

Global warming and climate change have created an urgency for change in the global system. This change is envisaged through regulations, financing, policies, technology and innovations related to all of them. In this chapter, I argue that such a techno-centric, piecemeal, mechanistic and transactional approach is bound to fail unless we have a spiritual foundation and a sustainable community building strategy. All work of the society ultimately aims for a group of people living together harmoniously. Thus, sustainability transition has to be founded on commonalities of consciousness often found in 'intentional' communities – a group of people bounded by a common aspiration/faith and living together. The chapter analyses the case of Auroville, located in Puducherry, India, and its 54-year history to draw conclusions about sustainable community building and discuss its implication for a low-carbon, equitable, net-zero society.

Keywords: Global warming; climatic change; regulations; financial policies; technology and innovations; transactional approach; spiritual foundation

INTRODUCTION

Sustainability and sustainable development have become the cornerstones of all global activities today. Countries, corporations, communities and individuals are

Strategic Corporate Responsibility and Green Management
Critical Studies on Corporate Responsibility, Governance and Sustainability, Volume 16, 99–110
Copyright © 2023 by Emerald Publishing Limited
All rights of reproduction in any form reserved
ISSN: 2043-9059/doi:10.1108/S2043-905920230000016007

exploring ways to reduce their greenhouse gas emissions on one hand and provide social and economic sustainability to the global citizens on the other. The scale and scope of such a global transition is unprecedented in human history. The COVID pandemic has shown that global challenges can change the dynamics of human life, but it is also possible to craft a global response to human existence. The approaches to a sustainable world are moving in two convergent directions – tackling climate change and providing just and equitable transition opportunities to poorer countries and communities. It is also clear that the emergent solutions need to come from the multiple realities of the developing world due to their concurrent needs for economic growth, demographic situation, inequal societies and political priorities. While it is tempting to think about new, green innovations in every sphere of human life, it is worthwhile to study the existing efforts to build sustainable communities and the lessons learnt from them. Over the last 100 years, several communities around the world have tried to design and live an alternative life inspired by philosophers and spiritual leaders. While the surface level looks of such communities vary around the world, they are similar in their search for a better world through cleaner, greener and a more conscious lifestyle. In this chapter, I draw upon the case of Auroville, India. Founded in 1968, Auroville is a community of seekers who have tried every aspect of sustainable living for the last five decades – urban design and land use planning, participatory governance, afforestation, green energy, sustainable mobility, organic food, sustainable fashion, local area development to name a few. All endeavours were guided by the vision of Auroville being a 'living laboratory' to achieve human unity. This study shows that there are several challenges in building sustainable communities even when their members are united by a common goal and faith: translating vision to practice, having enough number of committed individuals, resources for transition, balancing personal and communal growth and aspirations and the crushing pressure of the 'world as usual'. In this chapter I use sustainability and climate change interchangeably for the convenience of the readers though sustainability has a broader implication for human civilisation.

OBJECTIVE

There are many pathways to sustainable transitions – policy, technology, regulation, innovation – which need to work together if we are to move to a cooler and better world. While it is tempting to think of such tools as a silver bullet, we know from history that there are many uncertainties including human greed and ingenuity that prevent achieving sustainability at a global scale. Much of the challenges arise from the tension between growth and sustainability in emerging economies. Most developing countries point out the need to provide for the poor first (just transition). The objective of this short chapter is to draw lessons from the history of sustainable community building at Auroville. Auroville provides a rich history of 54 years in trying to build a conscious, sustainable community. It had adopted sustainability as an operating principle of community development long before the world knew the term and became cognizant of its challenges.

Some of the significant areas of achievement include afforestation, sustainable construction, building alternative economic and business models and governance approaches. The success and failure of various initiatives at Auroville can provide us lessons to keep in mind as India and the whole world try to pivot towards a greener future. The objective of this chapter is thus to tease out lessons from Auroville's journey which can inform readers about the challenges of building sustainable community. The broad research questions that inform this chapter include (1) How has Auroville done in terms of building a futuristic city and a sustainable community? and (2) What lessons can be learnt from Auroville's 54-year journey in terms of adopting sustainable practices and policies?

BACKGROUND

Auroville was founded on 28 February 1968, but its roots could be traced back to the philosophy of the Indian yogi, philosopher and thinker, Sri Aurobindo and his spiritual partner Mirra Alfassa, popularly known as The Mother. The place selected for the city was a barren patch of land in southern India. Auroville was designed to be a 'living laboratory', a 'future city', *a place where all human beings ...could live freely as citizens... a place of peace, concord and harmony* (Majumdar, 2017, pp. 37–38). The guiding principles of Auroville were put down in The Auroville Charter (see Exhibit 1). Over time, it received recognition from the UNESCO as *an international cultural township designed to bring together the values of different cultures and civilizations in a harmonious environment with integrated living standards which correspond to man's physical and spiritual needs.* (https://auroville.org/page/statements-of-support-unesco-960). The Auroville Emergency provision Act (1980) provides the Indian government overall authority in managing the township. As of 2022, around 3,000 residents from 50+ countries stayed in Auroville. The noted French architect Roger Anger was entrusted in designing the township for a future population of 50,000. Many early inhabitants of this township were Europeans who were fed up with the materialistic and consumerist culture of the West and were searching for a new ideal and spirituality. Building a city in a barren plateau thus provided the material and spiritual challenge for the first inhabitants of Auroville.

METHODOLOGY

The chapter uses the case method which is suitable for emergent phenomena (Yin, 2011). Qualitative, longitudinal studies are suitable for providing us a granular view of a phenomenon. Given Auroville's location in India and its history of adopting community-wide sustainable practices, it is a suitable case for studying community level challenges in moving to a low-carbon, equitable and inclusive society in developing countries. Data have been drawn from the author's association with Auroville for the last two decades, several field visits, archives of the community newsletter AV Today, books and writings of

Aurovillians, semi-structured interviews with Aurovillians and published academic literature on Auroville.

LITERATURE REVIEW

The political and cultural challenge in achieving sustainable development has given rise to the idea that sustainable communities may hold the key to the current problems. Sustainable communities are tied to the local realities and provide glimpses of how social, environmental and economic development are inter-connected and what trade-offs are required to achieve a balance (Bridger & Luloff, 1999). Sustainable community development requires a new approach to planning and consideration of both poverty and environmental degradation (Roseland, 2000). Building such community requires building social capital first (Bridger & Luloff, 2001). When communities are formed by like-minded individuals with a clear goal, they are often known as intentional communities. Such communities are often driven by a common faith or philosophy like Findhorn in the United Kingdom (Forster & Wilhelmus, 2005). Communities set up with an environmental goal are also known as eco-villages. Several scholars in anthropology, sociology, religious studies and philosophy have studied such communities. However, studying the history of such communities to understand the challenges of sustainable development in developing countries are relatively rare. This chapter aims to fill this gap.

There is admittedly very few publications on Auroville (Kapur, 2018), one of the reasons being that Aurovillians themselves are primarily interested in their work as a 'sadhana', a spiritual practice that focussed on work as an expression of their self. They are not keen to market or publicise their work, efforts and projects. This trend has changed recently, during the 50-year celebration of the community, with some of them (Kapur, 2018; Majumdar, 2017) coming out with books that chronicle the journey of the community and its members. Management literature on Auroville is sparse with a few exceptions covering specific topics like sustainable fashion (Bandyopadhyay & Ray, 2020; Ray & Bandyopadhyay, 2020), menstrual health and social entrepreneurship (Cherrier, Goswami, & Ray, 2018; Ray, Goswami, & Roy, 2016) and marketing of hygiene products among rural women (Sivaramakrishnan, Ray, & Goswami, 2020).

FINDINGS

Economy

Sustainable Development has been conceptualised as a balance among the 3 p's: people, planet and profit, with the underlying idea that economic growth that exploits natural and human resources is not sustainable. Global warming from climate change provides adequate evidence and warning in this direction Thus, economy and economic growth that balance social and environmental needs and eliminate poverty have been seen as central to sustainability transition. It is questionable if the existing economic system can deliver anything beyond incremental benefits while transitioning to a low-carbon economy. One of the central challenges has been the need for continuous growth in the capitalist system. With calls for de-growth and new forms of capitalism like conscious capitalism (O'Toole & Vogel, 2011), scholars have already signalled the need to re-think the existing market-based and market-driven system. The pioneers in Auroville thought through this problem and suggested five strategic issues in organising an alternative economy: 'ownership, money, work, business and fundraising' (Thomas & Thomas, 2013, p. 297).

The Auroville charter is clear about *ownership*: 'Auroville belongs to nobody in particular. Auroville belongs to humanity as a whole'. (www.auroville.com) hence all economic activities and enterprises are owned by the community. Auroville initially envisaged an economy with no circulation of *money* as the very nature of money creates challenges in achieving a sustainable community: ...*for in this place money would be no more the sovereign lord. Individual merit will have a greater importance than the value due to material wealth and social position. Work would not be there as the means of gaining one's livelihood, it would be the means whereby to express oneself, develop one's capacities and possibilities, while doing at the same time service to the whole group, which on its side would provide for each one's subsistence and for the field of his work* (The Mother, cited in Majumdar, 2017, p. 38).

Although many efforts have been initiated like a debit account, Auroville card and others, it is clear that Auroville is far away from this goal. Today leading scholars of Circular Economy has called for an economic system that is less automated and more labour intensive. In its goal to create harmonious relationship with the neighbouring villages, Auroville has experimented with *work* in two ways: involving local community (instead of outsourced contracting) in all aspects of economy and looking at work itself as a goal of their sadhana or yoga. Combination of these two aspects means that most Auroville enterprises remain small. Because work is considered as yoga, Auroville entrepreneurs lack in the competitive spirit of the market and are often satisfied with whatever is the outcome of their efforts as 'the motivation for work...is the expression of individual creativity and the opportunity to serve the community' (Thomas & Thomas, 2013, p. 301). Such approaches have been tried in other parts of the world like in Mondragon, Spain, and pose a challenge to conventional growth of the economy and enterprises. Funding of Auroville has been mainly through grants and donations. Thus, ensuring a steady flow of funds for economic activities has been a consistent issue in the community. From a sustainability perspective, we can argue that Auroville has shunned the primacy of economy in building a future city and society and always considered economic priorities in tandem with social (housing, transport, education) and environmental needs (afforestation). Lack of a formal banking mechanism has also hindered the growth of the economy.

Within Auroville, economic activities are unique in many ways: work is seen as part of self-expression and self-growth and enterprises are owned by the community and surplus is ploughed back to the community fund. More than 200 enterprises operates within Auroville in diverse areas like transport, food, clothing, furniture, electronics, home accessories, stationeries etc. (see auroville.com for some of the products manufactured by the community). Thomas and Thomas (2013) have provided an exhaustive review of the economic activities of the community and this section draws upon their work.

The Auroville economy has played a key role, though with mixed results, in fulfiling the Auroville vision of a future city. Sharing economy is a popular term these days. Auroville has experimented with sharing of common resources (food, clothes) for five decades now. The Auroville enterprises have generally increased their turnover and surplus over the years. However, without a banking system within the community, all economic activities relied on grants and donations. The goal of integrated local development also means that most Auroville enterprises relied on labour from neighbouring villages. However, Auroville economy's performance has not been smooth and consistent. Faced with pressure from the external world, many enterprises could not survive, and thus the original idea of creating a self-sufficient economy is still a distant goal. The labour market wages that kept on increasing put a dent on revenue and profitability. In keeping with the community's idea of individual growth and self-realisation, there has been no central support or monitoring of Auroville enterprises.

The three core aspects of economy – production, distribution and finance – have played out differently over the last five decades in Auroville. Given its focus on conscious growth and development, production has not been able to generate consistent performance. This will create challenges for the city in the coming days if it wants to attract 50,000 people and also address the increasing urbanisation around its periphery. Several free goods distribution initiatives have been experimented (like Pour Tous) to meet the community needs to a reasonable level. As long as the distribution of basic goods and services are met with, Auroville will have the headroom to grow and experiment with alternatives. As discussed above, finance remains a recurring issue in management of Auroville.

To test the success of Auroville economy, one would need to look at alternative parameters like integrated regional development, township development, inclusive growth rather than growth and revenue numbers. The fact that the city has survived for five decades as an island of alternative thinking in the middle of a highly competitive global economy provides hope for sustainability scholars and practitioners.

Environment

Auroville started in a barren patch of land with no vegetation or water. Over the last 54 years, there has been a magical transformation of the land that now has been afforested and boasts of a rich flora and fauna. A 'green belt' now surrounds the city and provides natural resources and regenerative ecosystem for the entire region. The zone is now used for agriculture and farming, nature regeneration and recreation. Regenerative farming is now adopted by multi-nationals like Pepsico (Pepsico, 2021). Auroville has pioneered such practices for many decades now. The goal has been to create a model prototype for the entire bio-region for the benefit of all stakeholders and not just the residents of Auroville. We are today seeing an increasing number of climate change induced natural disasters like flood, cyclone and drought. Forest management practices at Auroville have created natural barriers and solutions to many such problems. Inbuilt in such systems are solutions for coastal erosion management, wastewater treatment and experiments in producing energy from waste and biomass. Finally, social capital is enhanced by using forest and farmland for leisure and recreation of the community and teaching local farmers techniques in sustainable farming. Such initiatives are linked to the economic bottom line by highly successful social enterprises like Upasana and Mason's, producing sustainable apparel and organic chocolates, respectively.

In the process of building the city, innovative approaches to water management, soil conservation, seed collection, organic farming, renewable energy and construction were adopted. The community skills in such activities have attracted attention of several stakeholders and many Aurovillians today provide consulting services to governments in the area of sustainable development. Low cost sustainable construction techniques using local materials and appropriate architecture first piloted in Auroville are now used around the world in developing countries. Such efforts at environmental sustainability is driven by the conviction of integrality, that nature and human beings form the same continuum of consciousness and need to work with each other.

People

Clearly, it's the residents and their belief in The Mother's and Sri Aurobindo's vision that drives Auroville and its activities. Unlike other communities, one cannot simply move in to Auroville but has to go through a waiting period as a newcomer to convince the current residents about one's suitability in gaining a permanent residence status. While all are welcome to settle down irrespective of their social or material position, consciousness and belief in human unity provide safeguard against touristic incursions and converting Auroville to a high-end residential community. Auroville's relation with surrounding villages has gone through ups and downs like most sustainable communities. Around 8,000 villagers get their livelihood from working in Auroville and many, attracted by the ideology and activities, have become permanent residents. Yet, there have been occasional reports of violence and perceptions of discrimination against local villagers. As discussed above, The Mother was very clear that Auroville's success depended upon developing a holistic and symbiotic relationship with surrounding villages. She insisted that early Aurovillians work side by side with local villagers in building the city.

From its inception, Auroville has tried to develop a sound *governance* model shaped by the philosophy of Sri Aurobindo. Initially, The Mother gave the broad guidelines for conflict resolution (for example, drugs were prohibited in the community). A major event in the community's history is its tussle with the Sri Aurobindo Society over the ownership of Auroville which ultimately led to The Auroville Act, 1980. Over a period of time the Residents' Assembly was formed to handle issues related to running the city. The Governing Council, managed by the Indian government, worked with the Assembly to arrive at operating principles. Most common decisions are taken in collective Town Hall meetings. To ensure smooth relationship with local villagers, Village Liaison Groups are formed. The overall goal is to resolve issues by dialogue and mediation.

Education in Auroville followed The Mother's direction and was provided free of cost to all residents. Integral education was conceptualised as a learning system without formal boundaries and based on the learning capacity of the students. Being a 'living laboratory' the scope of education was broad based. Some recent initiatives include creating a unique vocational education for local youth in the area of digital systems. There is no fee but learners sponsor future students once they are able to earn their livelihood. Free trainings are provided in mediation, meditation, leadership, yoga, arts and music for interested residents.

Auroville provided free *healthcare* to its residents. Alternative therapies like homoeopathy, Ayurveda and yogic treatments are popular in the community. Facilities include palliative care, mental health support and geriatric care for old residents. In line with sustainable *mobility* principles, cycles and electric vehicles are encouraged though some residents use conventional motor cycles for long distance travel. Food provided in the community kitchen was cooked using solar power and organic crops grown primarily in Auroville. Several free stores operated for sharing of goods. Art and crafts shows are regular features where residents exhibit their skills.

DISCUSSION

Sustainability and climate change have many dimensions – policy, regulation, technology and justice to name a few. In spite of several improvements in our living conditions some persistent issues continue to dog humanity: hunger, poverty and peace to name a few. The ongoing war in Ukraine shows that sustainability is not about a green technology or policy but the human willingness to live and flourish together. Different stakeholders like to point out the relevance and criticality of the aspect that matters to them most. Systems thinking, de-growth, circular economy-based thoughts emphasise the need to have big-picture thinking to address the 'grand challenges'. In this chapter I argue that we need to look at cases like Auroville to understand how different elements of sustainability connect and conflict in the context of sustainability community building. The answer to sustainability challenges are not in functional innovations like electric cars but rather conscious, community-based interventions like transport systems which may use electric vehicles as part of the solution.

Auroville's success on the environmental front was driven by sheer need to build a city in a desertified land. Difficult material and financial conditions provided the impetus to use resources with care. The European background of the early settlers helped in thinking out of the box: they lived in thatched huts and enjoyed concreting as part of their yoga. Thus construction, water management and farming are some of the community success stories that can inform the world.

Auroville lessons can be particularly useful in resource constrained developing world where growth and sustainability have to go together. The concept of local, small scale, integrated development promoted by economists like Schumacher (2011) and Gandhi has been implemented by Auroville for over five decades. Since most developing countries have a prominent rural–urban divide in terms of development, Auroville's effort to integrate its growth with local villages and bio-region can be particularly instructive. Mega-cities and urban sprawls are global challenges in terms of resource distribution and access within a country. Auroville provides some pointers in building new, sustainable cities. For example, a pre-decided number of residents (50,000 in the case of Auroville) based on the 'carrying capacity' of an urban system could be a pre-condition for avoiding urban poverty.

The results on the economic front have been mixed at the best. While several enterprises flourished in the Auroville eco-system, lack of regular funding and rules around ownership (all property and economic units belonged to Auroville) meant that many economic units had to close down. This aspect is similar to the current (political) debate about financing sustainability in developing countries and may require further studies including the role of central banks in guiding economic growth trajectories.

The 'failures' in Auroville are also important lessons for us. Several conflicts cropped up during Auroville's journey: with neighbouring villages, with financing organisations like Sri Aurobindo Society and intra-community conflicts. Conflicts exist in interpreting what The Mother wanted and wrote on several aspects. However, Sri Aurobindo's and The Mother's writings and the personal spiritual vision of the residents often help in coming to a solution for seemingly intractable problems. Such conflicts show that future sustainable communities need to invest in better governance and conflict resolution mechanisms.

Auroville started with a goal of having 50,000 residents but have only around 3,200 residents from 59 countries in 2022 (www.auroville.org). Close to half of the Auroville population are Indians. The small number of Auroville residents can be considered as an acknowledgement of the fact that true sustainable development can/will be embraced by only a few in the long run and will take time. However, the biggest success of Auroville is its existence for 54 years, carrying along like-minded citizens coming from 50+ countries and pursuing a higher order living and thinking in spite of severe difficulties of all sorts. It shows the possibility of humanity being able to live and flourish *together*.

Bridger and Luloff (1999) have identified five dimensions of a sustainable community: increasing local economic diversity, self-reliance, reduced energy use and improved waste management, natural resource stewardship and social justice. Study of Auroville history shows remarkable performance along all five dimensions. However, most scholars have not studied the longevity of such communities and what such longevity entails. Auroville's example shows two aspects: the need for a common platform (of spirituality/consciousness/belief/faith) and mechanisms to navigate existential challenges.

Flourishing of the whole society may require a different approach based on spirituality (as opposed to two prevalent modes – organized religion and politics) and the consciousness of human unity, rather than piecemeal solutions that does not suit all stakeholders. Having addressed environmental, economic and social challenges, the 50 years of Auroville throws up some pertinent points which could be useful in our quest for a sustainable world:

(1) Sustainable community building requires a common denominator: the consciousness that we are all equal irrespective of our race, religion, caste or creed. Divisive thinking will not allow us to tackle sustainability/climate change which has a disproportionate impact on the poor and marginalised.
(2) Economic sustainability, providing a decent livelihood to the world population (no poverty, as envisaged in Sustainable Development Goal # 1), will be the most difficult to achieve and may endanger efforts on other fronts.
(3) The process of just transition, providing resources to the vulnerable and marginalised, will be slow and conflict ridden.
(4) Having a common goal or charter like the SDGs/net zero/Auroville Charter is helpful in keeping track of our progress though interpretations of such goals will be contested on a regular basis.
(5) Organised religion and political parties may not be required for a sustainable society though democratic principles of governance and conflict resolution will be essential.
(6) Transparent, open and honest communication and education among and within communities is essential for progress. Only through communication and reflection can we make sure that we are in line with our charted path.
(7) We cannot expect a large number of committed changemakers in our effort to build a low carbon economy.
(8) Our approach to sustainability needs to be experimental and experiential, aided by a 'never ending education' (which aligns closely to the management concept of agility) given its varied dimensions and challenges.

LIMITATIONS

There are of course limitations in trying to condense the 54-year history of a community within a few of pages and draw lessons from it. The founders of Auroville have written thousands of pages explaining their integral yoga and how it manifests on earth and how a physical place like Auroville can provide seekers with an opportunity to use work as a way of manifesting a higher consciousness. Second, being an outsider, my interpretation of Auroville in terms of its activities and sustainability is likely to be biased and incomplete. Third, this chapter has focussed more on the Auroville economy. This is for two reasons: Auroville economy has been researched more than other aspects like environment and society and the economy's mixed performance cautions us about the difficulty of achieving sustainable development goal # 1: no poverty. However, the purpose of this chapter is to throw some light on such unique socio-spiritual experiments in a developing country and provide some probable lessons to all stakeholders. Future researchers can dig deeper into each of these aspects.

CONCLUSION

The world today is looking for alternative solutions and pathways in every sphere of human life. Fifty plus years of Auroville's existence shows that it is possible to have an alternative system with excellence and sustainability at its core. However, that would require a common denominator of faith, good will and consciousness of human unity. Sustainability in the material plane will only succeed when it has been achieved in the mental and psychic plane. Transformation of the external environment has to be preceded by the transformation of the internal environment, i.e. the mind and spirit of world citizens Without such platforms, we may end up grappling with the complex challenge of climate change and sustainable development. Reflecting back on the Auroville history, one can conclude that economic growth and sustainability will remain a contested area for the world as it readies to change course towards a low carbon economy. The current debate about sustainability financing shows that economic means to achieve sustainability is still unclear and unresolved, much like the Auroville economy discussed in this chapter. As Auroville shows, creating economic sustainability outside of the conventional monetary and financial system will need significant rethink about sustainability financing and the role of financial institutions. Finally, it will be naïve to evaluate Auroville's success in terms of numbers and dates – neither speed nor size drives the social experiment at Auroville. Rather, it is 'quality of everything, especially the quality and consciousness of its participants' (https://auroville.org/page/frequently-asked-questions-on-the-city) that defines its success. Such journeys are never complete but always a work in progress. It is this focus on consciousness, perfection and aesthetics that may be missing in the (developing) world's current efforts to achieve sustainable development.

REFERENCES

Bandyopadhyay, C., & Ray, S. (2020). Finding the sweet spot between ethics and aesthetics: A social entrepreneurial perspective to sustainable fashion brand (Juxta) positioning. *Journal of Global Marketing, 33*(5), 377–395.

Bridger, J. C., & Luloff, A. E. (1999). Toward an interactional approach to sustainable community development. *Journal of Rural Studies, 15*(4), 377–387.

Bridger, J. C., & Luloff, A. E. (2001). Building the sustainable community: Is social capital the answer? *Sociological Inquiry, 71*(4), 458–472.

Cherrier, H., Goswami, P., & Ray, S. (2018). Social entrepreneurship: Creating value in the context of institutional complexity. *Journal of Business Research, 86*, 245–258.

Forster, P. M., & Wilhelmus, M. (2005). The role of individuals in community change within the Findhorn intentional community. *Contemporary Justice Review, 8*(4), 367–379.

Kapur, A. (Ed.). (2018). *Auroville: Dream & reality: An anthology.* Gurugram: Penguin Random House India Pvt. Limited.

Majumdar, A. (2017). *Auroville: A city for the future.* Noida: Harper Collins.

O'Toole, J., & Vogel, D. (2011). Two and a half cheers for conscious capitalism. *California Management Review, 53*(3), 60–76.

Pepsico. (2021). PepsiCo announces 2030 goal to scale regenerative farming practices across 7 million acres, equivalent to entire agricultural footprint. Retrieved from https://www.pepsico.com/our-stories/press-release/pepsico-announces-2030-goal-to-scale-regenerative-farming-practices-across-7-mil04202021. Accessed on October 18, 2022.

Ray, S., & Bandyopadhyay, C. (2020). *Upasana: A social entrepreneur's dilemma in positioning sustainable fashion.* Bedfordshire: The Case Centre. Case number 520010001.
Ray, S., Goswami, P., & Roy, P. S. (2016). *'Wings to fly'* – But to where? Menstrual hygiene, marketization and vulnerability among subaltern women in India. Presented at *the macromarketing Conference*, Dublin, Ireland.
Roseland, M. (2000). Sustainable community development: Integrating environmental, economic, and social objectives. *Progress in Planning, 54*(2), 73–132.
Schumacher, E. F. (2011). *Small is beautiful: A study of economics as if people mattered.* New York, NY: Random House.
Sivaramakrishnan, S., Ray, S., & Goswami, P. (2020). *Ecofemme cloth pads: Reaching rural women.* Ontario: Ivey Publication.
Thomas, H., & Thomas, M. (2013). *Economics for people and Earth: The Auroville case 1968–2008.* Auroville: Social Research Centre.
Yin, R. K. (2011). *Applications of case study research.* Thousand Oaks, CA: Sage.

APPENDIX 1

AUROVILLE CHARTER

(1) Auroville belongs to nobody in particular. Auroville belongs to humanity as a whole. But, to live in Auroville, one must be a willing servitor of the Divine Consciousness.

(2) Auroville will be the place of an unending education, of constant progress and a youth that never ages.

(3) Auroville wants to be the bridge between the past and the future. Taking advantage of all discoveries from without and from within, Auroville will boldly spring towards future realisations.

(4) Auroville will be a site of material and spiritual research studies for a living embodiment of an actual human unity.

(*Source:* www.auroville.org accessed on 18 October 2022).

CORPORATE SOCIAL RESPONSIBILITY IN MSMES IN INDIA

Rajesh Batra

ABSTRACT

The establishment and nurturing of Micro Small and Medium Enterprises (MSMEs) is a resourceful input leading to the rapid development of economic and social prospects. MSMEs could be the steroid which the Indian economy needs at this moment. As global competitiveness rises, the concept of Corporate Social Responsibility (CSR) is proposed as an impressive strategy to rejuvenate MSME operations and competitiveness. The outcomes of CSR activities can help to a greater extent in improving the survival rate of MSMEs and may offer great opportunities for business competitiveness, locally and globally. It helps in creating and developing the entrepreneurial foundation of the nation by supporting enterprises through supply of raw materials and a range of components required for production. Sustainable entrepreneurship is incomplete and inequitable without being given a standing ovation of the small and medium enterprises as engines of inclusive growth and development.

The prime aim of this chapter is to examine the strategies of CSR in MSMEs and its impact on the cexpansion of these sectors. The chapter also purports that CSR activities are not only contributing to large businesses but also creating evidence in enrichment of the competitiveness of MSMEs.

Keywords: Corporate social responsibility; socio political and legal environment; entrepreneurship; inclusive growth; competitiveness; Small and Medium Enterprises; Indian Companies Act

The distinctive feature of Small and Medium Enterprises (SMEs) are less capital investment and high labor absorption which has created unprecedented importance to this sector. As per the Development Commissioner of Micro, Small and

Strategic Corporate Responsibility and Green Management

Critical Studies on Corporate Responsibility, Governance and Sustainability, Volume 16, 111–116

Copyright © 2023 by Emerald Publishing Limited

ISSN: 2043-9059/doi:10.1108/S2043-905920230000016008

Medium Enterprises (2001), the sector has the credit of being the second highest in employment, which is next to the agricultural sector. In India, SMEs form the backbone of industry. There are to date more than 12.34 million SME units contributing 6% to the GDP of India. SME development agencies such as Small Business Administration (SBA) of the United States, Small Business Service (SBS) of the United Kingdom and SIDO (Small Industries Development Organization) in India are the intermediaries set up by the Government. Some of the important organisations that are associated with SMEs in India are: National Small Industries Corporation Ltd. (NSIC), Small Industries Development Bank of India (SIDBI), Confederation of Indian Industry (CII), Laghu Udyog Bharati (LUB) and Small Entrepreneurs Promotion and Training Institute (SEPTI). According to a study by the European Commission in 2007 (Corporate Social Responsibility (CSR) in SMEs – SMEs Good practice), CSR can positively influence SMEs' competitiveness in numerous ways. SMEs can provide improved products, high customer loyalty, motivated employees, innovative and creative employees, cost savings, increased profitability due to optimum resource utilisation, enhanced networking with business partners and improved company image.

The SME sector is a significant contributor to the Indian economy, and its contribution towards economic development is highly remarkable in comparison to any other sector of the economy. Its role towards investment, employment generation, export, GDP, industrial production etc. in every area is highly significant. The annual report of the Ministry of MSME (2010–11) shows that, in terms of value, the sector accounts for about 45% of the manufacturing output and 40% of the total exports of the country. The sector is the *International Journal of Latest Trends in Engineering and Technology* (IJLTET) Vol. 5 Issue 1 January 2015–277ISSN: 2278-621X estimated to employ about 59 million people in over 26 million units throughout the country. There are over 6,000 products ranging from traditional to high-tech items, which are being manufactured by the Micro, Small and Medium enterprises in India.

CSR is commitment by businesses to integrate social and environmental concerns in their business operations. It means the activities undertaken by a company in pursuance of its statutory obligation laid down in section 135 of the Companies Act. Section 135 covers the essential prerequisites pertaining to the execution and management for successful project implementation.

On 1st April, 2014, India became the first country to legally mandate CSR. Section 135 applies to 'Every Company' including private, public, small, government, unlimited, joint venture, new and one-person companies.

CSR is a Board-driven process and the Board of the company is empowered to plan, decide, execute and monitor CSR activities of the company based on the recommendation of its CSR committee. The CSR committee means the Corporate Social Responsibility Committee of the Board referred to in section 135 of the Act.

There is a growing realisation that long-term business success can only be achieved by companies that recognise CSR as part of the process of wealth creation and as a source of competitive advantage.

CSRs coordinate social responsibilities on economic, legal, ethical and discretionary dimensions. The concept of CSR was introduced in India to encourage social welfare activities by companies. This initiative was taken to push India towards achievement of sustainable development goals and public–private partnership in transforming the nation.

The activities undertaken to pursue CSR ought to be in conformity with Schedule VII of the Companies Act 2013.

CSR activities must not be activities that are:

(1) Undertaken in the normal course of business
(2) Undertaken outside India
(3) Only benefiting the employees of the company
(4) Carried out in violation of any statute
(5) On sponsorship basis to derive marketing benefits
(6) Carried out for fulfilment of any statutory obligation
(7) Carried out with contribution from any political party

CSR practices in India are mostly traditional and based on culture. These include activities that benefit the local communities. The responsibilities of businesses towards society have been mentioned even in ancient Indian scriptures like the Bhagavad Gita and advocated very strongly by the father of the nation, Mahatma Gandhi, whose thought became the leading vision and philosophy for nation building after independence.

Some of the activities covered by Schedule VII are as follows:

(1) Eradicating hunger, poverty and malnutrition
(2) Promoting health care including preventive health care
(3) Empowering Women
(4) Promoting gender equality
(5) Animal Welfare
(6) Protection of Flora and Fauna
(7) Agroforestry
(8) Conservation of natural resources
(9) Making available clean drinking water
(10) Livelihood enhancement projects
(11) Training to promote rural sports
(12) Contribution to Prime Minister's Citizen Assistance and Relief in Emergency Situations Fund (PM CARES Fund)
(13) Contribution to Prime Minister's National Relief Fund
(14) Disaster management including relief, rehabilitation and reconstruction activities.

The National CSR Awards instituted by Ministry of Corporate Affairs, Govt. of India, have been conceived as an official recognition at the highest level of outstanding contribution made by Corporates and SMEs by way of CSR activities in the areas of health, education, gender equality, research and development, innovation etc.

The main objective behind this initiative is to encourage companies to fulfil their CSR obligations, maximise the impact through competition and innovation and fully integrate CSR into their business philosophy.

Since India is a type of society that focusses on collectivism than individualism, more importance is given to social values.

CSR PRACTICES IN THE MSME SECTOR

MSMEs are micro, small and medium-sized companies. The basis on which the size of an organisation is defined and classified in the MSME landscape is the Investment in Plant and Machinery/equipment and Annual Turnover.

The SME sector is one of the fastest growing industrial sectors in the world economy which plays a key role in economic development. The emergence of CSR over the past decade quickly gave rise to the expectation that SMEs would tackle some of the world's most pressing economic, social and environmental problems. In the MSME landscape, CSR practices are mainly on Productivity issues, Environmental Responsibility and Social Domains.

Under section 135(1) of The Companies Act 2013, every company is required to spend minimum 2% of its net profit over the preceding three years on CSR activities as per the CSR policy.

Big companies can easily spend a minimum of 2% of their net profit on CSR activities and even micro, small and medium sized companies can do so with the help of collaborations.

Several SMEs have to spend the amount mandated under CSR. However, the small size of the funds available with SMEs and lack of capacity to conceptualise and implement projects is a major barrier. In order to address this gap, the handholding support to SMEs at affordable rates needs to be provided. SMEs' limited human resources and fluctuating performance makes them look at short-term projects. SMEs' growth is constrained by limited availability of managerial skills and specialised skills.

In order to propagate and facilitate compliance of the section 135 of Companies Act, 2013, MSMEs need handholding in CSR-related activities such as:

   i. Designing of new policies and review and revision of existing CSR policies;
   ii. Preparation of projects based on the CSR policies of the company;
  iii. Undertaking baseline surveys in local areas and assess the needs and gaps for developing projects;
   iv. Real-time evaluation of ongoing projects;
    v. Impact evaluation of completed projects;
   vi. Training and capacity building of executives/managers/Professionals and
  vii. Enabling SMEs to pool their resources with other SMEs and entrust responsibility to a single agency for implementation will reduce costs and lead to selection of long-term projects.

Besides, there is a need for preparation of separate communication material developed focussing on specific needs and requirements of SMEs in their CSR obligations.

The challenges faced by MSMEs in CSR projects and improvisation mechanisms are essential in the following areas:

  i. Lack of holistic view of local context – design and target;
 ii. Funds allocated annually instead of long term;
iii. Selection of appropriate projects;
 iv. Capability of implementation agency;
  v. Shortage of human capital and
 vi. Lack of data availability.

IN ENSURING SUCCESS... CONCERTED EFFORT IS IMMINENT!

Government Role:

- Facilitate
- Act as Catalyst
- Provide conducive business environment
  MSMEs need to:
- Innovate
- Automate
- Adopt ICT
- Reskill and Upskill
  Large size Private Sector Role:
- Support MSMEs
- Mentor MSMEs

The concept of CSR has changed over the years depending upon the changes in social, political, economical and legal environments. It includes many aspects which come under the fulfilment of CSR like charity, development of educational institutions, hospitals and temples, ethical functioning, respect to human rights and inclusive development which requires the companies to produce qualitative products up to the mark of international standards and adherence of laws relating to the business, etc. SMEs have played a crucial role in India's economic growth. With over 30 million units, SMEs accounted for 17% of the country's GDP in 2011 and employ around 60 million people, the second largest workforce in the country after the agricultural sector. SMEs always represent the model of socio-economic policies of the Government of India which emphasised judicious use of foreign exchange for the import of capital goods, labour-intensive mode of production, non-concentration of economic power in the hands of few and discouraging monopolistic practices. The small-scale industry accounts for 40%

of gross industrial value addition and 50% of total manufacturing exports. It is estimated that SMEs account for almost 90% of industrial units in India and 40% of value addition in the manufacturing sector. It can thus be said that the SMEs play a pivotal role in ensuring overall development of a country. But when it comes to the question of shouldering CSR only a handful of small firms are seen as successful. The chapter is an endeavour to examine the contributions of SMEs in societal development and benefits of CSR to SMEs.

It is important to foster the growth of the micro, small and medium enterprises and thereby greater job creation and productivity in the economy. The mandated 2% CSR investment in the Indian Companies Act is a novel solution to India's social problems. This will propel India towards the path of equitable and sustainable growth.

Hope, this short chapter will invite and motivate others to extend their skills, resources and services towards well-organised CSR initiatives that contribute towards nation building.

SMEs must adopt CSR for innovation, creativity, and flexibility which enable them to respond more quickly to structural changes and to adapt the dynamic demand patterns of consumers. The government must look into policies and legislations for the benefits of SMEs adapting CSR and take up initiatives aimed at encouraging SME involvement in CSR. Moreover for SMEs to fully utilise their potential, it is essential that the entrepreneurs along with the government support take necessary steps for further development.

GREEN GROWTH AND REGROWTH: PLEADING FOR PROGRESS WITH SUSTAINABILITY AND RESPONSIBILITY

Kuruvilla Pandikattu, S. J.

ABSTRACT

Basing himself on the premise that present economic progress cannot follow the 'Business as usual paradigm' and hope for continued and unlimited progress, the author holds that we need to look into the larger dimensions of growth and development, which include social, environmental and other complex factors. So in this chapter, the author makes some pertinent suggestions for a sustainable growth model inspired by green growth and degrowth.

The first section evaluates the salient features of green growth and its drawbacks. It is followed by a discussion on the notion of degrowth, with its challenge to change the direction of growth (economic, ecological, social and cultural), without which human civilisation, as we know it today, may not survive. Finally, in the concluding chapter, based on these two notions of green growth and degrowth, an all-inclusive and sustainable regrowth model is propounded.

By creating an awareness of the need to shift development goals and Corporate Social Responsibility (CSR), the author argues that we could use economic regrowth strategically and responsibly to make the world more sustainable and viable. Responsible corporates will make their contribution to such an organic, resilient and sustainable regrowth and their CSR activities could be the starting point for this change, without which humanity's future is seriously threatened.

Finally, the author acknowledges that humanity has profited from the tremendous technological and economic progress we have made in the last four

Strategic Corporate Responsibility and Green Management
Critical Studies on Corporate Responsibility, Governance and Sustainability, Volume 16, 117–141
Copyright © 2023 by Emerald Publishing Limited
All rights of reproduction in any form reserved
ISSN: 2043-9059/doi:10.1108/S2043-905920230000016009

centuries, learnt from its mistakes and are ready to reorient ourselves indi-
vidually and collectively towards a sustainable economic regrowth.

Keywords: Economic regrowth; economic degrowth; CSR; sustainability;
ESG; stakeholder; protection of environment

INTRODUCTION

Gone are the days when we could refer to economic prosperity apart from
morality (Dionne, 2019). Several questions have been raised about the unbridled
growth of the economy and the feasibility of green economy. It becomes
increasingly difficult to maintain this equilibrium when a country grows at a very
rapid rate. This fact helps to explain why no emergent economy has been able to
cut down on emissions, while sustaining an economic growth. Green growth is
possible, but necessitates effective governance and stern climate regulations. To
create a green and sustainable economy, we also need to tap into our society's
moral and social resources.

To make prosperity viable and sustainable we need to look into the larger
dimensions of growth and development, which include social, environmental and
other complex factors. So this chapter looks at the suggestions made for a sustainable growth model inspired by green growth and degrowth.

The first section evaluates the salient features of green growth and its drawbacks. It is followed by a discussion on the notion of degrowth, with its challenge
to change the direction of growth (economic, ecological, social and cultural),
without which human civilisation, as we know it today, may not survive. Finally,
in the concluding chapter, based on these two notions of green growth and
degrowth, an all-inclusive and sustainable regrowth model is proposed.

By creating an awareness of the need to shift development goals, Corporate
Social Responsibility (CSR) could be used more strategically and responsibly to
make the world more sustainable and viable.

LEARNING FROM GREEN ECONOMY

A green economy is one that is low in carbon emissions, resource-efficient and
socially inclusive. Growth in employment and income in a green economy is
driven by the infrastructure and resources that enable reduced carbon emission
and pollution, increased energy and resource efficiency, and sustained preservation of biodiversity and ecosystem (Environment, 2018).

It is vital to facilitate and support these green investments through targeted
public spending, policy modifications and changes to tax and regulatory laws.
UN Environment promotes a development route that regards natural capital as a
key economic asset and a source of public benefits, especially for disadvantaged
people whose survival depends on natural resources. Sustainable development is
not replaced by the concept of a green economy; rather, it is given new focus

along with the region's economies, capital and infrastructure investments, employment opportunities and positive social and environmental outcomes.

Bases of Green Economy

Resource conservation, environmentally friendly consumption and production, and green economy play an important role in promoting sustainable development. Resource efficiency refers to the methods in which resources are utilised to limit emissions, bring down waste production, per unit of product or service, and provide value to society. The goal of sustainable consumption and production is to enhance production techniques and shift consumption habits to lower resource consumption, reduce waste creation and emissions over the course of a process or a product's whole life cycle. The green economy proposes a macroeconomic approach for attaining sustainable economic growth, with a major focus on investments, jobs and skills (OECD, 2011).

The three main focus areas of the Green Economy's current activities are (Environment, 2018):

(1) Using regional, sub-regional and national fora to promote the macroeconomic approach
(2) Concepts associated with Green Economy will be expounded, with a focus on investments, technology and financial accessibility
(3) Assistance will be provided to nations in creating and putting into effect macroeconomic policies to aid nations in making the switch to a green economy

Green Growth Strategies for Human Betterment

The first United Nations Conference on Environment and Development Summit held in Rio de Janeiro in June 1992 had propounded the concept of sustainable development and advocated its attainability. Even after the massive effort made by the international organisation the world still faces two major challenges: expanding economic opportunities for everyone in the context of a growing global population and addressing environmental pressures, that, if not addressed adequately, may limit our chances of leveraging opportunities. Green development, which emphasises on utilising opportunities to solve both concerns at once, sits at the confluence of these two issues.

Green growth refers to fostering economic growth and development without the depletion of natural assets that provide resources and environmental services crucial to human well-being. This requires encouraging investment and innovation, which will sustain long-term growth and open up fresh business opportunities (OECD, n.d.).

Sustainable development cannot be supplanted by green growth. Instead, it should be viewed as a practical and dynamic roadmap for achieving measurable, tangible progress in both economic and environmental spheres. It also takes into account the social impact of the development dynamics of green economies. Ensuring that promotions natural resources may sustainably realise their full economic potential is the core objective of green growth initiatives. Besides promoting strong biodiversity necessary to sustain food production and human health, this economic potential also includes the capacity to provide the basic needs of a healthy life, such as clean water, fresh air, etc. Green growth strategies take into account the limited nature of natural resource replacement.

Green growth policies are a crucial part of the structural reforms needed to encourage a strong, sustainable and equitable growth. They may open up new growth possibilities by boosting productivity by creating incentives for more resource-efficient usage, reducing waste and energy use, spotting chances for innovation and value creation and diverting resources for high-value returns, boosting investor confidence by having the government handle important environmental concerns in a more predictable manner, lowering the likelihood of negative resource bottleneck to growth and adverse, perhaps, permanent environmental effects. These activities can also contribute to the creation or release of funds for pro-poor projects such as water supply and sanitation programmes and other anti-poverty initiatives.

When creating green growth plans, the unique demands of each nation must be taken into consideration. Careful thought should be given to the strategic handling of trade-offs and to extract benefit from establishing links between green growth and poverty reduction. Examples of the latter include addressing poor health conditions due to environmental degradation, providing people with more utilitarian infrastructure (particularly in the areas of energy, water and transportation) and introducing efficient technologies that can lower costs, increase productivity and reduce environmental pressure. Green growth strategies could mitigate the livelihood risks of the underprivileged by lowering their sensitivity to environmental threats, given the importance of natural resources in emergent economies.

Green growth strategies are recognisant of GDP being the prime measure for economic development which subdues the importance of natural resources to prosperity, health and well-being (OECD, n.d.). As a result, it must explore a wide range of development indicators that would take into account the environmental aspects and the quality of growth as well as its impact on people's income and well-being.

To implement green growth in a way that fosters job opportunities, eradicates poverty and strengthens a sustainable economy, many international organisations and governments across the world are working to identify policy combinations and measuring tools that countries in diverse contexts may apply.

The foundational idea of green growth is that there is no one strategy that fits all, and hence the approach to fostering an environmentally friendly growth needs to be dynamic. Social structures, resource endowments, institutional and regulatory frameworks, as well as environmental pressure points, all have an impact on an economy's capacity to expand sustainably. The advanced, emerging and emergent economies face distinct challenges and can explore different possibilities. The policies may differ across countries, but the three main pillars of action to promote social equity – intensified human capital investment, inclusive employment development and well-designed tax/transfer redistribution policies – must always be linked to green growth measures.

A recent study by Organisation for Economic Co-operation and Development (OECD), an international organisation focussed on creating better policies and improving lives, on green growth and developing nations locates regions where there is a strong possibility of attaining green growth objectives alongside implementing policies, regulations, finance possibilities, technology transfers and establishing potential new markets. It examines the main barriers and provides guidelines for a policy framework and a set of benchmarks that emergent economies may consider while draughting their green growth plans (OECD, n.d.). Additionally, the procedure for assessing progress will begin.

Based on discussions with emergent economies, the report was created. It seeks to provide the developing country partners a forum where they can express their interest in collaborating with the OECD to define an agenda for green growth that is workable, relevant and takes into consideration the aspirations of their population.

Green Growth Scenarios in India

Economically India is expanding quickly, and economic expansion is necessary for development. But does it really have to cost more in terms of deteriorating air quality and other negative environmental effects? According to a recent World Bank study, focussed policy changes can considerably lower environmental deterioration with minimal impact on GDP.

For instance, in the simulated scenarios, a tax on PM10 emissions – particles with a diameter of less than 10 μm – could significantly lower air pollution without impacting the GDP. The tax could also have positive effects on health (World Bank, n.d.).

In the last 10 years, India's economy has grown by more than 7% annually thanks to strong investment, improved productivity, increased corporate earnings and robust exports (Nikolova & Shibuya, 2006). Due to this progress, more people have access to employment options and can escape poverty. But does expansion, which is so necessary for progress, have to be accompanied with negative effects on the environment like worsening air quality?

According to a recent World Bank study, focussed policy changes can considerably lower environmental deterioration at a low cost to GDP. While observing India's economic development and environmental sustainability, the study focusses on the harmful health effects of particle pollution caused by the burning of fossil fuels, costing up to 3% of India's GDP. The study evaluates the effects on GDP, health indices and CO_2 emissions of various policy options, such as tax on coal or particle emissions (PM10).

Senior environmental economist at the World Bank and the report's primary author Muthukumara S. Mani stated the findings 'indicate that there are low-cost policy solutions that may drastically decrease environmental harm without jeopardising long-term economic objectives'. 'Additionally, they would significantly improve health. On the other side, failure to take action while the environment continues to deteriorate might reduce future opportunities for productivity and growth'.

Three Alternatives

Business as Usual Scenario: The IMF's most current GDP estimates for the period 2011 to 2015, together with projections up to 2030, and economic performance for the years 2007–2010 provide the foundation for the 'Business as Usual' scenario (World Bank, n.d.). The model computes the investments required and the quantities of various fuel types needed to achieve the predicted growth. Some emission reduction occurs under 'Business as usual' in relation to recent policy initiatives to reduce the sulphur content of diesel in the transportation sector, the use of compressed natural gas for public transportation, emissions-limiting performance standards for passenger vehicles and stricter enforcement of existing environmental laws (See Table 1).

The Green Growth Scenario: It aims to cut PM10 and other minor emissions by an additional 10% by 2030 than would be feasible under the current situation. A tax on coal or PM10 contributes to lowering emissions, converting to a cleaner fuel mix and increasing energy efficiency.

The Green Growth Plus Scenario: This incorporates a more aggressive 30% reduction in PM10 and other airborne small particles by 2030 compared to what may be achieved under business as usual. A price on coal or PM10 is once more utilised to cut down emissions.

In contrast to the Green Growth scenario, the Green Growth Plus scenario suggests that as the economy grows, customers will start to appreciate the benefits of cleaner, more efficient production. Market-driven 'pull' policies will be replaced by environmental command-and-control 'push' policies resulting in cleaner and more effective output. So if the new advanced coal technologies

Table 1. Comparison of Three Growth Scenarios (Worldbank, n.d.)

No	Business as Usual	Green Growth	Green Growth Plus
1	Oriented on unlimited growth	Growth with environmental concerns	Growth with focus primarily on sustainability
2	Market driven	Market plus environment driver	Environmental command-and-control push
3	Reducing polluting emissions	Increasing energy efficiency	Cleaner and efficient production
4	Enforcement of environmental laws	Environmental laws plus tax on coal and PM10	Emerging environmental protection
5	Focus on shareholders	Focus on environment	Focus on stakeholders and environment
6	Decrease in fossil fuel use	Decrease in particle emission	Further reduction in emission
7	Not much health benefits	Health benefits	Improved health benefits

become more competitive, then the older, less efficient plants will be replaced (World Bank, n.d.).

Results for Each Scenario

According to the 'business as usual' scenario, the usage of fossil fuel, which is the primary cause of pollution, is predicted to decrease giving way to cleaner coal. Although coal will still dominate our economy till 2030, its share of total energy consumption is declining and CO_2 emissions are captured at a higher rate (World Bank, n.d.). But there will be a considerable increase in demand for energy and goods derived from refined oil. Thus, it is expected that the percentage of emissions, comprising PM10 emissions, from productive activities will triple as a result of fast-rising economic activities, such as manufacturing, construction and transportation. Under current conditions, it is expected that the total PM10 emissions would rise from 8.7 million tonnes in 2010 to 16.8 million tonnes in 2030.

According to the green growth scenario, a 10% decrease in particle emissions can cause a modest drop in GDP. When compared to such a 'business as usual' scenario, a PM10 tax reduces conventional GDP by around $46 billion in 2030, or 0.3%. A tax on coal has a much greater impact on GDP.

According to the green growth plus scenario, a 30% reduction in particle emissions results in a $97 billion, or 0.7%, decrease in GDP. The scenario suggests that, if sufficiently backed by least-cost policy measures, even a considerable reduction in emissions may be achieved without having a materially negative effect on GDP. It may be noted that the coal tax is actually underperforming, resulting in a 1.07% drop in GDP.

Both scenarios offer significant health benefits. The derogatory health effects from PM10 are reduced by $105 billion in the 30% scenario and by $24 billion in the 10% case. The predicted GDP loss under the green growth plus scenario is offset by this.

An additional big advantage would be a large reduction in CO_2 emissions. The PM10 tax cuts these emissions more than the coal tax does. Even with a value per tonne of CO_2 of just $10, calculations show that the drop in CO_2 for the 10% PM10 reduction case is worth $59 billion, or just more than the loss of GDP. About $83 billion is the reduction for the 30% case, which is just somewhat less than the GDP loss.

Our Findings

Environmental taxes may help preserve the natural resources, without disrupting the Indian economy. The research shows that tackling 'public evils' using particular policy tools need not lead to substantial losses in GDP growth.

The model used in this work may be used to compare the benefits of various pollution-control strategies, as well as to assist, develop and choose the most focussed intervention programmes (such as an SO_2 tax, a CO_2 tax or emission trading schemes). After the impact of a plan, focussed on reducing particulate emissions, on air quality is calculated, the approaches used to measure the health risks associated with particle emissions may also be used to compute the welfare implications of doing so.

Comparisons across different scenarios suggest that a low-carbon, resource-efficient greening of the economy should be possible at a relatively low cost in terms of GDP growth. A more aggressive low-carbon plan called 'green growth plus' promises more benefits, but comes at a little higher economic penalty.

The model may be used for future studies to calculate how much GDP growth would be influenced by more severe cuts on harmful emissions. For the minimal consequences on GDP that this research implies, low-cost mitigation strategies must exist and be used (energy efficiency improvements, embodied technological improvements, improved daily operating practices of boilers). Therefore, while evaluating the environment-growth trade-offs, a choice must be made about the size, accessibility, suitability and appropriateness of such 'low-hanging fruit' and suitable incentives.

India: Green Growth Both Necessary and Affordable
India should be able to achieve green growth for as little as 0.02%–0.04% of its average annual GDP growth rate by putting environmental protection measures in place. According to a new World Bank report, this will allow India to maintain a strong rate of economic progress without jeopardising long-term environmental and economic sustainability (Viaggi, 2018, p. 153).

The report titled 'Diagnostic Assessment of Select Environmental Challenges in India' (World Bank, 2013a) contains the first-ever national-level economic assessment of environmental degradation in India. It analyses the trade-offs between economic development and environmental sustainability, the actual and monetary depletion of the environment's resources and quality, and it provides an estimate of the worth of India's biodiversity and ecosystem services (World Bank, 2013b).

In the report the authors estimate India's annual cost of environmental degradation to be more than Rs. 3.75 trillion ($80 billion), or 5.7% of GDP. It focusses on the impact of particle pollution (PM10) brought on by the burning of fossil fuels, which poses serious health risks and drains up to 3% of India's GDP in addition to losses incurred from lack of access to clean water supplies, poor sanitation and unhygienic living conditions, as well as depletion of natural resources.

Out of the estimated costs 1.3% is the price of indoor air pollution, whereas 1.7% is the cost of outdoor air pollution. The fundamental reason for the rising costs for both outdoor and indoor air pollution is the increased exposure of the young, productive urban population to particulate matter pollution, which contributes significantly to adult mortality from cardiac and chronic obstructive pulmonary disease. Additionally, a significant portion of the diseases caused by poor sanitation, hygiene and lack of access to water affect children under the age of five. The report claims that over 23% of infant deaths nationwide may be attributable to environmental degradation.

The debate between growth and the environment is rife in India, as it is in many other countries. This research suggests that there are low-cost strategies that might significantly lessen environmental harm without jeopardising long-term economic objectives, according to Onno Ruhl, director of the World Bank's India operations. Not only are the long-term costs of green growth reasonable, but the significant improvements in productivity and health would more than offset its cost.

The report suggests that a delay in action might reduce future productivity and, as a result, affect India's capacity for economic development.

Muthukumara S. Mani, senior environmental economist at the World Bank and the report's first author, believes that India cannot sustainably grow today and clean up afterwards. We believe that a low-emission, resource-efficient greening of the economy is feasible at a very low cost in terms of GDP growth.

Multiple simulations are used in the research to show that green growth is economical (Dale, Mathai, & Oliveira, 2016). The estimate shows that a 10% reduction in particle emissions by 2030 will only lead to a little 0.3% GDP drop in comparison to business as usual. Whereas, a 30% reduction in particle emissions lowers GDP by around $97 billion, or 0.7%, with minimal impact on growth rates (World Bank, 2013b).

Both scenarios offer significant health benefits. Savings from reduced health impacts range from $24 billion with a 10% decrease to $105 billion in the event of a 30% reduction. This fact further offsets the predicted reduction in GDP.

The study emphasises the value of measuring green growth and points out that India is home to some of the rare species and a diverse ecosystem. The study carried out the first comprehensive assessment of the value of ecosystem services from various biomes in the country.

Conservative estimates place its GDP contribution at 3.0%–5.0%. Conventional growth measurements do not adequately account for the environmental costs, which have been shown to be particularly severe given the present rates of fast expansion. Current technologies may also be used to quantify the sizeable contribution of natural capital in the form of ecosystem services. As a result, it is crucial to calculate green GDP – gross domestic product that accounts for environmental costs and services – as a gauge of economic advancement (World Bank, 2013b).

Greening Work

The creation of jobs is essential for promoting social inclusion, raising tax revenues and guaranteeing the economic stability of (welfare) governments. The Sustainable Development Goals (2015), the Paris Agreement (2015), the European Green Deal (2020) and Environmental, Social and Governance (ESG) Perspectives call for the simultaneous greening of our economy and labour markets. As a result, we must put in place labour market rules that encourage employment in the green sector. Eight categories are included in the Taxonomy of Sustainable Employment: conversion of plants and businesses, environmental labour law, climate decommodification, socio-ecological job guarantee, vocational guidance and retraining, distribution of employment time, alternative income sources and income equalisation. Katharina Bohnenberger examines the probable impacts of these characteristics on various policy initiatives. Despite the eight solutions' various degrees of intensity in each of the four dimensions, they are all capable of promoting green employment. This involves better protection of the workers and responsibility for the larger society. In light of the environmental issues, the findings suggest extending the toolkit of labour market solutions for a just and green transition (Bohnenberger, 2022).

Critique of Green Growth

All are not fascinated by the viability of green growth. George Monbiot, a regular *Guardian* columnist, claims that 'green growth' doesn't exist – less of everything is the only way to avert catastrophe. Simply put, maintaining the current level of economic activity would result in environmental destruction (Monbiot, 2021).

Politicians address the climate situation in a box with the label 'climate'. The biodiversity crisis is discussed under a box titled 'biodiversity'. In the lost property section of our world, there are other boxes that are gathering dust, such as those for pollution, deforestation, overfishing and soil loss. However, they are all a part of a single, more complicated catastrophe that we have broken down into smaller, more manageable pieces. Immanuel Kant noted that the categories the human brain develops to make sense of its environment are not the 'thing-in-itself'. Instead of describing the world, they describe artefacts of our perceptions.

There are no such divides in nature. Every stressor amplifies the others as Earth systems are shaped by everything at once. Consider the North Atlantic right whale, whose population increased briefly after whaling ended but is currently declining once more, with only 95 females of reproductive age left. The majority of the deaths and injuries brought on by whales being hit by ships or becoming entangled in fishing gear are the direct causes of this reduction. But because they were forced to move down North America's eastern seaboard into crowded seas, they have grown more susceptible to these effects.

Due to sea surface warming, their primary prey, a small swimming crustacean known as Calanus finmarchicus, is migrating north at an average rate of 8 km each year. Simultaneously, a commercial fishing industry has sprung up, utilising Calanus to produce fish oil supplements that are erroneously thought to be good for our health. The potential effects of fishing in Calanus have not even been attempted to be evaluated. We also don't know how this and many other important species may be affected by ocean acidification, which is also brought on by rising carbon dioxide levels.

Right whales in the North Atlantic have declining birth rates as their mortality rate increases. Why? Perhaps as a result of the contaminants that are building up in their systems, some of which may affect fertility. Or because of the stress and communication-disturbing effects of ocean noise from ship engines, sonar and oil and gas development. So, you could classify the decline of the North Atlantic right whale as a catastrophe involving shipping, fishing, the environment (including acidification and pollution), the climate or noise. However, it is all of these things in reality – a global crisis brought on by human activity.

Consider moths in the United Kingdom instead. We are aware that herbicides are harming them. But as far as I can tell, only one of these poisons' effects on moths has been studied. Bee research demonstrates that when pesticides are used together, their effects are synergistic, which means that the harm each chemical causes is doubled rather than added (Monbiot, 2021). The effects are increased once more when insecticides are mixed with fungicides and herbicides.

Moth caterpillars are also losing their food sources as a result of fertilisers and habitat loss. The adult organisms' reproductive cycle has also been thrown out of whack by the upheaval caused by the climate. We now know that light pollution has a terrible impact on the success of their reproduction. Energy is saved by switching from orange sodium streetlights to white LEDs, but insects find their wider colour spectrum to be terrible. Even in protected regions, light pollution is fast increasing and negatively harming wildlife practically everywhere.

Whole biological systems are being destroyed by cumulative effects. Coral reefs are less equipped to endure major climate events, such as tropical storms, which our fossil fuel emissions have also worsened, when they are undermined by the fishing industry, pollution and the bleaching induced by global warming. Rainforests are more susceptible to the droughts and fires brought on by climate change when they are divided by cattle grazing, logging and imported tree diseases.

Mobiot (2021) asks: What would we discover if we overcame our conceptual limitations? A full-spectrum assault on the living world would take place. Now, almost nowhere is safe from this ongoing attack. According to a recent scientific study, only 3% of the planet's geographical area should be regarded as 'ecologically intact' right now (Monbiot, 2021).

The sheer amount of economic activity is the common denominator behind all the different effects. The world's biological systems cannot sustain what we are doing because we are doing too much of practically everything. But because we can't see the whole picture, we can't properly and systemically deal with this situation.

When we compartmentalise this situation, we only make one facet of the dilemma worse. For instance, if we were to construct enough direct air capture devices to significantly lower atmospheric carbon concentrations, this would necessitate a vast new wave of steel and concrete mining and processing. Such construction pulses have an international impact. Sand mining, to name one component, destroys hundreds of priceless habitats in order to produce concrete. It's particularly harmful to rivers because its sand is greatly valued in construction. Drought, the melting of mountain glaciers and snow, water extraction by humans, and pollution from sewage, farming and industry are already having an adverse effect on rivers. Sand dredging might be the ultimate, irreparable blow after these attacks.

Or consider the materials needed for the electronics revolution, which is supposed to save us from a catastrophic climatic collapse. Already, habitat destruction and new pollution concerns are being brought on by the mining and processing of the minerals needed for batteries and magnets. Today, firms are using the climate catastrophe as justification for mining minerals from the deep ocean floor, long before we have any idea what the effects might be (Monbiot, 2021).

This is not a defence of direct air collection devices or other environmentally friendly technologies. The overall effect will be more harm to the living world if they must keep up with an ever-increasing level of economic activity and if the expansion of that activity is justified by the existence of those machines.

Governments all throughout the world are attempting to increase the economic burden by referring to 'unleashing our potential' and 'supercharging our economy'. According to Boris Johnson, 'Green growth must be at the heart of a worldwide recovery from the pandemic'. However, green growth does not exist. The earth is becoming less green due to growth.

Without a significant reduction in economic activity, we have little chance of escaping this full-spectrum disaster. A limited earth cannot support the increasing number of super-wealthy billionaires; thus wealth must be shared, but it must also be decreased. Maintaining our life-support systems requires reducing practically all of our activities. However, this idea – which ought to be at the heart of a new, environmental ethics – is considered secular blasphemy.

Climate Change and Economic Disparity
Climate change and growing wealth disparity are increasingly threatening modern living standards, peace and democracy (Fouquet, 2019). These two topics are frequently discussed separately on the policy agenda. A new generation of radical ideas have been put out to manage a just low-carbon transition. To study the long-term consequences of three scenarios – green growth, social equality policies and degrowth – a dynamic macrosimulation model can be developed in this way. The green growth scenario, which is based on technological development and environmental legislation, dramatically lowers greenhouse gas emissions at the cost of increasing economic disparity and unemployment. Additional direct labour market policies that improve social circumstances at the cost of a greater public deficit and environmental repercussions approximating those of green growth are included in the policies for social equity scenario (D'Alessandro, Cieplinski, Distefano, & Dittmer, 2020). The degrowth scenario, which imposes a wealth tax but also sees a decline in consumption and exports, reduces emissions and inequality more drastically while running a larger public deficit. We can show that radical, innovative social policies may combine social prosperity with low carbon emissions, and that they are both politically and economically feasible.

Indian Response
The Future We Want, a slick 53-page declaration, reaffirmed everything that must be done in the years to come. It was the result of the Rio+, or Earth Summit 2012. The Earth Summit in 1992 also echoed similar sentiments. To lessen the

global impact of the Brown Economy model of growth, the 'Green Economy' concept was the only thing added in 2012 (Kadekodi, 2013). The Green Economy model is presented as a chance to improve ecosystem services, permit growth and provide the poor with sustainable means of subsistence. However, this well-intentioned vision lacks a framework for developing global Payment for Ecosystem Services (PES) market prospects without jeopardising the fundamental right to subsistence as well as a design to enable green investments to reduce carbon intensities. According to Gopal K. Kadekodi (2013) writing in *Economic and Political Weekly*, the study shows a complete disconnect between a vision and the viability of a green economy (Leal Filho, Pociovalisteanu, & Al-Amin, 2017).

PROMOTING DEGROWTH

It is in the context of this disconnect that we take up the theory of degrowth, popularised recently. We take this notion to complement green growth, so that together they can create a viable life style, especially for the emerging economies.

Understanding the Notion

Degrowth is a term used to describe economies that are shrinking rather than growing, allowing us to use less energy and resources while putting well-being before profit (Berger, 2011).

Degrowth policies aim to assist economies in becoming more sustainable, which will be advantageous for their populace, the environment and themselves (World Economic Forum, 2022).

Effective degrowth strategies, according to the website Economics Help, include buying less goods, growing your own food and renovating empty homes rather than building new ones.

The word 'Degrowth' was first used in 1972, claims the website Degrowth.info, by French-Austrian social philosopher André Gorz. The early 2000s saw the emergence of the degrowth movement. One of the most influential proponents of contemporary degrowth is the French economist Serge Latouche. He argues that the current social paradigm of economic expansion is unsustainable.

Degrowth has to be promoted for the sake of our own viability and sustainability for the following reasons:

- We know civilisation started to see economic advancement in the seventeenth and eighteenth centuries. At that moment, technological development started to propel an increase in wealth.
- Since then, the primary goals of government efforts have been economic expansion and growth.
- The debate for degrowth has gained momentum as public awareness of climate change has grown.

- The argument argues that there will be no possibility of preventing global warming to 1.5 degrees if economic development remains the major goal.
- The beginning of human-caused global warming in the 1830s, at the height of the first industrial revolution in history, according to scientists, is no accident.
- The key to the problem is to get away from the notion that development is always good and essential.

One of the objectives of degrowthers, according to *The Conversation*, is to end the practice of using GDP as a measure of economic advancement (Shaw, 2022). The entire amount of goods and services generated in an economy is today measured by GDP, which is an unfortunate development.

Some specialists are highly critical of this notion of degrowth There are several opponents of the degrowth idea. According to the news and opinion website *Vox* (Piper, 2021), the invention of insulin, neonatal intensive care units and cancer cures were all made possible by economic expansion. A higher standard of living, indoor plumbing, electricity and independence from poverty are other advantages of unrestricted growth.

The fact that many nations have cut their emissions while rising GDP is one of *Vox's* arguments against degrowth. They have accomplished this by utilising technologies such as renewable energy. Another response is that wealthy nations cannot scale back to the same level whereas impoverished nations advance 'Up to a certain degree of prosperity' and then halt.

Who gets to pick what people buy in terms of products and services with their money? *Vox* opines that in the coming decades, developing middle-income countries rather than industrialised ones like the United States will emit the bulk of the world's carbon emissions. These countries include India, China and Indonesia.

Supporters of degrowth also have strong counter-arguments. Sam Alexander, a proponent of degrowth and research fellow at the University of Melbourne in Australia's Melbourne Sustainable Society Institute, is quoted in The Conversation. Degrowth, in his words, 'doesn't mean we are going to be living in caves with candles', he asserts. Instead, it might entail residents of wealthy nations altering their diets, moving into smaller homes and taking fewer road trips (Masterson, 2022).

Degrowth, according to researcher at the University of London Jason Hickel, is not always a negative term. 'It is important to clarify that degrowth is not about reducing GDP, but rather about reducing [energy and resource] throughout'. So we may assert that 'A different kind of economic structure is needed for an ecologically constrained world' (World Economic Forum, 2022).

Aftereffect of the Pandemic

Caricature aside, degrowthers' views raise serious questions about how, how much and why we labour.

In the midst of the suffering and mayhem caused by the coronavirus epidemic, there is some momentary consolation. The substantial decrease in aircraft and car traffic has made the air cleaner and the skies more clear. Supporters of the Green New Deal (GND), a major, state-funded programme to create green infrastructure, including mass transportation systems and a complete conversion to renewable energy, have solid reasons to be optimistic. The global recession is becoming more severe, and the GND seems to be the best route to recovery (the IMF predicts a 3% global decline).

Prior to the epidemic, the GND was garnering support from establishment politicians. However, there is a strong, immediate economic justification for introducing some form of 'Green stimulus' given that 26 million Americans sought for unemployment benefits in just the previous five weeks and that green enterprises are more effective at creating jobs than ones that rely on fossil fuels. Even without taking into account the longer-term economic advantages of decarbonisation, the US economy would decrease by up to 10% by the end of this century as a result of the harmful impacts of unchecked global warming, according to a 2018 US climate assessment (Seaton, 2020).

However, COVID-19's economic implications have made the 'degrowth' part of the climate movement look more starkly. As their name suggests, degrowthers are popular among Extinction Rebellion activists, but mainstream politicians generally dismiss them as impractical. They argue that unfettered economic expansion is ecologically unsustainable and that we must limit both overall consumption and our reliance on fossil fuels in order to avert a worldwide disaster. Degrowth advocates contend that we must discover ways to live and work that do not require an unending expansion of our economy.

Degrowthers have been particularly susceptible to parody in recent weeks. According to *The Spectator*, 'The coronavirus pandemic underscores the misery of degrowth', which is foreseeable. But the manner of life we currently lead, which includes unexpectedly high rates of unemployment, confinement and isolation, as well as pervasive food and economic instability, does not really portend better days to come. The horror we're living through right now isn't the fulfilment of degrowth's secret goal; rather, it's a terrifying caricature of it that the movement's detractors are now likely to exploit against it.

To see the current state as a rejection of degrowth would be unwarranted and improper. It fails to see the difference between the unexpected, abrupt suspension of significant portions of economic and social activity we are presently witnessing and the planned, democratic, regulated and equitable contraction of the economy that degrowth proponents anticipate.

The bulk of degrowth supporters argue that we must adapt to the current, protracted global stagnation, sometimes known as 'Secular stagnation', rather than calling for economic contraction per se. It says much more about our political environment than it does about the actual status of the economy that the only alternatives we have to slow down our economies are recession and austerity, with the cutbacks in public expenditure, increase in inequality (Fiorino, 2018, p. 98) and drop in real incomes that follow.

The dramatic shift in the global economy brought on by the coronavirus lockdowns has, however, substantially confirmed one important argument against degrowth: the consequences on employment. Since it excludes a wide range of important variables, including as equality, energy availability, the quality of healthcare, education and social support networks, GDP is a notoriously inaccurate and incomplete estimate of a society's well-being. However, as a result of workers' incapacity to create goods or render services, unemployment rises as GDP falls or slows. The coronavirus has starkly illustrated this reality.

According to economist and energy specialist Robert Pollin, the immediate effects of any global GDP recession would be huge job losses and a drop in working people's and the poor's living standards. During the Great Recession, there were almost 30 million extra jobless individuals in the world. We have not seen a degrowth advocate provide a compelling case for how we would avoid a sudden rise in mass unemployment if GDP fell by twice as much (Seaton, 2020).

The twin crises that are affecting us, the public health emergency and the escalating economic trauma brought on by the attempts to contain it, have brought to light many aspects of the interdependence, fragility and stark inequalities of our world's structure that we already knew but rarely fully understood. These crises have also brought into stark relief that employment is the economy's lifeblood. We must be ruthlessly realistic when evaluating the limitations of green methods since we only have a concise window of time left to stabilise the climate. British economist James Meadway states that the current economic crisis threatens 'Capitalism's most fundamental institution of all: the labour market itself'. Degrowth is the same. The energy and transportation industries appear to require ongoing expansion to be completely rehabilitated, at least temporarily. Politically, it is hard to see a recovery without entailing urgent measures to restore growth – and not always by greener methods – by politicians keen to revive flagging ratings as long as a consistently increasing GDP remains a necessary political requirement.

Focussing only on the issue of growth, however, runs the risk of highlighting the differences between degrowthists and Green New Dealers. This elevates the latter as pragmatic technocratic capitalists who want a return to normal economic activity, albeit powered by a different energy source, and dismissing the former as abstemious, back-to-the-land utopians who want to rob us of the majority of the luxuries of modern capitalist life.

As a result, we might only use a portion of the opportunities provided by the current circumstance, and we might only retain a portion of its lessons. Both schools of climate thought to challenge us to consider what types of occupations we need and what kinds of work our world needs from us. The current crisis raises this dilemma with a unique, terrible force as phrases like 'important workers' and 'vital services' permeate everyday speech.

Which goods and services are absolutely necessary, and which can we do without in our daily lives? This issue is addressed by degrowth and the GND, both of which also raises important, broader questions about how, how much and why we labour. They all provide unique solutions, from the creation of green infrastructure to the care economy. Once it is safe to exit economic survival mode, I sincerely hope that we will have the discernment to carefully assess which sorts of creative activity truly improve our lives and which of these our planet can support.

The Implementation of Degrowth

Degrowth is a concept that opposes the growth paradigm, and it is really implemented in many different ways. Cooperatives with a degrowth orientation are among them; they are associations of producers and consumers that strive to keep their attention local and use more responsible economic practices to support socio-ecological sustainability. Despite their increasing significance, a complete understanding of how they operate is still missing. This is essential to comprehending how they differ from traditional cooperatives and to encourage their dispersion. Cunico G. Deuten, & Huang thus analyse the internal organisational dynamics in a degrowth cooperative through a case study. With the assistance of the cooperative's members, they used a participatory system dynamics modelling technique to develop a causal-loop model illustrating the cooperative's major processes. A number of internal cooperative dynamics appeared to be active, strengthening those that were supportive of its expansion and balancing those that were impeding it. While the dynamics of development and conflict generation are typical of cooperative behaviour, restraining mechanisms are predicted to prevent the cooperative from becoming overly expansive and losing its degrowth ethos. These strategies will be influenced by regional priorities and possible thresholds for income sufficiency. Additionally, it seems that the members were better able to understand the problems, find common solutions and communicate better as a result of the participatory modelling technique used (Cunico, Deuten, & Huang, 2022). This study's contribution can be broken down into two parts: first, it describes the organisational dynamics of a cooperative that engages in degrowth; second, it emphasises how participatory modelling can be a powerful tool in those situations to increase member participation and enhance communication.

CONCLUSION: PLEADING FOR REGROWTH AND INCLUSIVE GROWTH

In this concluding section, we take insights from both green growth and degrowth, so that we can think of a radical orientation in our understanding of growth, which may be termed regrowth, as degrowth gives a negative connotation. It involves forming a circular economy and fostering inclusive growth, especially of the underprivileged.

Moving Away From the Growth Addiction

We might address poverty and global warming simultaneously with the right global economic policy. There has been agreement on the aim of economic policy for the better part of three centuries. The goal has been to attain as rapid expansion as possible ever since the industrial period began in the eighteenth century.

It's not difficult to understand why this focus has existed. Growth has boosted living standards, extended life spans, enhanced medical services and led to populations who are better educated and fed (Elliott, 2022).

The fact that emergent economies want to have developed countries is proof of how effective wealthy western nations have been at rescuing people from poverty. The world's poorer countries want more growth if it results in cleaner drinking water, more kids in school and fewer moms dying during childbirth (Elliott, 2022).

But there is a clear issue. If emergent economies are to have living standards that are even remotely comparable to those of industrialised nations, this will result in significantly higher usage of resources and increased strain on the environment. It entails a rise in energy use and the possibility of catastrophic global climate change.

The idea that growth is desirable is being seriously contested by individuals who contend that policymakers should aim for zero growth or even degrowth economies, ones that are shrinking, given the grave threat posed by global warming. Do not be misled; it is a positive thing that conventional thinking is being challenged. It is no longer tenable to argue that the answer to all problems is more growth.

The discussion going on right now is nothing new. Thomas Malthus predicted that there would be a famine when population expansion outpaced food production. The phrase 'growth in wealth is not infinite', spoken by John Stuart Mill, helped establish steady-state economics. Herman Daly, who passed away in October 2022, had long argued that expansion was constrained by the laws of nature. Robert Kennedy is renowned for saying that the things that make life worthwhile are not measured by gross domestic product, and his sentiments still hold true today (Elliott, 2022).

Nevertheless, achieving degrowth or a steady-state economy is not always straightforward. It will be quite challenging and demands both imagination and hard work.

It will first require a shift in how we view financial success. Parties compete with one another to promise voters the best growth strategy during political debates. Because language matters, it is good news when the GDP increases and bad news when it decreases. Depending on where they rank in global league tables of growth, nations are evaluated. Any politician would have a difficult time persuading voters to embrace the recession, which is still in its early stages.

That's because, over many years, people have discovered that degrowth has not been beneficial to them, especially the most vulnerable. Recessions, which are a sort of degrowth, cause hardships, including homelessness, insolvency and unemployment. Politicians also frequently step up their growth initiatives during recessions out of concern for voter backlash should living standards decline. Governments have chosen to increase their use of fossil fuels rather than risk having their lights go out.

A steady-state economy can only be achieved by combining an anti-poverty approach with a pro-planet strategy. It's not impossible to picture western cultures where, after some serious redistribution, everyone has enough money, possessions and free time to live well. Even so, it won't be sufficient. A worldwide plan is required to help less developed nations to achieve their justifiable anti-poverty objectives in a manner that is least damaging to the environment.

China and India together contribute for 36% of global CO_2 emissions, compared to Britain's 1% annual emissions. The carbon footprints of African nations are significantly smaller, but they are expected to grow as the continent's population and energy needs grow. The governments could accelerate its transition to a net zero economy, but this would have no appreciable effect on rising world temperatures unless it was matched by significant reductions in the use of fossil fuels by far larger emitters of greenhouse gases. Western nations can and should lead by example by making a quicker transition to cleaner energy, but it is unrealistic to think that underdeveloped nations will ever opt for degrowth.

That does not imply that the concept of a steady-state planet is unattainable. It does, however, imply that making emerging country growth as clean as possible needs to be the top focus right away. And more is required than just kind words. One estimate puts the cost at $2 trillion annually between 2020 and 2030.

The goal should be to create a new Marshall plan, similar to the one that existed after World War II, in which private investment is stimulated by financing given by international financial institutions and governments. According to Avinash Persaud, the special climate envoy to Mia Mottley, the Prime Minister of Barbados, the International Monetary Fund and the World Bank could be doing more to provide emergent economies, many of which are burdened with high debts and punitive borrowing costs, access to less expensive financing to support climate mitigation and adaptation projects.

Although it would be terrible, it is regrettably all too conceivable that the necessary resources won't be mobilised. Western governments think they have a limitless amount of time to modify how they do things now. The terrible truth is that they don't (Elliott, 2022).

Towards Green and Inclusive Growth

Over the past 30 years, a set of economic presumptions has shaped global development, encouraging nations to pursue economic growth through the privatisation of important industries, reductions in public spending and lower corporate taxes. Trust in the power of the free market and the private sector to produce the best economic results for everybody was at the core of the Washington Consensus, as it came to be mockingly known, especially after the crisis of the 1990s (JRS2021, 2021).

Whatever consensus there may have been on these principles following the 2008 financial crisis has been permanently destroyed by the COVID-19 pandemic and the enthusiastic support for private institutions by governments in industrialised economies.

When world leaders met in the following months for the G7 and G20 meetings in Cornwall (June 11–13, 2021) and Rome (October 30–31, 2021), respectively, they had more pressing issues to discuss than simply the current economic recovery. Additionally, they needed to challenge remaining assumptions that have influenced global economic ties for many years (Mega, 2016, p. xi). To make decisions that will ensure more equitable access to vaccines globally and a long-term economic transformation that creates a more resilient, equitable and sustainable world, world leaders will need to re-think these assumptions about how value is produced and governed in our economies and reimagine what can be in the years to come.

Governments must actively influence markets, claim the authors of *Building Back Broader: Policy Pathways for a Post-Pandemic Transformation* (World Economic Forum, 2021), to encourage inclusive and environmentally friendly growth. Strong public sector and robust, symbiotic public–private partnerships with common 'missions' for guiding the economy are essential. This has been amply demonstrated by the COVID-19 pandemic and the rush to create and distribute vaccinations that followed (JRS2021, 2021).

There is a shared interest and need to increase investment in research and innovation (Fücks, 2015), scale sustainable and inclusive technologies and solutions, and rethink the balance of value that the public and private sectors generate for society in order to ensure that much of the knowledge produced remains open as a public good.

In the chapter, we argue that one must adopt a market-shaping and market-co-creating lens rather than a market-fixing approach in order to fundamentally shift course. In order to direct the economy towards a course of inclusive and sustainable growth, that necessitates the use of all the tools at the disposal of governments, such as procurement policy, grants, loans and the use of public funds like development banks. This isn't a battle between the market and the government; rather, it's a discussion about how best to bring together the many stakeholders to tackle today's most urgent problems, including climate change and subpar healthcare systems (See Table 2).

The stakes are clear: Rapid and radical changes in ecology and economy the globe is necessary. The COVID-19 pandemic exposed weaknesses in global health

Table 2. The Paradigm Change for Regrowth (JRS2021, 2021).

No	Old Paradigm of Unlimited Growth	New Paradigm of Regrowth
1	Small government	Dynamic governance with support from public sector
2	Government enables business	Ongoing collaboration between public and private
3	Minimum control	Necessary regulations
4	Everything has a price	Reformulation of values
5	Annual yield and result	Patient and sustainable finance
6	Business knows best	Organic production increase
7	Consumer knows best	Nudging and shaping demand
8	Business for profit	Sustainable business also for profit
9	Shareholders first	All stakeholders (including clients and environment) treated fairly and equitably

systems, such as the inability to produce the most fundamental PPE for front-line healthcare workers, missed opportunities to deploy an active testing and tracing system that could have slowed the spread of this pandemic early on and finally the failure to develop an ambitious and well-resourced global vaccine programme to achieve the necessary immunity to help the entire world.

An effective illustration of what works and what doesn't is the unfair vaccination campaign. On the one hand, an astounding amount of public funding has been used to speed up the development of the vaccine: close to US$10.5 billion from various governments has been invested in the research and production of top vaccine candidates developed by American and European companies, including Johnson & Johnson, Pfizer/BioNTech, Novavax and Moderna (JRS2021, 2021).

Only 2.1% of people in Africa, 20% of people in Asia and 26% of people in South America have, to yet, receive immunisations due to vaccine nationalism and unequal distribution. This is problematic from a moral, economic and medical standpoint since it puts both people who have got immunisations and those who have not at danger of further epidemics and economic slowdowns. We have proposed that the IMF provide another round of Special Drawing Rights (SDRs) this year and that wealthy countries work together to ensure that part of this liquidity is used to fund the immunisation campaign.

The COVID-19 vaccination predicament serves as a reminder of the need to develop and make available the knowledge and technology needed to solve pressing global issues, including impending pandemics, climate change, population ageing and inequality. In addition to vaccinations, these public goods may also include decarbonisation technology and pandemic prevention technologies.

Public health, education, transportation and other areas of our social and physical infrastructures that strengthen the resilience of our economy must also be actively supported by the international community. This will help us to be better equipped to deal with pandemics when they do arise. As Nick Stern noted in relation to climate change, it will be less expensive in the long term to make the essential investments today to advance the path of equitable and sustainable development (JRS2021, 2021).

This calls for an outcomes-based view of our financial systems (Crespo-Cuaresma, Palokangas, & Tarasyev, 2013). By putting conditions on public funding that require firms to improve working conditions, reduce carbon emissions and correct decades' worth of value extraction through the excessive use of share buybacks, we may strive to restructure the economy rather than providing cash for recovery bailouts.

Last but not least, we must remember that to accomplish the economic progress we desire, we must make investments today to establish future markets that will allow us to address societal and environmental challenges. This explains a method of approaching industrial strategy that emphasises problem-solving above assembling a list of 'key sectors'. Our chapter includes a section on long-term funding of technological transfer and innovation through organisations like national development banks, sovereign wealth funds and innovation funds. Especially venerable businesses like cement and steel manufacturing, which must discover ways to lower their material content over the next years, such finance must be subject to industry change.

The concept of stakeholder value is essential in this situation. In comparison to any corporate social responsibility or charity giving activities, it is considerably more important to comprehend how government money may combine with company investment to produce value in a fundamentally different way. Given how long many affluent nations have industrialised without taking into account negative externalities, it is now vital to properly establish the ability of countries to change their economies in order to be more sustainable (JRS2021, 2021).

The world ought to learn from this tragedy and put those lessons into practice more successfully than it did in the wake of the 2008 financial crisis. The development of the COVID-19 vaccine illustrates both the advantages and disadvantages of existing frameworks and modes of cooperation, as well as the potential for a dynamic public sector working with businesspeople to develop new markets and accomplish common 'missions'. People from all around the world are asking governments to invest immediately in the initiatives that will assist us in addressing concerns like climate change, inequality, ageing and looming health problems. These and many more objectives will be achieved through new investments and a novel approach to market expansion.

The current difficulties in the economy, environment and health should serve as a grave warning. As was the case during the epidemic, if we want to perform better and remain sustainable in the years to come, we must include the idea of green growth and degrowth into every financing mechanism and type of collaboration in the global economy. This includes the way we set up our budgets, handle intellectual property rights, encourage collaboration for a greener economy and enforce sincere solidarity between rich and emergent economies. We might not have another chance if we fail (again). This is actually required by morality!

All-Inclusive Regrowth

Our exploration so far has made it abundantly clear that:

- Our economic progress cannot follow the 'Business as usual paradigm' and hope for continued and unlimited progress (Stoknes & Hawken, 2021).
- Such industrial and economic progress of unbridled competition and progress, which originated mainly from the industrial revolution, has led us to the present scenario of progress.
- Every problem created by humans (including our current ones) has a human solution. But this can only be achieved if we can collectively raise ourselves to a higher level of moral and social consciousness, as Einstein reminds us. 'We cannot solve our problems with the same level of thinking that created them'.
- The progress we have achieved in the last four centuries has very many commendable effects. We need to protect and promote it.
- At the same time, we need to recognise the harm this unidimensional economic progress and rivalry has led to. It has made human life unviable in the long run.

- One way of gaining control of our economic and industrial progress is to approach the notions of green growth (Kureethadam, 2019, pp. 35–38) and degrowth critically and creatively.
- Further, we need to recognise the disparity in the economic affluence of the people, commonly expressed by the Gini coefficient. We need to apply this coefficient also among countries.
- So we have a moral responsibility to include all agents and stakeholders in the growth process that we are visualising. This includes the rich and poor and the developed and emerging economies.
- So when we foster all-inclusive economic and industrial growth, it shapes humanity's social, cultural and moral dimensions.
- So we can plan for a regrowth, drawing from both inclusive green growth (Mandle, Ouyang, Salzman, & Daily, 2019) and degrowth, that caters to the well-being of the whole, including the environment and governance factors (ESGs). Such a move alone can do justice to Sustainable Developments Goals (SDGs) formulated by the United Nations in 2015.
- We need to take a serious look at the progress that we aspire for and be ready to change the direction of some of the developments (e.g. arms manufacturing, fossil fuel usage, increased income inequality, etc.) and change the orientation of other developments.
- Responsible corporates will make their contribution to such an organic, resilient (Dhyani, Gupta, & Karki, 2020) and sustainable regrowth and their CSR activities could be the starting point for this change, without which humanity's future is seriously threatened.

Thus we can hope that humanity has profited from the tremendous technological and economic progress we have made in the last four centuries, learnt from its mistakes and are ready to reorient ourselves individually and collectively. 'Yet all is not lost. Human beings, while capable of the worst, are also capable of rising above themselves, choosing again what is good, and making a new start, despite their mental and social conditioning. We are able to take an honest look at ourselves, to acknowledge our deep dissatisfaction, and embark on new paths to authentic freedom. No system can completely suppress our openness to what is good, true and beautiful or our God-given ability to respond to His grace at work deep in our hearts. I appeal to everyone throughout the world not to forget this dignity which is ours. No one has the right to take it from us' (Francis, 2015, para. 205).

REFERENCES

Berger. (2011). *Green growth, green profit: How green transformation boosts business*. London: Palgrave Macmillan.

Bohnenberger, K. (2022). Greening work: Labor market policies for the environment | SpringerLink. *Empirica, 49*, 347–368.

Crespo-Cuaresma, J., Palokangas, T., & Tarasyev, A. (2013). *Green growth and sustainable development*. Berlin: Springer.

Cunico, G., Deuten, S., & Huang, I.-C. (2022). Understanding the organisational dynamics and ethos of local degrowth cooperatives. *Climate Action, 1*(1), 11.

Dale, G., Mathai, M. V., & Oliveira, J. A. P. de. (Eds.). (2016). *Green growth: Ideology, political economy, and the alternatives.* London: Zed Books Ltd.

D'Alessandro, S., Cieplinski, A., Distefano, T., & Dittmer, K. (2020). Feasible alternatives to green growth. *Nature Sustainability, 3*(4), Article 4. doi:10.1038/s41893-020-0484-y

Dhyani, S., Gupta, A. K., & Karki, M. (Eds.). (2020). *Nature-based solutions for resilient ecosystems and societies.* Springer Singapore. doi:10.1007/978-981-15-4712-6

Dionne Jr., E. J. (2019, June 16). Opinion | We don't usually put 'moral' and 'economics' in the same sentence. It's time we started. *Washington Post.* Retrieved from https://www.washingtonpost.com/opinions/we-dont-usually-put-moral-and-economics-in-the-same-sentence-its-time-we-started/2019/06/16/36c780c2-8eb8-11e9-8f69-a2795fca3343_story.html

Elliott, L. (2022, November 17). Kicking our growth addiction is the way out of the climate crisis. This is how to do it. *The Guardian.* Retrieved from https://www.theguardian.com/commentisfree/2022/nov/17/growth-addiction-climate-crisis-economic-policies

Environment, UN. (2018, January 23). *Green economy.* UNEP – UN Environment Programme. Retrieved from https://www.unep.org/regions/asia-and-pacific/regional-initiatives/supporting-resource-efficiency/green-economy

Fiorino, D. J. (2018). *A good life on a finite earth: The political economy of green growth.* New York, NY: Oxford University Press.

Fouquet, R. (Ed.). (2019). *Handbook on green growth.* Cheltenham: Edward Elgar Publishing.

Francis, P. (2015). *Laudato si': On care for our common home.* Huntington: Our Sunday Visitor.

Fücks, R. (2015). *Green growth, smart growth: A new approach to economics, innovation and the environment.* New York, NY: Anthem Press.

JRS2021. (2021, June 9). How governments can shape markets towards green and inclusive growth. World Economic Forum. Retrieved from https://www.weforum.org/agenda/2021/06/how-governments-can-shape-markets-towards-green-and-inclusive-growth/

Kadekodi, G. K. (2013). Is a 'green economy' possible? *Economic and Political Weekly, 48*(25), 44–49.

Kureethadam, J. I. (2019). *The ten green commandments of Laudato si'.* Collegeville: Liturgical Press.

Leal Filho, W., Pociovalisteanu, D.-M., & Al-Amin, A. Q. (Eds.). (2017). *Sustainable economic development: Green economy and green growth.* Cham: Springer International Publishing.

Mandle, L., Ouyang, Z., Salzman, J., & Daily, G. C. (Eds.). (2019). *Green growth that works: Natural capital policy and finance mechanisms around the world.* Washington, DC: Island Press.

Masterson, V. (2022, June 19). How do we save our planet? A radical economic theory born in the 1970s might have a clue. Retrieved from https://theprint.in/environment/how-do-we-save-our-planet-a-radical-economic-theory-born-in-the-1970s-might-have-a-clue/1003054/

Mega, V. P. (2016). *Conscious coastal cities.* Cham: Springer International Publishing.

Monbiot, G. (2021, September 29). 'Green growth' doesn't exist – less of everything is the only way to avert catastrophe. *The Guardian.* Retrieved from https://www.theguardian.com/commentisfree/2021/sep/29/green-growth-economic-activity-environment

Nikolova, A., & Shibuya, M. (2006). *Green growth at a glance: The way forward for Asia and the Pacific.* Bangkok: United Nations, Economic and Social Commission for Asia and the Pacific.

OECD. (2011). *Towards green growth.* Paris: OECD.

OECD. (n.d.). *What is green growth and how can it help deliver sustainable development?* Retrieved from https://www.oecd.org/greengrowth/whatisgreengrowthandhowcanithelpdeliversstainabledevelopment.htm. Accessed on December 10, 2022.

Piper, K. (2021, August 3). Can we save the planet by shrinking the economy? *Vox.* Retrieved from https://www.vox.com/future-perfect/22408556/save-planet-shrink-economy-degrowth

Seaton, L. (2020, April 24). In the midst of an economic crisis, can 'degrowth' provide an answer? *The Guardian.* Retrieved from https://www.theguardian.com/commentisfree/2020/apr/24/economic-crisis-degrowth-green-new-deal

Shaw, K. (2022, August 8). The case for degrowth: Stop the endless expansion and work with what our cities already have. *The Conversation.* Retrieved from http://theconversation.com/the-case-for-degrowth-stop-the-endless-expansion-and-work-with-what-our-cities-already-have-187929

Stoknes, P. E., & Hawken, P. (2021). *Tomorrow's economy: A guide to creating healthy green growth.* Cambridge, MA: The MIT Press.

Viaggi, D. (2018). *The bioeconomy: Delivering sustainable green growth.* Oxford: CABI.

World Bank. (2013a). *Diagnostic assessment of select environmental challenges in India, Volume 1. An analysis of physical and monetary losses of environmental health and natural resources.* Washington, DC: World Bank.

World Bank, T. (2013b, July 17). *India: Green growth is necessary and affordable for India, says new World Bank Report.* World Bank. Retrieved from https://www.worldbank.org/en/news/press-release/2013/07/17/india-green-growth-necessary-and-affordable-for-india-says-new-world-bank-report

World Bank, T. (n.d.). *'Greening' India's growth.* World Bank. Retrieved from https://www.worldbank.org/en/news/feature/2012/10/18/greening-indias-growth

World Economic Forum. (2021, June 2). *Building back broader: Policy Pathways for an economic transformation.* World Economic Forum. Retrieved from https://www.weforum.org/whitepapers/building-back-broader-policy-pathways-for-an-economic-transformation/

World Economic Forum. (2022). Degrowth: What's behind this economic theory and why it matters today. World Economic Forum. Retrieved from https://www.weforum.org/agenda/2022/06/what-is-degrowth-economics-climate-change/

EPILOGUE – BUSINESS, SOCIETY AND GLOBALISATION: AN AGENDA FOR CORPORATE LEADERSHIP

Ananda Das Gupta

ABSTRACT

Capacity of a business to deal with the political and economic climate of a region or a nation depends on its financial strength. This ability to influence often remains undisclosed and is put to practice as and when required. The Enron project in India has been able to influence different state governments of Maharashtra, but the details of negotiation have never been made public. The marketing, production and labour departments of an industry often take care of the demands of the international customer and the industry, and are often not viewed as components of corporate social responsibility (CSR). Growth of civil society organisations has led to increasing democratisation in the marginalised and impoverished communities creating local responses to the grand meta-narratives. Yet nation state needs to evolve a new role for itself in this fast changing world. A stable nation providing good governance is thus a basic requirement for developing countries in their attempt to safe guard rights and interests of their poor and marginalised people.

Keywords: Civil society; corporate leadership; sustainability; business; society; globalisation

I

Business ethics can be examined from various perspectives, including the perspective of the employee, the commercial enterprise and society as a whole. Very often, situations arise in which there is conflict between one and more of the parties, such that serving the interest of one party is a detriment to the other(s).

Strategic Corporate Responsibility and Green Management
Critical Studies on Corporate Responsibility, Governance and Sustainability, Volume 16, 143–157
Copyright © 2023 by Emerald Publishing Limited
All rights of reproduction in any form reserved
ISSN: 2043-9059/doi:10.1108/S2043-905920230000016010

For example, a particular outcome might be good for the employee, whereas it would be bad for the company and society, or vice versa.

Philosophers and others disagree about the purpose of a business ethic in society. For example, some suggest that the principal purpose of a business is to maximise returns to its owners, or in the case of a publicly traded concern, its shareholders. Thus, under this view, only those activities that increase profitability and shareholder value should be encouraged because any others function as a tax on profits. Some believe that the only companies that are likely to survive in a competitive marketplace are those that place profit maximisation above everything else. However, some point out that self-interest would still require a business to obey the law and adhere to basic moral rules because the consequences of failing to do so could be very costly in fines, loss of licensure or company reputation.

Social Responsibility and Business Ethics

Social responsibility and business ethics are often regarding as the same concepts. However, the social responsibility movement is but one aspect of the overall discipline of business ethics. The social responsibility movement arose particularly during the 1960s with increased public consciousness about the role of business in helping to cultivate and maintain highly ethical practices in society and particularly in the natural environment.

Corporations are increasingly being challenged to act in ways that serve the best interests of society. Many companies are aggressively seeking strategies that can allow them to 'do well by doing good', leaving a positive 'footprint' on the world and avoiding actions that could harm consumers, employees, investors, competitors, suppliers and the general public. Already an increasing number of companies are recognising that globalisation is transforming corporate responsibility from a choice into an imperative. A recent international enquiry into consumer expectations concluded, for example, that 20% of consumers surveyed had avoided products and services of particular companies because of their negative ethical profile, and a further 20% were considering doing so.

The fact is that in today's connected world there is no hiding place for poor corporate citizens and no excuse for poor corporate citizenship. Whether it is labour practices, environmental habits or human rights, companies today must be concerned about their global reputations because their actions can quickly become globally known. The internet is both the great advertiser and the great tattler – it can open doors faster than you would believe. But it can also close them faster than you'd imagine.

The Threshold of CSR

CSR is generally understood to be the positive role that businesses can play in a host of complex areas, including safeguarding employees' core labour rights (to non-discrimination, freedom of association and collective bargaining against child labour and forced labour), protecting the natural environment, eliminating bribery and corruption, and contributing to respect for human rights in the communities where they operate.

CSR is not new to the international agenda; it has been around for many years. It has been gaining prominence and momentum worldwide: conferences are held weekly, papers and articles are published almost daily; new and innovative partnerships are being developed. There is reason for optimism. Even if we look only as far back as the Battle of Seattle in the fall of 1999, since then numerous initiatives such as the Organisation for Economic Co-operation and Development (OECD) Guidelines for Multinationals and the Global Compact have been introduced, implemented and, in some cases, refined and implemented again.

The Global Scenario

The growing international and domestic interest in CSR stems largely from the concerns held by many in every society about the real and perceived effects of rapid globalisation. The interest has been reflected in the expectation that globalisation must proceed in a manner that supports sustainable development in all regions of the world. People insist that the activities of corporations should make a positive contribution not only to the economic development and stability of the countries in which they operate but also to their social and environmental development. Failure to respond to such an agenda satisfactorily will contribute to increased social tensions, environmental degradation and political upheavals. Good corporate conduct makes an important contribution to sustainable development in any community and thus goes a long way towards responding to the concerns that globalisation raises.

Many companies and business associations have recognised the importance of CSR. Not very long ago, the dividing line between business and society appeared to be clearly drawn. According to the economist Milton Friedman, 'There is one and only one social responsibility of business: to use its resources and engage in activities designed to increase its profits'. This view no longer prevails. The CSR agenda is a complex one, requiring co-operation among a wide variety of stakeholders to be addressed effectively. Improved dialogue between the private and non-governmental sectors is one positive pattern emerging from recent corporate social responsibility (CSR) trends.

Indian Context

India is also working to promote CSR through support for the development of Globalisation that is already a force for great change, not simply a spectre on the horizon. Through technology, communications and economics, globalisation and our increasing interconnection are inevitable. Time, distance and geography are disappearing: globalisation is a reflection of that reality. In this environment, companies can and do make an important contribution to sustainable development in communities where they operate. Certainly progress has been made in some areas. But we must temper our optimism with the awareness that there is still much to be done and many challenges for us to keep in mind as we strive to ensure that globalisation is for the benefit of all people, in all countries of the world.

II

During the last 20 years, human resource management (HRM) has become a common way of managing people. Such an approach involves human resource professionals partnering with other managers so that people are used in the most effective way. More recently there have been calls for HRM to demonstrate that it adds value to the business.

CSR and responsible capitalism pose a number of challenges for HRM and for leadership in organisations. The HRM paradigm is based on a rational strategic management framework which is consistent with traditional economic analysis. This paradigm is limited in circumstances where organisations seek to behave responsibly with regard to a range of internal and external stakeholders and seek to take a longer term perspective.

According to Milton Friedman, a business has no social responsibilities other than to maximise its profits. However, today there is a growing perception among enterprises that sustainable business success and shareholder value cannot be achieved solely through maximising short-term profits, but instead through market-oriented yet responsible behaviour. This responsible behaviour of corporations can be called CSR.

There are different approaches in explaining CSR. One of them is the classical theory stressing that the primary goal of company is to secure its shareholders' financial goals and to respond to their wishes relative to the corporation. Secondly, the social demandingness theory of CSR means to promote and protect the general public's interests. On the other hand, the social activist theory holds that there exists a universal standard for determining responsible corporate conduct that is independent from the stockholders' interests.

Finally, the stakeholder theory on CSR, influenced by the view that companies are also corporate citizens, seeks to balance among the competing demands of stakeholders that support a company. From the stakeholder perspective, CSR means a commitment by a company to manage its roles in a society as producer, employer, marketer, customer and citizen in a responsible and sustainable manner.

CSR and sustainable development are gaining increasing prominence in the global business culture, as many businesses attempt to accommodate the CSR agenda. The concept of corporate sustainable development is still the subject of controversy and therefore the indicators used to measure CSR continue to be the topic of debate. However, no matter what indicators are used, the notion of responsibility includes responsibility for people in the collective sense (such as communities) and also for individuals.

CSR certainly seems to be the emerging flavour of the month, but is it a reflection of a 'two-faced capitalism'? In some senses, it could be.

First, Porter argues CSR initiatives need to be undertaken not for 'feel good reasons' or as defensive actions to avoid scandals, but they should be integrated into an organisation's competitive strategy. Companies need to be clear about how CSR initiatives contribute to organisational success and efficiency. This view reflects an emphasis on the desired outcomes of one stakeholder: shareholders.

Second, many CSR initiatives could just reflect the intention of management and be no more than rhetoric. The intention to further corporate and social responsibility does not appear to be implemented in many cases. Research by Business in the Community (BiTC) found that 60% of firms are not living up to their values. In addition, a report by a charity, Christian Aid, cites Shell, British American Tobacco (BAT) and Coca-Cola as paying lip service to CSR, but in reality the community development projects they undertake are ineffective.

It appears that many CSR initiatives reflect the essence of HRM activities. So what is the role of HRM in CSR? At present, it appears human resource (HR) is falling down in this task. A survey by Cronin and Zappala in Australia revealed that HR played a negligible role in decision-making in corporate citizenship. However, CSR will become an even more widespread and accepted way of doing business and it should have a further impact on HR's role. Not only will HR need to see its role as strategic from the shareholders viewpoint but it will also need to accommodate this view with the need to create a situation in which the workforce and the organisation is sustainable over the longer term.

HR has a role in demonstrating the benefits of workplace practices that both reflect CSR and, at the same time, contribute to organisational efficiency and success. In order to do this, HR needs to be familiar with the latest research on work practices and employee performance and also the language of business. It requires HR to integrate CSR initiatives through its roles as business partner, employee champion, and administrative expert and change agent. It also requires HR to be an organisational advocate in the community and with other external stakeholders.

CSR provides HR with opportunities. It provides a further opportunity to contribute to business success and employee satisfaction and performance. It also provides additional opportunities to contribute to community well-being.

This is why CSR means a commitment by a company to manage its roles in a society in a responsible and sustainable manner. Especially since the 1980s, CSR has become an increasingly important part of the business environment. Today there is a growing perception among enterprises that sustainable business success and shareholder value cannot be achieved solely through maximising short-term profits, but instead through market-oriented yet responsible behaviour. The aim of this study is to present the main findings from a recent survey of Turkey's top companies on the HRM dimensions of their CSR.

Our overall hypothesis is that corporate citizenship contributes to competitive advantage. We argue that corporate citizenship is a potentially lucrative business practice, a position based primarily on the findings of two research projects that demonstrate the existence of a relationship between corporate citizenship and improved competitive advantage.

Despite the variety of stakeholder groups and their demands, CSRs can be classified into four broad categories: (1) economic, (2) legal, (3) ethical and (4) discretionary responsibilities. Corporate citizenship can therefore be defined as the extent to which businesses meet the responsibilities imposed by their various stakeholders.

As society's economic agents, businesses are expected to (1) generate and sustain profitability, (2) offer goods and services that are both desired and desirable in society, and (3) reward employees and other agents who help create success. To satisfy these expectations, businesses develop strategies to keep abreast of changing customer needs, to compensate employees and investors fairly, and to continually improve the efficiency of organisational processes. A long-term perspective is essential when establishing these strategies: A responsible business must continue to earn profits from its ongoing business in order to benefit its stakeholders.

Regardless of their economic achievements, businesses must abide by established laws and regulations in order to be good citizens. Because training all the members of an organisation as lawyers is impossible, the identification of legal issues and implementation of compliance training are the best approach to preventing violations and costly litigation. The establishment of strict ethical standards in the workplace may also be an excellent way to prevent legal violations by creating a focus on integrity in decision-making.

In addition, an organisation guided by strong ethical values may also be better able to satisfy ethical responsibilities, the third type of responsibility imposed by stakeholders. Two main types of ethical issues are likely to emerge in an organisational context: (1) decisions in so-called grey areas in which the right decision is debatable and (2) decisions in which the right course of action is clear, but individual and organisational pressures propel even well-intended managers in the wrong direction. A proactive corporate citizen develops precise guidelines that help organisational members deal with such pressures by stressing the importance of stakeholders' viewpoints relative to organisational achievements.

In addition to meeting economic, legal and ethical responsibilities, businesses are also expected to display a genuine concern for the general welfare of all constituencies. For example, society desires a cleaner environment, the preservation of wildlife and their habitats, as well as living wages for employees, but it also demands low-priced products. Companies must balance the costs of these discretionary activities against the costs of manufacturing and marketing their products in a responsible manner.

One of the dimensions of corporate citizenship is an ethical work climate that includes values, traditions and pressures exerted in the work environment to make legal and ethical decisions. An ethical climate involves formal values and compliance requirements as well as an understanding of how interpersonal relationships affect the informal interpretation of ethics. Loe (1996) examined the association between an ethical climate and improved organisational processes. When clear barriers are established to limit the opportunity for unethical activities, and when ethical behaviours are rewarded, an ethical climate prevails in an organisation. In an ethical work climate, employees are able to identify ethical issues as they arise and are aware of the company resources available to help them act ethically and according to organisational policy and culture. An ethical climate characterises businesses that are committed to ethical citizenship.

Before we examine the benefits of an ethical work climate, it may be useful to briefly consider the negative outcomes that may arise from a work climate that does not emphasise ethical conduct. Consider the case of Bausch and Lomb.

The company's operations were governed almost exclusively by strict sales and earnings objectives. Under stringent bottom-line pressures and with no counterbalancing values helping them to differentiate right from wrong, managers engaged in unscrupulous pricing and fraudulent billing. These practices translated into a series of lawsuits from customers and distributors, bad publicity and a sharp decline in the firm's market value.

Thus, a major benefit of an ethical climate is the avoidance of negative consequences that may result from unscrupulous conduct in the workplace.

The Linkages Between 'Business' and 'Society'

The linkages, relationship and interface between 'Business' and 'Society' are from their inception; however, over the years it has undergone spectacular changes. The survival and effectiveness of any organisational entity depend on the quality of support it gets from all stakeholders including the society at large. Although in the initial years of this interface between 'society' and 'business', CSR was confined to 'philanthropy' but there have been successive changes and developments in the understating of these stakeholders to make it more of 'business strategy' rather 'philanthropy'.

CSR is the continuing commitment by business to behave ethically and contribute to economic development while improving the quality of life of the work force, their families as well as of the local community and society at large. Business needs a stable social environment that provides a predictable climate for investment and trade. Understanding society's expectation is quite simply enlightened self-interest for business in today's interdependent world. The CSR, therefore, will be centred on (1) to treat employees fairly and equitably, (2) to operate ethically and with integrity, (3) to respect basic human rights, (4) to sustain the environment for future generations and (5) to be a caring neighbour in their communities.

Due to globalisation, corporations are no longer confined to the traditional boundaries of the nation state. On the one hand, globalisation has provided a great opportunity for corporations to be globally competitive by expanding their production base and market share. On the other hand, the same situation poses a great challenge to the sustainability and viability of such mega businesses. Labourers, marginalised consumers, environmental activists and social activists have protested against the unprecedented predominance of mulitnational companies (MNCs). The success of CSR initiatives, in future, will largely depend upon the relationship between the corporate system and the social and political systems. The notion of a generalised responsibility is not an operational concept any more than is the idea of profit maximisation. A company's goals, policies and strategies must be uniquely determined in the light of opportunities and threats sighted in its external environment, its internal resource strengths and weaknesses, and the values held by its principal managers.

III

Globalisation along with changed norms of production, labour and environment with conditions of best practice has influenced behaviour of businesses across the world. The success of the acceptance of these norms has been outside the letter of law and the adoption has often influenced state to adopt better/improved or at least changed role for itself. The norms of resettlement and rehabilitation as dictated by the Indian state are by law adopted by joint venture companies involved in extractive industries yet many other activities are also undertaken as CSR, which are neither detailed nor dictated by law. Growth of civil society organisations has also led to increasing democratisation in the marginalised and impoverished communities creating local responses to the grant meta-narratives. Yet nation state needs to evolve a new role for itself in this fast changing world. A stable nation providing good governance is thus a basic requirement for developing countries in their attempt to safe guard rights and interests of their poor and marginalised people.

Indian business has been actively involved in corporate philanthropy since the early 1900s. The charitable outlook of Indian businesses is progressively undergoing change under some external and internal influences. The increase in the momentum of CSR has created new routes or avenues via which issues of CSR are put to practice.

The success of the acceptance of these norms has been outside the letter of law and the adoption has often influenced state to adopt better/improved or at least changed role for itself. The norms of resettlement and rehabilitation as dictated by the Indian state are by law adopted by joint venture companies involved in extractive industries yet many other activities are also undertaken as CSR, which are neither detailed nor dictated by law. Growth of civil society organisations has also led to increasing democratisation in the marginalised and impoverished communities creating local responses to the grant meta-narratives. Yet nation state needs to evolve a new role for itself in this fast changing world. A stable nation providing good governance is thus basic requirement for developing countries in their attempt to safe guard rights and interests of their poor and marginalised people.

During the late 1960s and 1970s, CSR emerged as a top management concern in both the United States and in Europe, only to seemingly 'wither on the vine' during the 1980s. Today, it is back on the agenda of many CEOs. This time it is also on the agenda of governments, both national and local, as well as NGOs, consumer groups, investors and other actors in civil society. This book seeks to articulate and communicate what social responsibility means and why it makes good business sense to integrate it into business strategies and practices. It does this by:

(1) Outlining some forces at work and trends affecting corporations
(2) Explaining six key dimensions of CSR
(3) Making a case for integrating CSR into sustainable strategies
(4) Describing how CSR can be built into management practices
(5) Looking beyond social responsibility

The great changes of the last two decades have set the scene for a worldwide pattern of social organisation. It is based on the institution of public, for-profit and non-profit sectors working separately and together, within the context of the informal relationships that are the basis of family and everyday life. Only a few countries, such as North Korea and Cuba, resist this model of social organisation; for them the state dominates all aspects of economic and social life. Most other countries (industrialised and developing alike) have now rejected the dominance of the state and are increasingly fostering a large new for-profit sector through a wave of denationalisation and deregulation. The boundaries of the state have contracted in the social sphere as well. A dynamic non-profit sector is emerging around the world both to provide human services and to campaign for social and environmental causes.

Between the United Nations Human Rights Conferences in Tehran in 1968 and Vienna in 1993, as well as in other international fora, the organisation's Declaration came under fierce criticism. At times some have even publicly asked whether the 1948 document could be 'touched up', since it cannot be replaced altogether. They argue in favour of including the concerns of cultures overlooked by the text's original authors, blinded as they were by a Western world view. It would be the height of irony if the 1948 Declaration were made universal at last by taking into account specific cultural features of individual countries (World Bank, 1997).

Two sides soon confronted each other. The advocates of universality, who consider it dangerous to renegotiate the Declaration, have clashed with those who would introduce clauses relating to their specific cultures, some of which have only a distant kinship with respect for rights of the individual. The stand-off came to a head in the first half of the 1990s. In Vienna and elsewhere, several Asian countries that challenged the Declaration's universal character in the name of Asian values joined forces with the most conservative Muslim states to oppose the West's efforts to have the document accepted as universal.

Since the 1980s, the planetary interdependence stemming from globalisation has increased debate and media coverage of human rights in many arenas. The recommendations that came out of conferences held during the present decade – Rio de Janeiro, Cairo, Copenhagen, Beijing and Istanbul – have usually been based on an affirmation of rights: rights to a clean environment, socio-economic rights, the rights of women and the right to housing.

A growing number of people and organisations are involved in these issues, which is helping to raise awareness of human rights and to spread more information about them in specific areas of concern. But these sometimes powerful, sometimes weak, players have conflicting positions and interests and advocate strategies that do not always coincide. Interdependence does not necessarily mean establishing symmetrical relationships and equal opportunities. The various forms that globalisation is taking and their destabilising effects on social relationships may even explain the growing concern with human rights.

These 'new rights' are appearing in a particular context, which explains why there is an urgent need to defend them and accounts for certain problems relating to how they have emerged. For they must be defended without dividing up the issues and diverting attention from the political and social relationships that lead to violations.

Most economists argue that globalisation is the outcome of unavoidable adjustments to the new rules of international competition and to the laws of the marketplace which supposedly ensure the optimum distribution of resources around the world. But globalisation should be seen more as an eminently political process involving negotiations and struggles for influence and power engineered and institutionalised by players such as governments, transnational corporations and multilateral financial institutions.

What is more, the globalisation of financial markets and that of goods and services has different social, economic and political implications depending on the region. Even though they are all part of the same worldwide process, these different situations have their own special features, which must be taken into account when it comes to questioning human rights and the necessity of defending them.

The liberalisation underway goes hand-in-hand with a programmed withdrawal by the state from certain areas such as planning, production and social reform and a re-orientation of its involvement in others, such as redistribution, regulation and mediation. The aim is to encourage special economic growth strategies based on the promotion of private interests. That has helped to undermine the legitimacy of states already beset by fiscal crisis – especially in the South, where countries are struggling with 'structural adjustment'. That has special implications for human rights.

The growing politicisation of the globalisation process, and especially the politicisation of how the crisis is managed in the developing countries undergoing structural adjustment, has led to a redefinition of the state's role. But in both the North and the South, economic recovery based on the private sector involves special forms of integration with global markets and new relationships with transnational corporations.

Domestically, reform programmes that seek to create a set of economic and social relationships in accordance with international norms of productivity, capital returns and competitiveness are directly or indirectly attacking long-held rights, where they exist, such as employment and social security benefits. The aim is to help redistribute resources from 'less productive' sectors – social welfare, health and education, for example – to 'more productive' ones. That shift comes at an incalculable social cost because it involves dismantling rules by which society has operated over the last several decades.

During the 1990s, as the marginalisation and exclusion of certain social categories increased, the Bretton Woods international financial institutions gave some thought to the plight of 'target groups' – women, old people, children and the handicapped. Special measures were adopted in their favour, but without questioning the economic programmes which have helped to worsen their situation in the first place.

More recently, the World Bank's, 1997 World Development Report, which focusses on the redefinition of the state's role, contains a chart showing the different functions the bank thinks the state should fulfil. The role of 'ensuring social equity' is not presented as an end in itself – and even less as a social or economic right – but as a means to stabilise and consolidate a model of economic growth whose logical progress can only increase inequality and so lead to potential violations.

Poverty and the various dysfunctions of society worldwide are partly rooted in a selective and inequitable form of social and political regulation, which means that the battle to win new human rights is actually a struggle for the redistribution of power – an eminently political matter. By presenting economic and now institutional reforms from a purely technical point of view, the multilateral and national institutions are dodging key questions with regard to the control of the development process. Who controls it? What is their aim? It seems illusory to redefine measures for promoting social and economic rights, including the aspiration to broaden their scope, before the content and purpose of the growth those institutions recommend are made clear. In this context the major transnational corporations, especially those that sell consumer goods in wealthy countries, have been busy promoting the establishment of codes of conduct or ethics to avoid the kind of boycotts that have occurred in Europe and the United States. But most codes, when they exist, have major loopholes, including a lack of means to enforce them, of effective oversight and of sanctions in the event of violations. Consequently, the adoption of such codes can actually be a smokescreen for human rights abuses by large corporations.

At the same time, the process of globalisation and the questions raised about the state's role in redistributing resources, along with its withdrawal from many areas of political and social responsibility, has underscored the emergence of new players making their voices heard for the first time. They are mobilising and organising to demand new rights in new ways, including rights for the homeless, young people, the elderly and the handicapped, the right to breathe clean air, to drink uncontaminated water and to eat food that is not poisoned by pesticides. In some North American cities, car windscreen washers have formed groups to defend their right to earn a little money. In many respects, these demands update several articles in the 1948 Universal Declaration. Some of them – the right to access personal data, to a healthy life without genetic engineering and to a clean environment – reflect technological and scientific advances. But again, the question might be asked: who controls the benefits of such technology and science? Who decides how they shall be used? To which ends and in whose interests?

The impact of human rights on the current globalisation process is above all a political matter that requires identifiable players to build different power relationships at different levels. Emphasising the players and the responsibilities not only shows that development and defence of human rights are closely linked but also that the defence of new and old rights – which are inseparable – depends on taking back control of development strategies and of the power needed to defend them.

In an open global market, companies have to understand the importance of local 'roots' and cultural systems in the market or country or the community in which they operate. In order to be successful in this multi-cultural and multi-regulatory environment, companies also have to deal proactively with their image of 'rich outsiders', and put in place effective environment management plans and systems. Transparency, disclosure and corporate responsibility for managing risks imposed on communities and environment have therefore become a universal expectation and an important global corporate strategy. Business also faced issues of spatial distance, lack of market knowledge, communication cost and problems, increase in administrative costs, varied government policies, a need to reduce the 'liability of foreignness' and increase integration in the host country. Against this backdrop, CSR may often seem to hold the answer as business strategy. International companies attempting to address issue of public image, pressures from local rivals and from local stakeholders therefore started to take up CSR as a strategic effort than as charity in the early 1980s.

EMERGING PERSPECTIVES THAT ADDRESS CORPORATE SOCIAL RESPONSIBILITY

CSR is basically a new business strategy to reduce investment risks and maximise profits by taking all the key stakeholders into confidence. The proponents of this perspective often include CSR in their advertising and social marketing initiatives.

The second is an eco-social perspective. The proponents of this perspective are the new generation of corporations and the new economy entrepreneurs who created a tremendous amount of wealth in a relatively short span of time. They recognise the fact that social and environmental stability and sustainability are two important prerequisites for the sustainability of the market in the long run. They also recognise the fact that increasing poverty can lead to social and political instability. Such socio-political instability can, in turn, be detrimental to business, which operates from a variety of socio-political and cultural backgrounds.

Seen from the eco-social perspective, CSR is both a value and a strategy to ensuring the sustainability of business. It is a value because it stresses the fact that business and markets are essentially aimed at the well-being of society. It is a strategy because it helps to reduce social tensions and facilitate markets.

For the new generation of corporate leaders, optimisation of profits is the key, rather than the maximisation of profit. Hence, there is a shift from accountability to shareholders to accountability to stakeholders (including employees, consumers and affected communities). There is a growing realisation that long-term business success can only be achieved by companies that recognise that the economy is an 'open subsystem of the earth's ecosystem, which is finite, non-growing and materially closed' (Herman, 1996).

There is a third and growing perspective that shapes the new principles and practice of CSR. This is a rights-based perspective on corporate responsibility. This perspective stresses that consumers, employees, affected communities and shareholders have a right to know about corporations and their business. Corporations are private initiatives, true, but increasingly they are becoming public institutions whose survival depends on the consumers who buy their products and shareholders who invest in their stocks. This perspective stresses accountability, transparency and social and environmental investment as the key aspects of CSR.

Though the concept of CSR has only recently been formulated, there is a long history in both the East and West of a commitment to social philanthropy, in the belief that the creation of wealth is primarily geared for social good. This aspect of ethical business in modern times can be traced back to 19th-century philanthropists like Robert Owen and the various Quaker-owned businesses. The Quakers 'ran successful businesses, made money because they offered honest products and treated their people honestly, gave honest value for money, put back more than they took and told no lies' (Roddick, 1999).

In the traditional paradigm, most corporate bodies viewed CSR as the extension of a financial input for a humanitarian cause. However, the contemporary context is more complex: 'A company that undertakes activities aimed at communities (be they philanthropic, social investment or commercial initiatives) but does not comply with business basics cannot be termed socially responsible' (Srivastava & Venkateswaran, 2000).

Ethical business is the more fundamental, emerging trend on the international scene. It focusses on specifics:

(1) how a business is conceptualised,
(2) how a business is operated,
(3) the notion of fair profit.

In an ethical business, the essential thrust is on social values and business is conducted in consonance with broader social values and the stakeholders' long-term interests.

To understand the rise of CSR in the Indian context, it is important to understand the political and bureaucratic climate of the country since 1990. India, since the mid-1990s, is under constant political upheaval and no single party has achieved absolute majority in the parliament. This has led to formation of coalition governments, none of which have lasted a full term of five years, till date. Therefore, a highly cautious, nervous and speculative investment climate exists in India as the 'Swadeshi' fervour often sways the political parties. Due to the political instability, projected figures for foreign direct investment have not been achieved. Even approved proposals may be called for re-investigation in parliament. Financial caution related to investment is exercised not only by international business but also by Indian business. The Indian business sector, though, has the advantage of being intimately familiar with the Indian situation and makes attempts to proactively engage with the bureaucracy and the political parties. Under strict implementation of election guidelines, corporate donation to political parties at times of election have reduced drastically, but business now undertake activities supported by major political leaders or political parties to influence the bureaucracy and the political climate (globalcompact).

India has an extensive bureaucratic machinery, and even after liberalisation and reduction in 'licence raj' 'rule of the licence', each new industrial set-up may require 70–90 clearances from local, state and national government authorities, while the 'Swadeshi' fervour creates a fear of 'being asked to leave among the transnational corporations'. In an unstable political and rigid bureaucratic set-up businesses have to use caution when dealing with government and political parties. CSR in a situation where dealing with the stakeholders is imperative for survival, and the stakeholder stance may change overnight under political considerations, is thus gaining ground in becoming an important corporate strategy for survival (humanresourcesmagazine).

The time for unmotivated philanthropy seems to be coming to an end in the Indian context, and the usage of the term 'corporate social responsibility' is gaining currency since the 1990s. It needs to be mentioned that progressively businesses keen on CSR also want 'some visible benefits' identifying with the issue of 'mutuality' of CSR. Therefore, well-established business also may have a well-established strategy of 'corporate social responsibility' to (1) effectively deal with the instability of the Indian politico-economic climate, (2) proactively deal with all the other stakeholders and (3) meet the demands of international customer especially as regards to labour and environment.

Capacity of a business to deal with the political and economic climate of a region or a nation depends on its financial strength. This ability to influence often remains undisclosed and is put to practice as and when required. The Enron project in India has been able to influence different state governments of Maharashtra, but the details of negotiation have never been made public. The marketing, production and labour departments of an industry often take care of the demands of the international customer and the industry, and are often not viewed as components of CSR. CSR in the Indian context often gets translated as (1) 'social service', 'social development' or 'community development' etc. at the local level, (2) public image-building at the local and national level and (3) proactive engagement with the political and economic elite at the local, regional or national level. The engagement with the stakeholders at the local level has led to an increased interaction of the business and the development sector (Arora).

SUMMING UP

The time for unmotivated philanthropy seems to be coming to an end in the Indian context, and the usage of the term 'corporate social responsibility' is gaining currency since the 1990s. It needs to be mentioned that progressively businesses keen on CSR also want 'some visible benefits' (BusinessWorld, 1998) identifying with the issue of 'mutuality' of CSR. Therefore well-established business also may have a well-established strategy of 'corporate social responsibility' to (1) effectively deal with the instability of the Indian politico-economic climate, (2) proactively deal with all the other stakeholders and (3) meet the demands of international customer especially as regards to labour and environment (Business, 1998A).

The success of the acceptance of these norms has been outside the letter of law and the adoption has often influenced state to adopt better/improved or at least changed role for itself. The norms of resettlement and rehabilitation as dictated by the Indian state are by law adopted by joint venture companies involved in extractive industries yet many other activities are also undertaken as CSR, which are neither detailed nor dictated by law. Growth of civil society organisations has also led to increasing democratisation in the marginalised and impoverished communities creating local responses to the grant meta narratives. Yet nation state needs to evolve a new role for itself in this fast changing world. A stable nation providing good governance is thus basic requirement for developing countries in their attempt to safe guard rights and interests of their poor and marginalised people.

REFERENCES

Arora, A. S. Centre for Communication and Development Studies, Pune.

Business World, 1998A:80.

Herman, E. (1996). Daily in 'sustainable growth? No thank you'. In J. Mander & E. Goldsmith (Eds.), *The case of the global economy*. Sierra Book Club.

Roddick, A. (1999, August). *KLM Herald magazine*.

Srivastava, H., & Venkateswaran, S. (2000). *The business of social responsibility*. Bangalore: Books for Change.

World Bank. (1997). *The state in a changing world*. The World Development Report, Washington, DC.

http://www.humanresourcesmagazine.com.au/articles/22/0c01d922.asp.

www.globalcompact.org.

Printed and bound by CPI Group (UK) Ltd, Croydon, CR0 4YY

17/08/2023

08101598-0001